RITUAL AND REMEMBRANCE

RITUAL AND REMEMBRANCE

RESPONSES TO DEATH IN HUMAN SOCIETIES

Edited by

Jon Davies

Copyright © 1994 Sheffield Academic Press

Sheffield Academic Press Ltd
343 Fulwood Road
Sheffield S10 3BP
England

Typeset by Sheffield Academic Press
and
Printed on acid-free paper in Great Britain
by The Cromwell Press
Melksham, Wiltshire

British Library Cataloguing in Publication Data

A catalogue record for this book is available
from the British Library

ISBN 1-85075-469-1

CONTENTS

Acknowledgments

This book owes its origins to a series of public lectures delivered in 1993 at the University of Newcastle upon Tyne. The editor and the contributors wish to thank Dr Margaret Lewis, of the Public Lectures Committee, and Mr George Robb, Technician, for their assistance in making the lectures possible.

The editor and the contributors also wish to thank Sheffield Academic Press for their consistent support, and in particular Helen Tookey, desk editor at the Press, for her expert guidance in the preparation of the manuscript.

List of Contributors

ANDREW BARDGETT worked as an engineer before joining his family's funeral directing business. He holds the Diploma in Funeral Directing, and is involved at both national and local level with the National Association of Funeral Directors.

JOHN CHAPMAN is Senior Lecturer in Archaeology in the Department of Archaeology at the University of Newcastle upon Tyne, where he lectures on Prehistoric Britain and Prehistoric Europe. He is the author of *The Vienca Culture of South-East Europe* and editor of numerous other volumes. He is currently co-directing an archaeological project in north-east Hungary.

ERIC CROSS is Senior Lecturer in Music and Head of the Music Department at the University of Newcastle upon Tyne. He is the author of a two-volume study and numerous articles on the operas of Antonio Vivaldi. He is currently conductor of the Newcastle upon Tyne Bach Choir and the Director of Cappella Novocastriensis.

JON DAVIES is Head of the Department of Religious Studies at the University of Newcastle upon Tyne, where he lectures on death, marriage and religion in contemporary society. He has written and edited books on town and country planning, the family, religion and economics, and the sociology of sacred texts.

DAVID HARTE is Senior Lecturer in Law at the University of Newcastle upon Tyne. His particular interests are church law and environment law. He is the author of *Landscape, Land Use and the Law* (1985).

GRAHAM HARVEY is attached to the Department of Religious Studies at the University of Newcastle upon Tyne, where he is engaged on a study of the belief systems of pagan groups in the United Kingdom.

MARIA MANUEL LISBOA was formerly Lecturer in Portuguese and Brazilian Studies at the University of Newcastle upon Tyne, and is now at the Department of Spanish and Portuguese at the University of Cambridge, where she is a Fellow of St John's College.

JOHN SAWYER is Emeritus Professor in Religious Studies at the University of Newcastle upon Tyne, Honorary Professor at the University of Lancaster, and the author of many books and articles, the latest of which is *The Fifth Gospel*, an account of the book of Isaiah.

BRYAN VERNON was formerly the Anglican Chaplain at the University of Newcastle upon Tyne and the Chair of the Newcastle Mental Health Trust. He is now Lecturer in Medical Ethics in the Medical School of the University of Newcastle upon Tyne.

DIANA WHALEY is Lecturer in the English Department of the University of Newcastle upon Tyne and the author of a book on Snorri Sturluson's *Heimskringla* and other work in the field of Old Icelandic studies and skaldic poetry.

Introduction: Ancestors—Living and Dead

Jon Davies

> The symbols of death say what life is and those of life define what death must be.[1]

In 1941 W. Lloyd Warner and Paul Lunt published the first volume of the classic 'Yankee City' sociological series called *The Social Life of a Modern Community*.[2] The preface to the 1941 edition promised a fifth volume, to be entitled *American Symbol Systems*. When volume five actually appeared in 1959 it had changed its title. It had become *The Living and the Dead: A Study of the Symbolic Life of Americans*. In this volume Lloyd Warner described and analysed, in graphic and very moving ways, the day-to-day activities and processes, rites and ceremonies whereby an American community created a present and future for itself by constantly reinvoking and reinvigorating the great (and small) events, the shared troubles and triumphs of the past. The dead (both the heroic and the ordinary dead) of this community are, as the author shows, alive both in 'secular symbols which often emphasize the living present [and in] sacred symbols [which] appear to be more concerned with death, with the past of the species and the future of the individual'.[3] With both secular and sacred symbols, the members of a community invoke a moral, exemplary ancestry which locates their particular experience within all the possible histories of the species.

---

1. W. Lloyd Warner, *The Living and the Dead: A Study of the Symbolic Life of Americans* (New Haven: Yale University Press, 1959), p. 320.
2. W. Lloyd Warner and P. Lunt, *The Social Life of a Modern Community* (repr.; Westport, CT: Greenwood Press, 1973 [1941]).
3. Lloyd Warner, *The Living and the Dead*, pp. 4-5.

Lloyd Warner wrote:

> Human culture is a symbolic organisation of the remembered
> experiences of the dead past as newly felt and understood by the
> living members of the collectivity. The human condition of
> individual mortality and the comparative immortality of our
> species make most of our communication and collective activ-
> ities in the larger sense a vast exchange of understanding
> between the living and the dead. Language, religion, art,
> science, morality and our knowledge of ourselves and the world
> around us, being parts of our culture, are meaningful symbol
> systems which the living generation has inherited from
> those now gone... Communication between living and dead
> individuals maintains continuity of culture for the species.[1]

Lloyd Warner was an anthropologist whose first work was a
study of a Stone Age people in Australia,[2] and he was familiar
with the work of Malinowski, Durkheim, Frazer and Sapir, as
well as with the more 'urban' work of his compatriots in
Chicago such as Robert Park and Ernest Burgess. He was also a
subtle analyst of liturgy and theology, and *The Living and the
Dead* contains a detailed dissection of the logic and symbolism
of the Mass and of the communal significance of those age-old
stories of sacrifice, suicide and tragedy which are caught up in
the story of Christ's death. It is, as my own paper in this
volume shows, in the remembrance of that story that the
potency of the Christian message is to be found. Lloyd Warner
was also something of a classicist, and *The Living and the Dead*
concludes with a discussion of Oedipus Rex and the claim that
all people, those of Ancient Greece and of Yankee City, could
'walk in pain with Oedipus since we share common feelings
and a common conscience with him'.[3]

The enduring and particular value of the Yankee City series
lies not so much in the excellence of its empirical data on social
class or employment patterns but in the contents of the final
volume, that is to say in its finely argued insistence that the life
of a community is comprehensible, subjectively and objec-

---

1. *The Living and the Dead*, pp. 4-5.
2. W. Lloyd Warner, *A Black Civilization: A Social Study of an Australian
Tribe* (New York: Harper & Brothers, 1939).
3. Lloyd Warner, *The Living and the Dead*, p. 506.

tively, only when it is understood as grounded in a covenant of mutual loyalty between the living and the dead. This covenant with the ancestors is the covenant which, beyond all others, makes sense of, makes moral and validates all the lesser covenants and contracts within which our communal life is enmeshed. Religion, for example, is never communally experienced as 'theology', but as the record of a religious historical journey, expressed in the lives of men and women no longer with us in the flesh, but speaking to us in handed-down and handed-on hymns, ceremonies, buildings. These hymns, ceremonies and buildings endlessly, insistently and helpfully present to the living the authoritative transcendental ideas and example of the dead. Cities may seem busy; but the busy life goes on in streets named after the ancestral dead and around monuments giving us vital uses of and for the example of the dead.

Political theorists may try to create visions, and politicians models, of societies abstracted from the weight of the past; they create utopias and dystopias from which the past is either excluded or anathematized or reduced to a mere quaint relic. Yet the relics are alive. They return as a vital lesson, for better or for worse, insisting on the primacy of the relationship between the generations that were and those that are and those that are yet to come. The voices of the dead delimit the political options and provide a practical civic ethic.

Family life, with all its curses and blessings, is the paradigm of community living, a perpetually unravelling revelation of and to the new and the old generations, in which the once-new become by example the long-since or about-to-become dead. It is within family life that one first encounters those forms of death which unstructure one's own self. We are literally deracinated by such deaths—and then re-racinated. It is indeed the case that children are the death of their parents, as well as the life of the family. The trajectory of an individual towards his or her death, and via the death of loved or hated others, is precisely what makes possible the construction for that individual of a proper moral pilgrimage. 'What do you want to be when you grow up?' is a valid question only when it is realized that 'growing up' means nearing death and that it also entails the death of parents, those people who knew that life for you meant death for them. What you will be when you grow up is a person with dead parents. Parents who have to bury their own children know what a blessing that is.

Seen in this way, it is the fact of death that creates the necessity for and the possibility of a basic human covenant which both transcends and envelops all other social bonds. No civic morality, no altruistic ethic, no community aesthetic, no view of the purposes of human life and of the place within that of me and you and the community of which we are part, as friends, strangers or even enemies, can ignore the vitality of death as the prior validating ground of the community between the living and the dead, a base community which makes possible the day-to-day utilitarian contracts and lesser covenants between the various groups of the living. A community without a properly incorporated relationship with its dead ancestors can be destroyed.

To make this point in a stark way we can perhaps look briefly at a society which deliberately set about destroying the covenant between the living and the dead, and in so doing destroyed itself. From 1933 onwards the National Socialist government of Germany set about trying to transform its Jewish citizens into non-persons, people who were simply *not there*, whether alive or dead. The very existence of the Jews was to be denied or ignored, in this life and the next. Simply killing them was not enough, because, as I have already stated, the dead as memory, as internalized spiritual inheritance, are a vital part of the bonds of the community of the living. The German government was determined to destroy these bonds. The story of the actual killing—on a mass and anonymous scale—has been often told, as has the story of the continuing efforts of the surviving Jews to deny that non-being in monument, memorial, proclaimed history, film, and above all in the adamant existence of the State of Israel. All of this effort proclaims that the Jewish dead were and are dead, *our* dead, *our* ancestors, and not the non-persons into which the Germans sought to transform them. The Jewish non-persons must be made livingly dead by being *named*. In this way they will be restored to the community of the living and Hitler will be denied his victory.

As part of the process of transforming the Jews of Germany into non-persons, the German government after 1933 had first to detach them from the larger German Christian community of which they were part. Whatever was true of the leaders of the National Socialist Party, it is doubtful whether the majority of Germans at the time could consciously have comprehended that their relationships with 'their' Jews were not simply to be restructured in a more or less radical manner, but were to be reduced to a total practical and spiritual oblivion. Government policy to this end was therefore introduced slowly and incrementally, and arbitrarily, designed from the beginning to produce not simply dead Jews, but non-persons, whose death would be irrelevant because non-persons, not being alive anyway, and neither being nor having ancestors, would have no conceivable way of dying or need for memorial.

The German city of Bamberg had, in 1932, a long-established Jewish population of 821 persons.[1] By 1943 there were none left. In October 1932 Rabbi Katten of Bamberg led the prayers for the Fatherland, in particular for the President of the Reich, Hindenburg, praised as 'the true representative of the Fatherland'.[2] By March 1933 there were worries about the intentions of the new regime. In April 1933 two members of the congregation lost their right to practise law because they were Jews, with exemptions only for non-Aryans who had served at the front or who had lost a son or father in the war. In the same month there was a boycott of Jewish shops and a prohibition of all ritual slaughter. In May of that year there was a lecture on the use of the commentaries of Rashi. Also in May a compulsorily sealed coffin containing the body of 27-year-old Wilhelm Aron was returned from Dachau, where he had been

---

1. See K.H. Mistele, 'The End of a Community: Jews in Bamberg, 1930–1942' (trans. J. Feuchtwanger for the Leo Baeck Institute, New York; unpublished; n.d. [German original 1988]). See also the unpublished lectures of Dr H. Loebl given in the Department of Religious Studies at the University of Newcastle upon Tyne.

2. Mistele, 'The End of a Community', p. 21.

killed, and there was a wedding of one of Bamberg's daughters to a doctor from Wurzburg, the couple having decided to emigrate to England.

A rather expensive shipment of kosher meat arrived from Denmark, five girls emigrated to Palestine, and Ernst Simon lectured on Jeremiah and his message for the times. In August 1935 all Jewish schoolchildren had to be registered as such, their parents being made responsible for doing so. In September 1935 the celebration of the 25th anniversary of the synagogue was to be the last time the Jews of Bamberg celebrated as citizens of the German Reich. In December 1935 the congregation acquired a property known as the White Dove Inn to serve as a centre for activities which they were no longer allowed to share with Bamberg Aryans. The White Dove Inn, the Jewish community centre, was later used as the collection point for deportation 'to the east'. In August 1936 the state prohibited all Jewish instruction in state schools. The Goldschmidt family emigrated to the USA. In November a school for Jews only opened, in the synagogue, but within the state system, the state paying the salary (no pension rights, four months' notice). The teacher was arrested in 1937. In the same year a Gentile teacher hired to teach needlework was forced to resign because Aryans were not allowed to teach Jews.

In November 1938 the synagogue was burnt down, the classroom with it, and on November 18 Jews were expelled from any connection with the state educational system. This was part of the systematic exclusion of Jews from any form of contact with their Bamberg neighbours and their reduction to a total dependence upon the Gestapo as their only link with the city in which they had been born. Jewish doctors had their titles revoked and were allowed to treat only Jews (the newly renamed 'Jewish Medical Attendants' were forced to remove their own shingles). In order neither to offend nor embarrass, leading Jewish non-doctors would cross the street to avoid their quondam Aryan colleagues. Jews were forced to transfer their property to Aryans with a small reimbursement if they emigrated (until 1941 when all emigration was stopped). They were restricted to certain occupations, forced to hand in their jewellery, were curfewed and 'advised' not to use the street in numbers of more than two, to give up their place in queues to Aryans and to be self-effacing in public places. They were forbidden to buy shaving soap or to have ration coupons to buy clothes, denied the right to use any form of transport other than (with permission) a bicycle. An edict of 1941 required all Jewish typewriters to be registered, and all Jewish war veterans to give up all their privileges, including the right to their war medals. Jews were forbidden to use telephones, to buy flowers or German folk costume, and they had to hand in their surplus shaving equipment, combs and scissors. They were forbidden to have domestic pets. In October 1941 the Bamberg Gestapo was ordered to begin preparation for the transportation of the by now much reduced population. The Jewish leadership was forced to cooperate.

On November 14 1941, 114 Jews left Bamberg on a transport, allegedly for a labour colony in the east. As they did so, yet another decree (there were hundreds) removed from all Jews who 'emigrated', including to the Ostmark to which the train was heading, their remaining rights as German citizens. A midwife checked their bodies for hidden valuables and the ID cards they handed in were stamped 'Evacuated'. The 'colonists' were asked to buy their own tickets, arranged by the local Gestapo with the state railway authority, at special rates for single-journey tickets. After the first transport there were about 126 Jews left in Bamberg. Thirteen of these left on another transport in March 1942, and another 61 between February and September 1942. As the train pulled out of the station, it passed the Jewish cemetery. The Jews on the train were, whether they knew it or not, passing ancestors to whom they were never to be joined in a city in which they themselves were never to become ancestors. By the end of 1942 there were no Jews left in Bamberg: the city was *Judenrein*, both of the living and the dead.

This story, no doubt repeated throughout most of German-dominated Europe in the middle of this century, is one of the rare examples of an attempt to destroy death: this was war on the dead, war on the ancestors. There have, clearly, been many examples of cultures or people being overwhelmed or wiped out, but even the memories of such violent transactions have usually been retained, even boasted about, as part of some kind of record of events. The Nazi project was different: it was to make both the lives and the deaths of Bamberg's Jews a non-event, to deny them a place—even a place as victims—in the history of the city. The Jews, alive or dead, were simply not to be there and their dead were simply those who never were. The endless violent flow of petty restrictions, as well as the most radical forms of violence, tore up all forms of community; of the Jews with the Aryans, and even of the Jews among themselves. The sister of Max Sussman, who was murdered at Dachau in 1939, agreed to 'adhere strictly to the rules of the law'[1] when warned to stop enquiring about her brother, and it was the leadership of the Jewish community which warned women to be self-effacing when shopping to avoid 'provoking' the Gentiles.[2] The Jews became neither the living nor the dead, neither ancestors nor inheritors, simply not there.

In recent years, the 'Remembrance' effort of Holocaust writing has sought to restate the reality of what happened, in Bamberg as elsewhere, by giving names and biographies to the Jews of Europe, both as people who lived and as people who were killed and died there: *Yad VaShem*, 'A Place and a Name', as the Israeli Holocaust Centre is called. In both their life and death, and only in both, do the Jews of Bamberg become people again—too late, perhaps, given the horror of what happened. So strong is the need to die properly within the life of the living that one can see in this story of the middle of this century something which is true for all communities, that the living need the dead if the culture is to survive and perhaps flourish. To destroy a culture, destroy its dead, deny its ancestors.

The essays in this collection do not, generally, approach the subject of the living and the dead through the records of an event as terrible as the Holocaust. I have introduced it because it is such a graphic demonstration of the truth of Lloyd

1. Mistele, 'The End of a Community', p. 100.
2. Mistele, 'The End of a Community', p. 154.

Warner's evaluation of the necessity and function of the bond between the two worlds of humans. These essays deal with the more normal manifestations of this bond, and derive from a rather lugubrious calculation (which no doubt has an element of error in it) that since the last Ice Age about ten thousand years ago approximately one hundred billion people have died (in the American sense of 'billion').

This ten thousand years represents all of our history. Human history, when seen as a parade of the ancestors, takes on a distinctive perspective. Most history is clearly the story of the records and (in terms of social action) the remains of the important or very important dead. Darius, king of the Persians, insisted on having a splendid tomb precisely because he had been so important. Archaeological evidence for the humble dead is of a very different order to the great mausolea or tombs of such personages as Darius, so that the history of, for example, the ordinary Neolithic Orcadians must be constructed from a rather mixed up collection of bones found in the Tomb of the Eagles[1] (a name which is itself a twentieth-century conceit) on South Ronaldsay in the Orkneys.

It has been argued that language and therefore social processes and culture itself arose out of our ancestors' attempts to understand death and to provide their dead with appropriate forms of farewell. It is probably the case that funerary ritual liturgy preceded and led to theology. No doubt, the greatly complex visions of life, death and the afterworlds which we find in the records of ancient Egypt and early Christianity had their equivalent in expressions of funerary thoughts and actions in the minds of our less literate ancestors on the Orkneys and elsewhere, these now being lost to us. Obviously, we will never be able to comprehend the full articulation of the spiritual worlds of our ancestors, and even the physical artefacts are sparse and difficult to interpret. Yet within what may be rather a naive assumption—that there is indeed a common human experience of death and a common human urge to locate a sense of self in both individual and

1. J.W. Hedges, *Tomb of the Eagles: A Window on Stone Age Tribal Britain* (London: John Murray, 1984).

collective ancestries—we can perhaps take the essays in this book as a genuine part of the study of the lives and deaths of a hundred billion ancestors. The essays are widely spread, both in the range of cultures on which they draw and the types of data to which they refer. They cover war, funerals, the masculine and the feminine, law and liturgy, music, art and literature; and attempt throughout to give a reasonable representation to 'ordinary' or mundane forms of death, rather than dealing only with the more prominent styles of heroic death—the subject of so much of our art, music and literature.

The law has a lot to do with and to say about death. Much law has to do with the property rights of the dead and their living relatives; indeed, the very matter of 'relationship' emphasizes the centrality of ancestry in the determination of rights and obligations in such matters. Many of the more poignant matters with which law and ethics have concerned themselves have derived from those disputes between generations over access to and use of scarce resources, or between rival cultures engaged in settling similar disputes at times of war or geographical expansion. Here again, ancestry and ancestral rights are powerful affective forces claiming allegiance and fuelling enmities which seem quite impervious to sense and good reason. Wars usually involve either a dispute about ancestry or a conflict between ancestors. Within the family, of course, the law is increasingly being involved in that most delicate of all death-decisions, the determination of the end of life. The great covenant between the generations is essentially one of and for life. How, then, do we locate this covenant in a deliberate consideration of death, be this a good death ('euthanasia') or a bad one?

Art has always been full of death. For some time, scarcely a work of art was produced, on no matter how vital or erotic a theme, which did not have tucked somewhere a gaping skull to remind both viewer and viewed that death was inherent in all life and that the sure and certain joys of the urgent flesh would be followed by the equally sure and certain journey to the grave. Our own modern, or postmodern, culture has to a large extent managed to separate its artistic treatment of life and death, and popular culture insists on such a separation. At the same time, our own culture, throughout most of my lifetime, has had to live with the possibility of mass death, whether through war or through 'accidents' and environmental degradation. In the event, Europeans have in the main been spared the actual experience of such death, but more recently the advent of AIDS has restored the intimate connection between lovemaking and deathmaking, graphically depicted in a Ugandan Government anti-AIDS poster, where the lovemakers' bed is the inside of a skull (Figure 1).

Figure 1. *Ugandan government anti-AIDS poster.*

War at the end of this century has returned to Europe, ironically to where it started in 1914, and continues to be a major provider of death. In this century war has been the occasion of that most democratic form of all art works, the war memorial; every village now has its own collective mausoleum, in which the mysteries of war and religion achieve a very distinctive artistic expression. Indeed, in war and war remembrance we find a major source of religious survival and expression in a generally secular age.

In poetry, music, art, film, in newspapers, on street names, in monuments, in the concerns of the great, and in their monuments, and in the day-to-day lives of the ordinary people and their monuments, death is to be found for those who would choose to see the world through its eyes. The essays that follow, many of which were given as part of the University of Newcastle's Public Lecture series, illustrate how widely the sense of death permeates our lives, when by 'our' is meant the accumulated legacy of the one hundred billion dead. As the essays make clear, death is both a seriously tragic and a seriously cheerful part of our lives, a blessing and a curse from our ancestors.

Part I

The Politics of Ancestry

One Hundred Billion Dead: A General Theology of Death

Jon Davies

In the last ten thousand years—what we know as history—one hundred billion people have died. In mass this is the equivalent of Halley's Comet and in numbers the equivalent of ten thousand First World Wars.

Of those that have died some, relatively very few, had and retain a degree of personal fame; their death is to some extent transcended in memory and monument, poem or song. It is only in the last hundred years or so that death, usually of men who died in battle, has been democratized in monument and word in a somewhat similar way. Similarly, it is only in the last hundred years or so that the general population has been able to 'individualize' their own dead in a ritual over which they have a large degree of control. In our cemeteries now, all our ancestors are thus individualized.

Most of the hundred billion, however, have passed into oblivion, remembered as generalized ancestors, not as individuals. We will never know much about them. The evidence of archaeology seems however to indicate that within the limits of their technology, our ancestors went to very considerable lengths to provide appropriate and lasting burials and burial chambers for their dead. No society that we know of has been uninterested in death, and while not all theology is about death and death rituals, no theology worthy of the name excludes a more or less detailed explanation of death and its attendant mysteries—where do we come from, where do the dead go?

As a matter of record, theological speculations about death have in general regarded it with fear and terror. Maurice Bloch feels that human beings fear death because 'all human beings understand the processes of life and duration in ways which are universal, [and death rituals are] nothing other than a secondary transformation of that experience'.[1] Yet if this were the case then human theories and rituals about death would surely have taken on a naturalist or humanist cast. 'We are,' said a humanist friend of mine cheerfully, 'nothing more than putrefying protein'. Such a view would compare the hundred billion human dead with the associated life and death of flaura and fauna and realize that if our ancestors had *not* died, things would be very much more difficult—perhaps impossible. Life on the planet would be squalid and fractious indeed if no one had ever died.

Theologies and rituals of death do indeed have naturalistic elements in them, but cannot be regarded as *simply* natural, although they certainly seem to be universal. All human societies mobilize a death theology and ritual which recognizes the ecological truth that there must be death if there is to be life. Death is the major legacy of the dead to the living. All death is sacrificial and no one dies in vain. This is, however, a dangerous truth, for if *all* death is sacrificial then life itself can too easily be regarded as exploitable and the way is open to 'holy' suicide or genocide. Theologies and rituals of death seek to limit death, that is, to diminish its naturalness, but in so doing run into the need to discriminate between the value of each and every life. This is what death theologies and rituals have historically done.

Death has never been taken for granted, taken as simply natural. All cultures, in separating themselves out from the generality of the human race and in creating both inter-group and intra-group hierarchies, in creating a history of and for themselves, have woven a view of death into it. The idea of death as a necessary sacrifice made by all human beings is at the centre of this view—but is paradoxically overlain with a depiction of death as the result of sin. This is paradoxical until one notes that it is only via the idea of sin that a species

1. M. Bloch, *Prey into Hunter: The Politics of Religious Experience* (Cambridge: Cambridge University Press, 1992), p. 23.

theology of sacrifice made by everyone can become a particular doctrine of forgiveness for the chosen few. Even those theologies which appear to be most concerned with punishment are inherently concerned to find reasons to forgive—but not to forgive everyone. The ontological and unifying sense of death as sacrifice has been turned into a sense of death as necessary and proper punishment for the sins of enemies. This then makes possible the political annexation of death as an instrument of terror.

There must be sin before there can be forgiveness. Sin 'sells' forgiveness, and makes it possible to root death rituals in an expression of judgment. An indiscriminate sense of sacrifice is of no more political relevance than an indiscriminate sense of sin.

The logic of death theologies and death rituals therefore becomes, and certainly became in our society, a semi-political argument about the calculus of sin and forgiveness, in which the notion of general or species sacrifice became obscured and replaced by a politicized notion of Judgment.

Sin or Sacrifice?

In most of the world's cultures death, self-evidently a necessary and usually benign event, enters human life through evil or sin. 'Death is the ultimate consequence of sin',[1] says the *New Catholic Encyclopedia*. As Saint Paul puts it, 'By one man sin entered into the world, and death by sin; and so death passed upon all men, for that all have sinned' (Rom. 5.12).

One of the indigenous cultures of what is now called New South Wales says that in the original and timeless society created by God, men and women lived in a garden in which there was a hollow tree. This tree, said God, was not to be touched. One day, a swarm of wild bees occupied the hollow tree. The women developed a hunger for honey and wanted to open up the tree. The men tried to dissuade them, but one woman went and took a tomahawk to the tree. Out of the

---

1. 'Death', in *The New Catholic Encyclopedia* (New York: McGraw–Hill, 1967), IV, pp. 688ff.

wounded tree flew a huge black bat, called Death. The bat flew, and whoever it touched with its wings died.[1] Many thousands of miles and years away the English poet Milton used remarkably similar language to describe the same event:

> So saying, her rash hand in evil hour
> Forth reaching to the fruit, she plucked, she eat:
> Earth felt the wound, and Nature from her seat
> Sighing through all her works gave signs of woe,
> That all was lost.[2]

There are some quite obvious similarities between the Aboriginal myth and the seventeenth-century English poem, and between both (not surprisingly in Milton's case) and the Creation story in Genesis: there is the tree, the agency of woman and the concomitant separation of and hostility between men and women (see Manucha Lisboa's essay in this volume), and the description of becoming human via an act of disobedience against God—an act, that is, creating the very notion of enmity. It would appear that few of the cultures of the hundred billion dead have been able to conceive of death as anything other than a punishment, a built-in destabilizing factor destroying not only each individual life (on its own a reasonably acceptable idea) but also the very possibility of stability or permanence in human affairs. After the honey, after the apple, death has never been seen as natural, neutral or benign.

The religious response has been to offer immortality as an antidote to death. Whether of the body and the soul, or simply of the soul, immortality claims to negate the finality of death.

However, the origin of death in an act of sin or disobedience has meant that access to this immortality can only be accomplished through some form of trial, a Judgment.[3] In Egyptian, Buddhist and Christian literature and art there appear paintings and descriptions of various Judges and Judgment

1. J. Hastings (ed.), *The Encyclopedia of Religion and Ethics* (Edinburgh: T. & T. Clark, 1911), IV, p. 411.

2. J. Milton, *Paradise Lost*, Book IX, ll. 780-84.

3. See S.G.F. Brandon, *The Judgment of the Dead* (London: Weidenfeld & Nicolson, 1967).

Days and of the decisions and consequences of those judgments. Christians have to look no further than the paintings of Hieronymous Bosch or the great medieval poem written by Dante. In these works we have displayed or described a map of the afterlife, with (in the Christian tradition) a threefold division into heaven, hell and purgatory. Such a division is the necessary corollary of death seen as the result of sin, as of course is the idea of judgment.

This essay will centre on that feature of the afterlife which has, since the Reformation, been rather despised and rejected, the Christian idea of purgatory. By the thirteenth century the doctrine of purgatory had become an established part of the theology of the medieval church, surrounded with a great complexity of doctrine, liturgy and iconography.[1] In the present context, however, the key aspect of the notion of purgatory is that it is the only post-death option which retains, indeed strengthens and enhances, friendly relationships between the living and the dead, because it comprehends the notions of sacrificial living and sacrificial dying without turning either into a dogma of terror. The doctrine of purgatory is a sociable doctrine. It recognizes the nature of death as sacrifice, a sacrifice made by all humans, not just a chosen few, and was generated by a determination to create human space in a medieval world increasingly dominated by professionalized theologies of sin and judgment. In this article I will illustrate the ways in which the idea of an afterlife in which the living and the dead can and do maintain their relationships keeps its vitality in spite of being played down and anathematized by ecclesial established religion. Purgatory belongs to the basic anthropology and archaeology of our religious culture, a genuinely populist construct, and I will later illustrate this by reference to the 'Family Announcements' or 'In Memoriam' pages of local newspapers, which function in this respect as a kind of mass media chantry.[2] Before dealing with this directly,

1. See J. Le Goff, *The Birth of Purgatory* (Chicago: University of Chicago Press, 1981).

2. See E. Duffy, *The Stripping of the Altars* (New Haven: Yale University Press, 1992).

however, I will have to deal with the larger topic of death and judgment, and the funeral liturgies which express such ideas in words, movement, poetry and music.

Sinners, Saints and Judgment in Christian Origin Stories

Judgment would be meaningless if its outcome were the same for everyone. There must be sinners if there are to be saints, and there can be saints only if there are sinners. Since the story of Origin has death and sin intertwined in our collective memory, there are likely to be more sinners assured of punishment at the moment of death than there are saints assured of forgiveness and salvation—or, to put it more realistically, all of us would be sensibly advised to think of ourselves as actually damned and only potentially saved. (Again, Manucha Lisboa's paper shows how the calculus of sin has over the centuries been imposed upon and internalized by women.) Sinners we are, saints we may be allowed to become—there are very few saints, and very few people who know any.

At the very least, sainthood is not something one can arrogate to oneself; there are very few people who would lay claim to such a title. Sainthood is not, of course, something one can apply for. Indeed, the division of humanity into saints and sinners, the loved and the hated, friends and foes, us and them, targets and comrades, has always been regarded as the absolute foundation of both religious and political sovereignty. How else could a government order its subjects to kill?

To the ordinary problems of finite physical decay and death, then, we have added the near-certainty of post-death judgment; an existential anxiety about its outcome; a terror of perpetual pain, misery and suffering, and the sense of a ubiquitous censorious Power growling at our every little foible and act of self-indulgence.

To cope with this we rely not simply upon ourselves but on other people; ordinary, unpredictable other people, who must manage our transition towards the Day of Judgment and the afterlife with appropriate rituals and benign concern (see the essay in this volume by Andrew Bardgett on the complex etiquette of funeral directing). For their sakes, as well as our own, we cannot be allowed to die 'naturally' or 'by ourselves'. Our own death solves nothing. No proffering of salvation to me makes sense without the simultaneous evocation of the terrors which may be on offer to you, or vice versa. No imagery of the Day of Judgment can exercise dramatic power without being seen to punish at least as often as it rewards. Hell must be known to exist before heaven becomes believable, or vice versa.

Religion and Violent Ritual

It is in this substratum of terror and anxiety that Maurice Bloch locates the inner meaning of many forms of religious death ritual, as the title of his book *Prey into Hunter* makes very clear. It is, for example, not so much the fear of physical death on its own but the anxiety about everlasting life or punishment that makes the death of ordinary people so dreadful and dependent upon the ritualized (that is, non-arbitrary) ministrations of other people. These ministrations are never disinterested, because the death of one person advertises the mortality of all and proclaims the irreducible fragility of all human institutions. Death must be conquered; the use of such military language underscores Bloch's insistence that the 'irreducible core of the ritual process'[1] is an interpenetration of religion and violence. In many of the world's cultures death is generally an occasion for the unleashing of (among other emotions) anger and aggression.[2] The sharing out of the dead person's possessions, for example, which is a standard part of our funeral practice, can be seen as just as final a dismembering of the dead person, whose death has so terrified and therefore angered us, as were earlier practices of the burning or burial of possessions. Funerals insist on the dreadfulness and deadness of the dead. Funerals kill the dead.

Bloch insists that religion and violence are ritual coexistents,

1. Bloch, *Prey into Hunter*, p. xi.
2. See P. Rosenblatt, *Grief and Mourning in Cross-Cultural Perspective* (St Paul, MN: University of Minnesota, Human Relations Area Files, 1976), p. 29.

as the frequent employment of the words 'conquer' and 'victory' in death ritual indicates. Bloch sees death rituals and other rituals as constructed around the oppositions of permanence and impermanence, of mortality and immortality, of vitality and transcendence, of this-worldly fleshly physicality and other-worldly never-dying spirituality. These antinomies can only be handled through the use of empowering, powerful rituals. At the very moment of physical death the power of the immortal spirit, the 'Word which was in the beginning and is now', must be reasserted, and this is done in a way which expressly proclaims and even enhances the passivity and vulnerability, the *deadness*, of the dead.

This can be seen in the older version of the Anglican Order for the Burial of the Dead.[1] This liturgy opens with an absolute insistence on the primacy of the Word, the non-flesh: 'I AM the resurrection and the life, saith the Lord: he that believeth in me, though he were dead, shall he live'. The coffin-occupant is failed flesh, a 'vile body...[which] worms destroy'. The physical coffin-occupant, whose vile body is to be exchanged for the 'glorious body' of the Lord Jesus Christ, is made totally dependent upon the power of the Word. At the conclusion of the liturgy the vulnerability of the physical and the precariousness and conditionality of salvation are again emphasized:

> Man that is born of a woman hath but a short time to live and is full of misery. He cometh up and is cut down, like a flower... Of whom may we seek for succour but of thee, O Lord, who for our sins art most justly displeased... Make us acceptable in thy sight.

The last sentences in the above quotation are spoken by the attendant laity, who had earlier beseeched the Father 'to raise us from the death of sin unto the life of righteousness that when we shall depart this life we may rest in him, as is our hope that this our brother [the corpse] doth'.

In denying the moral worth of their own human vitality, and in identifying themselves with the corpse and its hoped-for

---

1. In *The Book of Common Prayer* (Oxford: Oxford University Press, n.d.).

salvation through death, these participants in this formal ritual have turned themselves into potential corpses, passive suppliants to and dependants upon the all-powerful Word, a Word which may of course conquer or reconquer or punish them just as it has conquered the 'death of sin unto the life' of the departed brother (or sister—but see below).

Bloch notes that such a ritual formulation may represent a collective (or 'democratic') reassertion of vitality—the general hope of new life for the whole society may well be realized[1] (Bloch's data are mostly taken from small-scale societies)—or the formulation may be annexed by superordinate powers and used as a device to maintain or extend social hierarchy. Those who speak for the transcendent Word speak with the power of the transcendent Authority. The authoritative figures or leaders of most religious establishments conquer death by allying themselves with the death-deciding God. Much of the analysis of the social functions of such ritual formulations has concentrated on their use either in constructing legitimations for ruling strata (including the domination of men over women—women are totally ignored in the Anglican funeral service—and of humans over other animals and plants) or in the radical inversions of such legitimations, that is, in the spasmodic democratization of death rituals in millenarian eschatological movements, when *everybody* lives or dies in one hugely exploding Last Day. These liturgies are too terrible.

A Death Ritual for the Market Place

A low wind creeps along the fern,
And makes a murmur in the furze.
The path at every sunny turn
Is populous with grasshoppers.

I cannot tell the words they say,
Yet sure the burden of their speech
Is just that life is good today,
And Heaven within our easy reach.

---

1.   Bloch, *Prey into Hunter*, p. 98.

Far off, no doubt, great men of State,
Diplomatists and Chancellors,
Discuss explosives, and debate
Of bloodshed in the Common Cause.

But I must think, do what I may,
We're wiser here among the furze,
For if mankind is what you say,
Then God is for the grasshoppers![1]

In our society, a 'free market' in so many ways, in which neither radical social conflict nor the more violent outrages of nature are to be found, we find relatively prosaic forms of death liturgies and rites. In death liturgical matters, as in so much else, the citizens of a liberal, pluralistic market economy, free of both the authority of tradition and of the authority of authority, are for the first time in our history free to choose their own modes of dying. Oddly enough, perhaps, they choose a somewhat old address of death, updated in keeping with the general rational optimism of capitalist culture.

I am interested in the ways in which certain ideas about the afterlife, of judgment and salvation, of the meaning of death, have been made 'matter of fact' in the day-to-day lives of ordinary people, and in the way in which such matter-of-fact solutions have been used, by such ordinary people at ordinary times and by ordinary people at extraordinary times such as war (see the articles on war remembrance in this volume). It has to be said that our own funeral liturgies, such as the Anglican Order, as they have been revised seem to me to have lost their way as a ritual system for the celebration of death. The Order itself had moments of considerable callousness; and there is now no follow up to it in the way of repeated rededications at specific times (as in pre-Reformation practices such as the bede-roll or funeral anniversaries), and there is now virtually no formal post-funeral system of mourning. The perfunctory crematorium service ('as moving as a Tesco checkout') is the not illogical end product of this liturgical failure.

I will therefore look at an aspect of death and the afterlife

1. O. Baker, 'Grasshoppers', in B. Lloyd (ed.), *Poems Written during the Great War 1914–1918* (London: George Allen & Unwin, 1918), p. 21.

which seems to me to try to compensate for the evident short-comings of death theology and death liturgies in our own culture. In the common-sense experience of the 'common people' there seems to me to be a version of the medieval idea (rather than the theological *doctrine*) of purgatory, and I see this expressed in the daily Family Announcements (including obituaries) page of the *Evening Chronicle*, a typical British local newspaper,[1] and indeed in pretty well every local newspaper that I have looked at. A rather different, but clearly related expression of this idea is exemplified in the thousands of war memorials created in villages and towns of Britain by or in response to pressure from ordinary people (for which see the articles on war remembrance in this volume).

I am not centrally interested in the idea of purgatory as part of systematic theology—as it is analysed in Le Goff's fascinating book—but in its utilization in powerfully underpinning death rituals by providing for, indeed insisting upon, building death and the remembrance of the dead into the very foundation of society, as the vital, transcendent continuance of relationships, a celebration of common humanity, the fundamental social contract between the living and the dead.

The Anglican 'settlement' of the Reformation arguments—arguments which were more about death than anything else—included a dismissal of the doctrine of purgatory as a Romish doctrine, a 'fond thing vainly invented',[2] and it has always been too closely associated with corrupt activities such as the sale of indulgences to be unembarrassedly proclaimed by the post-Reformation Catholic church—Vatican 2, for example, barely mentions it. Yet the idea of purgatory has three main advantages which make it a vernacular favourite.

First, it avoids and rejects the dread notion, most bleakly presented by Calvin, of being *predestined* to be either a saint or a sinner, fixed in those categories by God, out of human time and therefore beyond human control. As I have already indicated, most people sensibly regard themselves as being

---

1.   The *Evening Chronicle* is the daily afternoon paper on Tyneside.
2.   Article XII of the Anglican Articles of Faith, in *The Book of Common Prayer*.

neither saints nor sinners but mixtures of both, the mixture varying from time to time for reasons over which we have little control. Those of the dead who become saints are as alien to the living as are those of the dead who become sinners. Purgatory is an egalitarian idea.

Secondly, implicit in the idea of purgatory is the notion that the people of this world retain an intercessionary interest and competence in the next world. Thirdly, the people in purgatory (and not just the saints in heaven) retain an interest in and intercessionary competence for the people of this world, and as people rather than saints they are rather more approachable.

These three premises reinforce and reinvigorate the absolute experiential predication of community life, that is, the inter-dependence of the living and the dead; again, Calvinistic ideas of predestination and of mutually exclusive categories of saints and sinners totally destroy this community. So strong is the practicality of this vernacular version of purgatory that it could and perhaps should be claimed that everyone believes in purgatory and no one believes in heaven or hell, because we do not really believe ourselves to be either saints or sinners, preferring to see ourselves as now and then saintlike, now and then sinful. In medieval theology, of course, purgatory was depicted as terrible enough in its own right—but it seems clear that the church authorities did this in order to counter its inherent practical utility and popularity.

The obituary page of the *Evening Chronicle* demonstrates this; it is noteworthy that most local newspapers have such a page, where one can find a kind of populist, latter-day mass media chantry. The page is written primarily by the relatives and loved ones of the deceased, although many local newspapers maintain a set of poetic 'modules' which can be personalized. The fact that it is chosen 'in the market' is as salient as what is actually said; there is no priesthood in the *Evening Chronicle* obituary page. This means, of course, that the living can avoid such obstructionism as that encountered by a Chopwell family whose memorial poem, written by three young daughters of a dead mother, was rejected as unacceptable for the headstone by the Durham Diocesan Office because it was 'unchristian'.[1] It also means that the family (it is usually the family) can avoid the ministrations of bureaucrats, who in Gateshead for example were planning to restrict the use and display period of memorial plaques at the local crematoria.[2]

Every day many ordinary people write in to greet their dead and, by doing so in a *public* place, a newspaper, they advertise the fact to their dead that they are doing so—and they tell the living what they are doing. They are talking to the dead in the face of the living.

The notices are short; like the inscriptions on war graves they have to be paid for by the word and line, and like all such lapidary texts they are terse but not, in these cases, epigrammatic. They are often in poetic form, or at least in blank verse; that is, they aspire to something other than mere day-to-day utilitarian conversation. They express, and advertise, the particular, personal virtues of the dead; they often insist ('never forgotten', 'always in our minds') that the dead are not dead, and they not infrequently invoke the range of kinship to which the remembered person is (not *was*) related. These are not the formal encomia which we find in, say, the obituary columns of the *Times*, but are essentially conversations with the dead.

There are often references to heaven but never a mention of hell. Most people are virtuous, but seldom saints or sinners, just human beings, remembered as if in life, and mostly for their good points, by people whose evident sorrow at their death is in itself an intercessionary mediation. The style of these obituaries is conversational; they presuppose the reality of dialogue between the living and the dead, and they expect the dead to be conscious of the continuing complexities of family and communal relations in this life. They assert the continuing vitality of those relationships:

> The passage of time does not diminish the love and affection which you bestowed upon us all. A devoted husband and father... Dad, you might be gone in body but in spirit you are always with us (4.1.1993).

1.   The Newcastle *Evening Chronicle*, 10.12.1992.
2.   The Newcastle *Journal*, 29.3.1993.

The *Chronicle* letters ask the dead to be active in responding to the expressions of memory and love:

> We loved you so much Colin,
> why did you have to go? (4.1.1993)

and at times they treat the dead as still relevant to the living:

> The brightest star in the sky tonight is our grandad saying goodnight, from grandsons (5.12.1992).

God is asked, in a firm and familiar way, for particular care:

> Wrap your arms around her Lord and give her the special care, to make up for her suffering and all that was unfair (5.12.1992).

The writers express and seek love and unity:

> A quiet thought, a silent tear keeps you close Brian, and oh so near. You won't come back, I know it's true, but in God's own time I will come to you. Sadly loved and missed, Mum and Dad, Mandy, Thomas, Allan, Eileen, John and Families (5.12.1992).

> Those special years will not return when we were together but with love in our hearts you will walk with us for ever (7.12.1992).

God is treated as friendly and available—see the above request to him to compensate for the sorrows of the deceased's life on this earth—and is occasionally rebuked:

> One year ago today my life was torn apart, God took from me my darling son and nearly broke my heart (12.12.1992)

In another approach to God, he is asked

> To pick a bunch of roses and place them in her loving arms and tell her they're from us (12.12.1992).

The power of the relationship between the living and the dead is occasionally shown in words that God would no doubt understand:

> Since you left me, home has never been the same, all the world would be like Heaven, just to have you back again (12.12.1992).

Time and time again, the writers spell out their highly particular, familiar and familial relationships with their dead interlocutor in a way which retains the centrality of the ties between the living and the dead:

> We miss your smile,
> your face, your touch, we miss your love so much. We shared so much together, laughter, joy and tears, for us who loved you dearly, But they are very special years. To have you for my dad was the greatest gift of all (12.12.1991).

Better theologians than I am could no doubt claim that these letters are rooted in a view of the afterlife which is more heavenly than purgatorial, and there is some truth in this; but then there always was a dispute as to whether the medieval purgatory was an antechamber of heaven or a gateway to hell, with popular pressure always pushing in the direction of heaven. Purgatory gives space for the continuance of relationships between living and dead human beings, *qua* human beings, whereas God and the Devil filled up all the space in the other two sections of the afterlife. Purgatory alone creates the possibility of meaningful conversations about important matters between the living and the dead. It also makes sense, as I have already said, of the commonplace idea that we are all mixtures of sinfulness and saintliness, and that if judgment, even the Final Judgment, has to be made, then it should err on the side of fairness by keeping the options open—open, that is, to a continuance of forms of association and amity between the living and the dead, the very basis of community life.

One local evening newspaper is perhaps a rather parochial note on which to end a general discussion of death theology! However, the sentiments expressed in the *Evening Chronicle*'s In Memoriam pages are to be found in much of this century's re-writing of funeral liturgy and in results from many wider social surveys indicating how increasingly dismissive ordinary people are of the kinds of theologies and philosophies in which death, power, judgment and hell are all run together as one set of dreadfulness. The purgatorial view of death begins to move away from the meagre and death-diminishing punitive liturgies of most official theologies, and begins to re-create a proper sense of the nature of death as a benign, common and necessary sacrifice made by our ancestors so that we—who will in turn become ancestors—can live in cheerful and respectful harmony with our own being, that is to say in a form of life with an ending which reunites us.

The Living, the Dead and the Ancestors: Time, Life Cycles and the Mortuary Domain in Later European Prehistory

John Chapman

Introduction

If Jon Davies is correct in the calculation of 100 billion dead humans from 10,000 cal BC[1] until this century, it may be estimated that some 1–2 billion of the deceased are the proper concern of prehistorians. Museum curators charged with the storage of cultural property must be greatly relieved that only a tiny fraction of this total of skeletal remains has ever passed into their care. For prehistorians, however, this shortfall poses one of the most intriguing problems of our discipline—namely why so few remain from so many. Attempts to resolve this issue lead directly into debates on archaeological and anthropological theories concerning the mortuary domain—the land of the dead in both literal and metaphorical senses. We shall see that, in this field, it is as hard to explain relatively few presences as to account for almost unquantifiable absences.

In the end, it is the few presences which command more attention. While the sample they comprise is biased, very incomplete and almost certainly unrepresentative, the mortuary record invites varied forms of analysis—biological, demographic, palaeopathological, cultural and social—from many fields. Since the basic dimensions of human existence are time and space, this article will focus directly on the social aspects

1. The abbreviation 'cal BC' refers to calendrical dates before Christ, where 'cal' refers to the calibration of radiocarbon dates necessary for their conversion to historically more accurate dates, and 'BC' is the archaeologically standard term for 'before the Christian Era'.

of time and space. It is curious that, although archaeology is justly proud of its great time-depth (Greene 1983), prehistorians have tended to consider time in the limited, chronometric sense of dating sites, events and artifacts, rather than making an assessment of other aspects of time as the basis for social action. Similarly, until recently, more attention has been paid to geometric or physical aspects of space than to the inter-relations between social action and spatial patterns. These interests have, for the most part, inhibited analysis of power relations in prehistory, especially insofar as they relate to time–space fundamentals. In this essay, an attempt is made to explore the relations between time, exchange and life cycles, on the one hand, and space and arenas of social power on the other. The mortuary domain plays a vital part in this explicitly ideological exploration.

One data-set will be interrogated in search of long-term changes in the form and structure of the mortuary domain. These data derive from Eastern Hungary, where a long-term sequence of tells, barrows and other cemeteries is known from the periods of the Neolithic, Copper Age and Bronze Age. In this regional data-set, contrasts are drawn between the domestic and mortuary domains and the uses to which each is put in the creation and establishment of power relations and in social reproduction—the process of establishing continuity of community groups across individual and generational life cycles. In particular, the concept of the human life cycle is used as a metaphor for understanding temporal and spatial patterning in artifacts, structures and settlements.

The Formation of the Archaeological Mortuary Record

Discovery of burial remains is heavily dependent upon past and current strategies of archaeological investigation. While the size of the context of preservation and its associated features will affect the likelihood of discovery, the geological context of simple buried features may affect their likelihood of being discovered from the air, through differential accessibility to aerial photography (Riley 1987). Intensive systematic field survey is more likely to find remains with which burials are associated than haphazard grab samples across predetermined portions of the landscape. While upstanding monuments may be easily found, flat cemeteries may be harder to discover. No cemeteries coeval with the Bulgarian Copper Age settlement sites known as tells were found until systematic radial trenching outwards from the tells was initiated (Todorova *et al.* 1975). But in addition to planned campaigns, the possibility of finding what was not being looked for can never be discounted (for example, the discovery of that rare site type, a Late Iron Age cremation cemetery in Britain, during work on the Westhampnett Bypass in Hampshire [Fitzpatrick 1992]).

Underlying both the thermodynamic and contextual approaches to archaeological formation processes, however, is a more fundamental question: why did some societies create the conditions for the preservation of the bodies of their dead while other societies clearly did not? Even a cursory examination of the anthropological literature on death and burial will indicate the surprisingly wide range of possibilities for disposal of the remains of the dead (Monty Python were guilty of serious oversimplification when they declared in the undertaker's sketch: 'we can burn her, bury her or dump her' [cited in R. Chapman, Kinnes and Randsborg 1981: 1]).

My starting point is to situate disposal of the dead in the full sequence of mortuary practice (Figure 1). While not all steps in Bartel's iconic model are utilized by every society (Bartel 1982), there is a wide range of opportunities available for making statements about the deceased and their relation to social groups and to particular survivors. Thus, mortuary rites involving tree- or platform-burial can be complex (cf. O'Shea 1981: 41-42) but the mode of disposal of the corpse ensures non-incorporation into the archaeological record. By contrast, non-permanent mortuary rites of comparable elaboration are known to precede and surround the burial of individuals whose remains are ensured survival, albeit in a simple, unfurnished grave (Trinkhaus 1984). Thus elaboration of mortuary non-burial rites does not necessarily constitute an alternative to preservation of bodily remains.

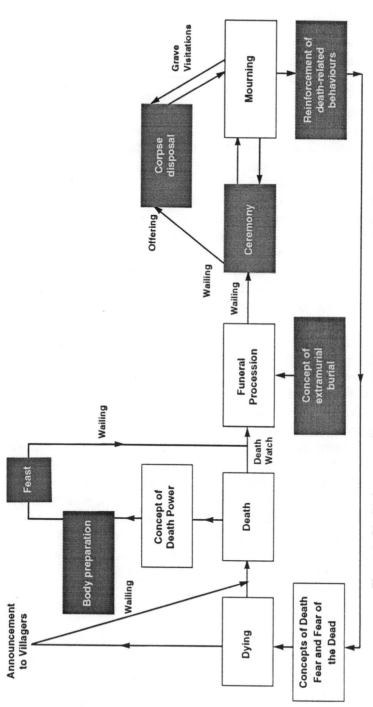

Figure 1. *Idealized sequence of mortuary behaviour (after Bartel 1982, with modifications). Shaded boxes indicate areas of potential archaeological visibility.*

Any attempt to answer such a large question as why only some societies were concerned with the preservation of the dead requires cultural and historical grounding, especially in view of the likelihood of widespread variations in palaeo-eschatology, or the prehistoric concepts of the afterlife (cf. Graslund 1993). If we accept that death creates an opportunity for the re-negotiation of the social reproduction of the group by making statements about its cultural core and most significant relationships, a close relationship would be expected between attitudes to the individual, the mode of social reproduction and the form of mortuary rites, including the preservation of remains. In those communities with a concept of the individual as distinct from society, deaths are more likely to be memorialized and the achievements of individuals commemorated; by contrast, in societies where individuals *qua* individuals are not so significant, the dead tend to pass into a generalized dreamworld, where personal memorials are unnecessary. It is also important to note that, in his study of four immediate-return hunter-gatherer groups, Woodburn (1982) found little elaboration of death ritual where social adjustments involved no reallocation of authority nor of assets but were focused on personal feelings. Glazier's (1984) study of the changing mortuary practices of the Mbeere of Kenya supports Woodburn's assertion; attempted government rural land reform through the provision of land title to individuals led the Mbeere to use burials of the newly-dead in support of land claims rather than continuing their traditional, impermanent disposal of the dead in the wilderness, which they had followed when they were mobile shifting cultivators with communal land-holding. There would appear to be a relationship between the use of permanent burials and land tenure (while groups without tenurial or other claims over assets may not incorporate physical remains into their landscapes), as well as a relationship between attitudes to the body and the way it is disposed of.

This notion is supported by Criado Boado's (1989) study of the ideology of foragers and farmers, in which he proposes that the world-view of the former relies on the denial of the new dead through the absence of formal burial, in an attempt to portray a timeless world in which the living maintain significant relations only with the ancestors. By contrast, farmers are vitally concerned with kinship reckoning and time, so their burial rites are dominated by classifications concerned with the new dead (Criado Boado 1989).

However, any suspicion that subsistence practices and land tenure would have a strong influence on disposal of the dead must take into account the archaeological evidence for the burial of only a small percentage of the total population in complex foraging groups or farming societies, whether in southern Britain (Atkinson 1968), the Balkans (Chapman 1983) or the Netherlands (van der Velde 1979). The first inference is that, while an ancestral presence in the landscape is important to many communities, a minority of ancestors would be able to stand for, or symbolize, communal relationships with their land. The second is that incorporation of any individual into a context of preservation signifies the special status of that individual ancestor-in-transit. Permanent retention of only a selection of the bones of the newly-dead is a common feature in megalithic burial in Britain (Shanks and Tilley 1982).

A further general observation concerns the availability of alternative arenas for communication of messages which may be delivered through mortuary ritual and permanent burial. Goldstein's (1981) reworking of Saxe's (1970) Hypothesis #8 concerning the relationship between bounded mortuary areas (cemeteries), descent groups and scarce resources indicated that the formation of cemeteries was but one pathway to the symbolization of corporate group formation; others include the creation of settlement enclosures and the increased emphasis on ceramic decoration exclusive to the group.

Cannon (1989) has advanced a persuasive case for a cyclical movement between increasingly elaborate expressive displays in competitive mortuary strategies and restrained displays in which status is achieved through moderation and understatement of funerary rite. In response, Bradley (1989a) proposed that restraint in the mortuary sphere may be part of a wider cultural strategy in which competitive consumption is transferred to other social arenas (for example, hoarding, votive deposition [Bradley 1990]). Furthermore, Rothschild (1989) speculates that mortuary behaviour may be visible in the archaeological record only in cases of a sustained cycle of expressive elaboration. These notions imply the existence of several alternative pathways to competitive elaboration, only one of which may create permanent mortuary remains in the archaeological record. While preference for non-mortuary expressive displays can explain why burials may not be common in such periods, this does not explain the reasons for such a choice. Is there something quite specific about bodily remains which may provide further clues?

The bodies and the bones of the deceased are widely believed to be a special resource, which can symbolize many fundamental aspects of a society's belief system. Howell (1989) directs our thinking with her insight that, in our notion of indigenous society, we must include the dead, the ancestors and the supernatural beings along with the living. This can be exemplified in Strathern's (1980) recognition that, once the occasion of death had been used to redefine social relations amongst the Melpa of highland New Guinea, future exchange relations included not only the paternal and maternal kin of the deceased but also the spirits of the dead and their living kin. In one of his recent studies of the Merina of Madagascar Bloch characterizes the principle of descent as 'the merging of living, dead and ancestral land in order to produce an enduring, ideally eternal entity' (1985: 640). In an attempt to overcome the problem of individual death, the Merina symbolize group immortality by the construction of monumental tombs for the ancestors, who fertilize the land for the growing of rice. One of the most specific and intensive uses to which the bones of the newly-dead are put is seen in the Bimin-Kuskusmin of Papua New Guinea, whose life cycle rituals all focus on the relation between bone and spirit and who have developed a lengthy sequence of bone-centered mortuary rituals culminating in ritual empowerment of all surviving bones (Poole 1984).

Living–ancestor relations are often mediated through the use of human bones, typically after phases of exposure burial, defleshing, disarticulation, sorting and re-storage of the bones. The transformations made of the dead into the ancestors define attitudes to both the pollution brought into a community by the deceased and the purity contained within their physical remains. While final incorporation of human bones into the domestic or the mortuary domain (either household shrines or tombs) signifies the revitalization of that resource often conceived to be essential to the reproduction of the social order, prior exposure burial of dead bodies allows removal of those polluting constituents which may be of potential hazard to the living. Hence, a general proposal which may explain why human remains find permanent burial places is the cultural centrality which human bones symbolize at times of death, both in terms of their representation of individual personalities and the essence that they contain.

In this section, I have attempted to characterize some of the main reasons why human skeletal remains, whether complete or partial, have survived to be incorporated into the archaeological record. Although matters of environmental degradation and strategies of archaeological research are important, the critical underlying question was found to be why such contexts of preservation were created or were never created in the first place. The attitude to the person as distinct from the community was found to be an important first difference. Questions of flexible resource reallocation at death were also found to be important for immediate-return hunter-gatherers, while land tenure was found to influence the location of some permanent burials.

The principle of the few symbolizing the many could very probably explain the small fraction of burials selected from complex foraging and early farming groups. However, the main reason advanced for the creation of permanent burial facilities concerns the cultural centrality of the physical remains of the dead, in terms of their representation of individuals and the socially vital essences of reproduction which they contain. Here I would stress that a Cartesian dualism of mind–body and materialism–idealism is not helpful for the understanding of ancestors, the dead and the living. We now need to set the living and the ancestors in a broader context of time and place before we can consider the mortuary record in eastern Europe.

A Brief Prehistory of Time

The key question in the agenda of social time has been raised
by Berger (1984: 9-10) in his philosophical exploration of time
and space. He contends that humans constitute two events, the
event of the biological organism and the event of consciousness,
and that these two times coexist. The first time understands
itself, as do animals, while the second time, that of human
consciousness, understands itself in different ways. Therefore
the first task of any culture is to propose an understanding of
the time of its consciousness, of the relations between past,
present and future. The notion that time is socially constituted
and multifacetted provides us with a starting point for our
discussion. For it means that there is no justification for an
automatic mapping onto the prehistoric past of the characteristically nineteenth-century concept of time as abstract, uniform, irreversible and unilinear, by which consciousness is,
quite implausibly, treated as an event like any other.

Indigenous concepts of time tend to embody a plurality of
lived experience, an idea with which Einstein would have been
quite at home. Just as individuals experience time as faster or
slower depending on the intensity of the activity in question,
different rhythms of time are thought appropriate to various
activities, different ages and genders and contrasting status
positions. It is not uncommon to find different concepts of time
applied to short-term actions and long-term processes within
the same community. Within this phenomenological jungle,
there are common themes of the overarching nature(s) of time.
Insofar as each theme has its own local rules of meaning, its
structure and its dynamics, time can be seen as a cause of social
behaviour, not just one of its emergent properties (Hazan 1984).

There are three common ways of conceptualizing time in
indigenous groups: alternating, cyclical and linear. Edmund
Leach advances the case for the primacy of the alternating
concept in the sense that, while the other two notions are
founded on an abstract, geometric idea (line, circle), series of
alternating states—night and day, winter and summer—are
fundamental to human experience (Leach 1961: 126, 132-34). He

goes on to propose alternating states of sacred time and profane time in which secular life is created by establishing intervals (often sacred intervals) in social time.

While it is readily appreciated that such a binary view of time would find favour with a structuralist theoretician, we should recall that extra terms are often inserted into binary oppositions; so it is with human lives, for example age-grade systems (Bernardi 1985), the division of the day into many phases and the Lapps' division of the year into eight seasons. A combination of several alternating states can, in another time perspective, become a cycle of events, especially if the intervals are marked by different ceremonies (for another critique of Leach 1961, see Layton 1989). However, the two concepts can be combined, as in the Avatik village on the Sepik river in Papua New Guinea, where the villagers' concept of time is a succession of repeated alternations (oppositions) between an annual cycle and a generation cycle (annual: yam cultivation, age-grades and the displacement of elder by younger brothers; generational: male cults, initiation grades and the replacement of fathers by sons [Harrison 1982–83]).

While the Cartesian concept of unilinear time is not necessarily appropriate to the study of past social time, the concept is valuable in its recognition of that basic property of time, its irreversibility. This is particularly true during periods of intense social change, as Riesman's variant on Heraclitus reminds us: 'one can never step into the same culture twice' (Riesman 1986: 106). Nevertheless, irreversible time makes people face the reality of death, loss and bereavement so directly that a cyclical concept of short-term time is often adopted. Thus, among the Nuer, ecological time is perceived as cyclical, structural time as progressive (linear) and both times are in phase with each other, moving to the same *tempo* (Evans-Pritchard 1940).

We have seen that each of the three indigenous concepts of time can be used independently or in combination. However, since the cyclical concept can be adapted for a greater variety of time durations and a wider range of successions of events, I shall investigate this notion further, using the life cycle as a metaphor for other cyclical behaviour. At this juncture, I shall make a preliminary partition between the cycles of individuals and social groups, on the one hand, and the cycles of material remains on the other. The interconnections between the two kinds of evidence necessarily raise the most interesting questions, for it is these cycles that intersect and cross-cut, framing the quotidian, Bourdieu's (1977) *habitus*—the everyday basis for social reproduction.

I have already indicated that the notion of an individual's life cycle is problematic to the extent that reincorporation of the deceased individual's bones maintains their presence among the living and the life of the deceased's spirit continues in the spirit world. Nevertheless, the basic notions of birth, maturity, ageing and death point to a process of biological 'expansion' and 'contraction' in terms of faculties and capacities. An obvious social parallel to the personal life cycle is that of the household cycle, a notion theorized by Chayanov (1966) and Fortes (1949), refined by Sahlins (1972) and developed by some archaeologists in the 1980s and 1990s (Wilk and Rathje 1982; Samson 1990; Tringham and Krstić 1991). Fortes identified the household as the nodal mechanism for social reproduction in many agrarian communities, arguing that reproduction of the public domain was critically dependent on the developmental cycle of domestic groups (Fortes 1949). However, Mosko (1989) has criticized Fortes for ignoring the equal significance of contraction, dispersion and dissolution in households in favour of expansion and extension in group reproduction (for other critiques of Fortes, see Bohannan 1958 and Worsley 1956). Mosko also theorizes the existence of developmental cycles among public groups which run parallel to, and interact with, domestic groups. For the public groups, the nodal mechanism of social reproduction is mortuary ritual and exchange. This operates in two ways: (1) although involving a small segment of the social whole, mortuary ritual and exchange stimulate the configuration of the entire sphere of public relations, and (2) despite representing a small portion of the individuals in a community, they activate the whole group (Mosko 1989). In this context, it is important to underline Mauss's (1974) insight that the person, the group and time itself emerge in part as the products of a system of exchange (cf. also

Lambek 1990). Exchange relations cannot be ignored in the exploration of the constitution of the social self through time.

Hence, alongside the individual life cycle we can set two social cycles, the household and the public (Table 1), whose various expansions and contractions are directly related to social reproduction through the media of exchange and mortuary ritual. It is an empirical task to discover whether it is the household or the public groups which play a more significant role in the social reproduction of specific communities.

Individuals	Birth	Life	Death
Artifacts	Manufacture	Use	Deposition
			Accidental loss
			Destruction
Houses (annual)	Construction	Occupation	Abandonment
			Destruction
Houses (daily)	Waking	Going out to work	Evening return
Sites	Construction Reoccupation	Occupation	Abandonment
Monuments	Creation	Use	Destruction
			Survival

Table 1. *The metaphor of the life cycle*

Just as we can define biographies of people and households, it is possible to characterize artifacts, sites and monuments in terms of their respective biographies. Not only do artifacts have their own material cycle of manufacture, use and disuse (Table 1) but they also bear qualities of their past history and associations with previous owners. It is their biography which allows some objects to be inalienable and some to be commoditized (Kopytoff 1986). Howell (1989) reminds us of one of Mauss's neglected suggestions, that in total prestations between clan and clan, things are related in some degree as persons and persons in some degree as things. An example of this notion is the Maori belief that, because of their antiquity and history, valuables form a focus of ancestral power and link people to their own past (Howell 1989: 420). Thus not only can the value of artifacts be characterized in terms of raw material, craft and rarity but also in terms of their past biography. The meanings of past contexts can be brought into the present (in Ray's

[1987] term, 'presencing'), just as Gothic brooches bore the associations of a Roman imperial past into the early medieval period (Greene 1987). Both Bradley (1990) and Rowlands (1993) have noted that things may be considered to have lives and essences and can be 'killed' as easily as humans, or instead of them, through special deposition. The deposition of grave goods is, of course, an act of death for the artifact as much as for the deceased.

The life cycle of structures which archaeologists interpret as 'houses' may be divided into a daily and a whole-life cycle. The house as home implies an ontological grounding; for Eliade (1960), the home is a place from which the world was founded, the centre of the world, the untold story of a life being lived. In his discussion of the living house, Bailey (1990) takes up the theme of the multidimensionality of houses, stressing the varied perceptions of residents, kin and strangers to the wide range of meanings contained in the house. As a centre for production, reproduction and consumption, whether social or physical, the house is an active component in the construction of social reality. Like the artifact, the house has its own biography: construction, use and disuse in the long term, inhabitants' waking up, working there or going out to work, and returning to eat and sleep on a diurnal scale (Bailey 1990); the residents all provide their particular associations to the house, whether in the form of internal fittings and decorations or in the manner of the spatial ordering of the household. The frequent comparison between houses and tombs, the latter being seen as houses for the dead, reinforces the biographical symbolism of the living house; the architecture here mediates between the living and the dead as liminal zone.

Finally, sites and monuments may be compared in terms of their respective biographies. While sites and monuments share a basic cyclical biography of creation, use and disuse (Table 1), the prominence of monuments in the landscape provides a stronger link to the ancestral world than do the often insignificant remains of previously occupied flat sites. Nevertheless, the frequency of reoccupation of some flat sites in areas such as Eastern Hungary (see below) may be related as much to cultural memory and accumulated place-value as to maximization of local ecological potential. The longer a site or monument is occupied, the stronger the place-values which attach to that place. However, the reoccupation of sites and monuments can bridge the gap since their last occupation or use by a process analagous to presencing; there is much ideological significance in assuming the role of descendants to an unrelated group's ancestors, thereby legitimating the 'new' foundation. Thus old sites can return to life, rather like the ancestral spirits of the deceased, to restart the cycle of occupation, disuse and reoccupation, in a way that should be related to the larger pattern of social reproduction at group level.

We have seen how the metaphor of the life cycle can without excessive distortion be applied to social groups, artifacts, sites and monuments. But before attempting to paint life cycles onto too broad an archaeological canvas, we should heed Barrett's words of caution: 'these cycles are not explanations of the past but unintended outcomes of routine practices of people who could have acted otherwise' (1990: 187). In the prehistory of routine practices, we have now considered only one of the two essential dimensions of social life. It is time to turn to questions of space, place and arenas of social power.

Space, Place and Arenas of Social Power

The process of social colonization of an unknown landscape has been summarized as the movement from space to place, in which a neutral, value-free, meaningless physical space takes on properties of meaning and value from those who colonize it (Chapman 1988). The creation of place led to the formation of those special areas termed settlements, the appearance of which attests to the emergence of a place-based world-view. The appearance of settlements, especially those with upstanding remains ('monuments'), gives rise to the idea of place-value, or the nexus of stored meaning of past activities and traditional usage associated with a significant place. This idea can be more generally expressed in terms of the history of a settlement and its occupants as stored in collective memory—a site's 'biography'. These notions which link time and place are basic to the development of a socially meaningful landscape.

An integral part of this process of spatial differentiation in the landscape is the matching of place-based activities with those people and groups who are empowered to be in the places that matter, to carry out significant activities and organize the participation of others not so empowered. This process begins from Foucault's (1984) idea that the control of space lies at the heart of social power. Since most of the social groups under study are small-scale communities with restricted hierarchical differentiation, networks of social power are most readily related to the social space which they have created. Individuals take the inherently risky step of creating and maintaining social power through their propensities to take action on their own behalf or on behalf of the group. Social activity *per se* produces power reflexively, just as power provides the opportunities for further action. The more varied, differentiated or specialized the activity or the place where it occurs, the greater the potential social power accruing to the individual concerned.

The term 'arena of social power' has been coined to identify those places where ideological, economic, military and political power (Mann 1986) can be spatially identified. Arenas of social power mark a conjunction of a specific place, with its functions and meanings, and the social actors who have the power (including knowledge) to perform the activities in that place. The reasons for the creation of a new arena of social power are often related to the development of contradictions in the social order, where new developments are incompatible with the traditional social structure. Thus, household or individual wealth accumulation may be impossible within the social framework of communal ownership of land and herds, yet opportunities may arise for private accumulation based on either exchange or local production. Alternatively, major changes in gender relations may lead to the elaboration of new arenas where the social power of one gender may be reinforced at the expense of the other. Yet again, the colonization of new landscapes may lead to the creation of new arenas which legitimize the social claims of leaders to the newly settled land. Hence, the identification of new arenas of social power is always a sign of fundamental social change which *requires* explanation in terms of the local landscape and the regional setting (Chapman 1991b, 1992).

Now that I have proposed a framework for the social reproduction of small-scale communities in which mortuary ritual, exchange, place, time and social power play their role, it is time to examine these ideas in the specific archaeological context of the mature farming groups in eastern Hungary. Particular attention will be paid to the existence of cyclical patterning and coincidences of different cycles, the uses which coeval communities make of the mortuary domain and the formation of arenas of social power in the landscape.

Tells, Barrows and Cemeteries in the Great Hungarian Plain

The settlement record for later prehistory in Central Europe is dominated by two classes of sites: flat sites, where one or several phases of occupation are found over an often large area, and tells, where occupation is restricted to a small area and develops vertically (Chapman 1989).

In contrast to Bulgaria, where tells are not the only site type but are certainly the dominant one throughout the Neolithic and Copper Age, settlement on the plains of eastern Hungary is mixed (Map 1). Tells were a relatively rare settlement type in the lowlands of eastern Hungary in the three millennia after the introduction of farming. An alternative settlement mode is based on long-term but not necessarily continuous occupation of valley segments but with frequent settlement shifts within preferred zones. On many of the sites, repeated occupation for up to six, seven and even eight phases is typical. In the Ko. Békés II survey region (Jankovich, Makkay and Szőke 1989), over 80% of all prehistoric sites were found in less than 20% of the region, with strong local settlement concentrations, termed site clusters (Chapman 1981).

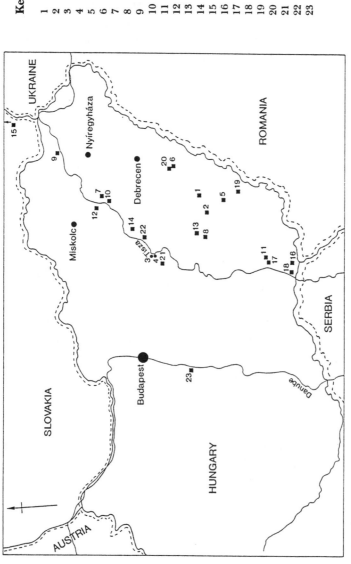

Map 1. *Location map of main sites mentioned in the text*

Only in the Late Middle–Late Neolithic (Raczky 1987) and the Early–Middle Bronze Age (Meier-Arendt 1992) were tells constructed in the Alföld plain and then only within the confines of these long-term site clusters.

Tell villages in these periods are distinguished from other, neighbouring flat sites by remarkable residential continuity. Once village houses became disused, they were reconstructed in more or less the same place. Since the fired clay rubble of the previous houses was often levelled before new building, the surface level of the settlements tended to rise, producing a distinctive mound shape (Figure 2) which is known by the Arabic term 'tell' (Mellaart 1975). The primary characteristic of the tell is that it represents the creation of an orderly category of living space. Since occupations are constructed directly over previous living surfaces, the tell is literally a power-full ancestral space, in which communities live where their ancestors had once lived. The tell is therefore a social landmark with a cumulative place-value achieved through long-term community participation, a habitus of stability and an active contribution to social identity. In descent-based groups where relations with the ancestors are critical for social reproduction, tells would have acted as a physical and social expression of continuity with the ancestors. In such settlements, it is the elders, with their deeper knowledge of the past and thus of the ancestors, who would have sought to maintain positions of power and authority.

While being central to the community's strategy for maintaining direct relations with the ancestors, the tell would also have been actively used for creating and maintaining social space for the living. The traditions of ancestral space were reinforced by tightly controlled principles of planning and architecture, both at settlement and household level. Neolithic tells are defined by a relatively high ratio of built to unbuilt space, rarely exceeding 1:2 (regarding built to unbuilt space ratios, see Chapman 1989: 35 and Table 1). This limits the possibilities for outdoor on-site action: activities such as outdoor ritual, dancing, group meetings, pyrotechnology, horticulture and animal keeping. The layout of the houses is generally regular, with structures separated from each other by narrow

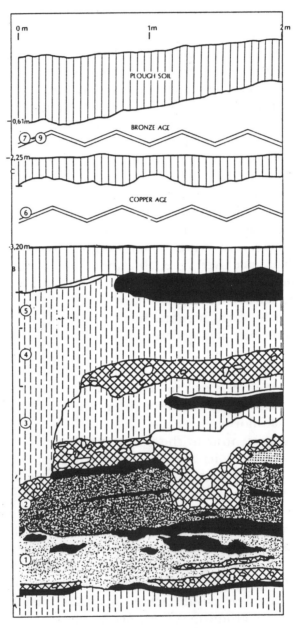

Figure 2. *Main profile of Vésztő-mágori halom*
(Hegedűs and Makkay 1987: Abb. 2).

lanes and often laid out on the same or similar orientation (for example, Herpály level 8: Kalicz and Raczky 1987b). The main visual foci are the houses themselves. The rooms, one, two or three of them, are rectangular, and of strikingly similar layout. The continual rebuilding of tell layers gives rise to the concept of cyclical, or reversible, time, in which both houses and the whole settlement are periodically rebuilt, renewed with the fertile earth of the land.

The other monument class found in the Alföld plain is the mortuary barrow (Ecsedy 1979), whose distribution rarely matches that of the site clusters. These barrows, often known by the Russian term *kurgan*, are composed of turf and fertile black earth and can reach diameters of 70 metres. The common feature of both tells and barrows is height above a lowland expanse whose modern flat relief conceals considerable ecological variability in the Middle Holocene. The dominant relief of tells and barrows, matched by their similar appearances, reinforces their significance as key places of social value in the landscape.

Now that the main site types have been outlined, let us turn to the settlement sequence to understand the dynamics of the region.

Early Neolithic (5800–5000 cal BC)

Small open settlements both near and set back from the main watercourses are characteristic for the first farmers; the sites showed frequent lateral relocation over areas up to 2 km long (for example Dévaványa-Katonaföldek: Ecsedy 1972). Total excavation of a satellite Körös culture site (Endröd 119: Makkay 1992; Bökönyi [ed.] 1992) indicated two houses each occupied over some 50 years, with nine intramural burials. A broad-spectrum economy with hunting, fishing and fowling as important as cereal cultivation or stockrearing suggests that the Körös culture may be rooted in the local forager population (Chapman in press). Although few Körös houses have been identified until recently, the domestic arena of social power is dominant in these settlements.

Four forms of mortuary practices may be defined for the Körös group: skull burial, inhumation of disarticulated and partial skeletons, inhumation of articulated complete skeletons and, rarely, cremation of partial bodies (Chapman 1983). Most inhumations are deposited within the settlement, in pits or on unoccupied parts of the site, so as to include some of the ancestors into the local settlement context of the living. However, burials inside the house have also been identified as a significant rite at two Körös sites: Szajol-Felsőföldek and Szolnok-Szanda-Tenyősziget (Raczky 1982–83). The excavator commented that the interior fittings and contents of the houses had been left intact as funerary offerings (for example, figurines, pottery, stone and bone tools). Here we have an instance in the Great Hungarian plain of the deliberate 'killing' of houses by fire in the same act as the final burial of the deceased. The intersection of the end of the life cycle of social actors, material culture and houses is deeply significant for the reconstitution of the social world of Körös settlements, marking either the death of a significant individual or a reordering of the whole community or both. In the Körös case, death is so absolutely polluting that all associations with the newly-dead must be destroyed before the re-emergence of the community becomes possible. This attitude to death may well be the cause of short-distance relocation of Körös sites, since social reproduction was not possible on sites polluted by recent deaths (M. Rowlands, pers. comm.). Since the transformation of the deceased into the ancestor takes place wholly within the settlement, the subsequent reincorporation of the ancestors into the social life that continues on an adjoining site is tightly structured to provide continuity between living, dead and ancestors.

Middle Neolithic (5000–4600 cal BC)
In the subsequent phase of Middle Neolithic settlement on the Alföld plain, a larger number of usually smaller sites is followed by the onset of settlement nucleation (Kalicz and Makkay 1977; Makkay 1982). Part of this nucleation concerns the creation of the first tells, which can with certainty be dated to the later, or Szakalhát, phase of the Middle Neolithic, from c. 4800 cal BC. The Vésztő mound was at least 1 m high by the end of the Szakalhát phase (Hegedűs and Makkay 1987).

The mortuary evidence from the Middle Neolithic shows continuity from the Körös period, with intramural burial of skulls, disarticulated partial and articulated complete skeletons (Chapman 1983). One burial is known from the Szakalhát levels on the Vésztő tell (Hegedűs and Makkay 1987: 91). The Vésztő burial is important in showing the typical path of future intramural tell burials—articulated but not buried in a burnt house. Thus the domestic arena maintains its ancestor focus, both on flat sites and on tells. However, the Hungarian tell burials comprise complete articulated individuals; it would seem that death has become less polluting in the Middle Neolithic, perhaps through the introduction of social bound-edness designed to contain and limit the dangers from death to the community. Since the ancestral traditions so distinctive of tells have hardly developed strongly yet in eastern Hungary, alternative modes of ancestral relations relating to mortuary ritual may have been more important.

Late Neolithic Tells (4600–4100 cal BC)

The first flowering of the tell tradition in Hungary dates to the Late Neolithic, c. 4500–3900 cal BC. Even then, fewer than 20 tells and tell-like sites are known from eastern Hungary, their number being exceeded by sometimes larger flat sites (Kalicz and Raczky 1987a). The height of the tells at 3–4 m indicates intensive building and rebuilding, with rubble from earlier houses flattened and reincorporated into new houses, a parallel strategy to incorporation of ancestors. The houses on the Hungarian tells are closely spaced, with a built-to-unbuilt ratio of around 2.3:1 for level 8 at Herpály (Figure 3: see also Chapman 1989: Table 1). The contents of tell houses are extremely rich in pottery, figurines and other ritual parapher-nalia. The houses are well-built, comfortable, full of life, fertility, possessions and furniture and fittings (for a full description, see Raczky 1987). There is little doubt that the domestic arena of social power is dominant on Hungarian tells. The question of hierarchical relations between tells and flat sites is still debated (Kalicz and Raczky 1987a); some smaller flat sites near tells may be satellite sites (for example, Szarvas 56:

Jankovich, Makkay and Szőke 1989: 423) but other, larger open sites (for example, Sárazsádany) appear to be distinct entities.

Figure 3. *Balloon photograph of Houses 5, 6, 8, 9 and 10, Level 8, tell Herpály (Kalicz and Raczky 1987b: Fig. 6).*

A frequent event on tells is the destruction of a house or whole group of houses by fire; the stratigraphy of many tells reveals a 'burnt horizon' of burnt clay fused by high-temperature firing. Three explanations of burnt horizons or houses have been advanced: (1) the traditional invasion hypothesis, usually involving long-range north Pontic arsonists (Gimbutas

1978, 1979); (2) accidental fires resulting from cooking, baking or other pyrotechnical activities; and (3) the deliberate destruction by fire of houses to complete the life cycles of the houses and their contents (Raczky 1982–83; cf. for Vinča houses, Tringham and Krstić [eds.] 1991: 584, 588).

The north Pontic invasion model of Kurgan waves can be dismissed summarily, since the radiocarbon dates for the tells are more than a millennium earlier than the earliest dates for the north Pontic barrows. Accidental fires cannot be ruled out, especially not on sites where houses often lie less than 2 m from each other. In the Zürich Lake-Village exhibition of 1990, a fire started by an arsonist in one house spread to the whole village within half an hour (Ruoff 1992), leaving no time to salvage the domestic artifacts. The third hypothesis is the hardest to test, despite the evidence available for deliberate house-burning in the Early Neolithic. The problem is that there is no example of a burial deposited as the penultimate act of the life of a Late Neolithic house. The situation is in fact quite the opposite—all the recently excavated Late Neolithic tells boast numerous burials of partial or complete inhumations, usually of articulated skeletons, on unoccupied parts of the tell but, *without exception*, outside the houses (Raczky 1987). The only example of a burial 'associated' with a house is the coffin burial inserted into the south wall of a shrine from a previous occupation horizon at Vésztő (Hegedűs and Makkay 1987: 96). It is of course still possible to argue for deliberate house destruction at the end of the social cycle of the household. In contrast to the fusion of deceased person and structure in the Hungarian Early Neolithic, the separation of dead human from dead house may represent a distancing of the newly-dead from the household or the distinction between a failed social grouping and a failed architectural structure. The notion that death had less potential for pollution seems to characterize the Late Neolithic, the period *par excellence* of extreme material and ritual boundedness.

The alternative mortuary rituals of on-tell inhumation indicate ancestral continuity in the realm of the living. This is best demonstrated by the preliminary results of serological analysis of the tell burials at Gorzsa, which indicate that the burials comprise the deceased of four successive units of the same genetic unit (Horváth 1987: 45). An innovation for tell burial is the provision of timber coffins for many of the tell burials (Figure 4). It is interesting to note that the proportions of the coffins at Vésztő match those of the shrine building in level 4; the form of the cult building for the living may have been implicated in the passage of the newly-dead to the ancestors. The small groups of burials on the tells represent the first spatial step in the distancing of bodies, if not ancestors, from the houses of the living. But still the ancestral values predominate on the tell and the ancestors are not excluded; rather, the passage from the world of the living to that of the dead is made more secure by the provision of coffins and fine grave goods.

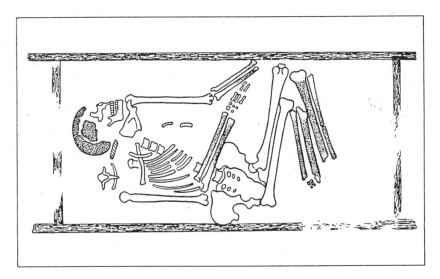

Figure 4. *Coffin burial no. 7, Late Neolithic level of tell Vésztő-mágori halom (Hegedűs and Makkay 1987: Fig. 33)*

In summary, ancestral values continue to dominate the Late Neolithic, not least because of the visual symbolism of the height of the tell in contrast to the flat sites of the other villages and hamlets and the surface of the plain itself. The higher the tell rises from the plain, the deeper the ancestral relations which tell-dwellers can claim, in contradistinction to the occupants of flat sites whose descent group memories are constructed in different and less visually impressive ways. For this reason, social relations between tell communities and those on flat sites may have been mediated primarily through the ancestor cult, privileged access to which was in the hands of the tell ritual specialists. Preliminary data from flat sites suggest that there are fewer burials and fewer objects of ritual paraphernalia there than on tells.

Early Copper Age (4100–3700 cal BC)
The first use of distinct, bounded cemeteries in the prehistory of eastern Hungary is dated to the Copper Age. Because of their small numbers in the Alföld, each Late Neolithic tell assumed a greater place-value, in a wider social setting, than in a landscape full of tells, such as Bulgaria. For this reason, there was a greater likelihood of inter-site tensions between tells and flat sites in a period of wide-ranging exchange networks, with their potential for wealth accumulation. The larger number of flat sites, each at an important node in the exchange network, made it harder for tells to exert the same control over prestige goods that they would inevitably have had in a tell-dominated landscape. Thus, at the time when the first cemeteries appear in the Early Copper Age, in the early fourth millennium cal BC, tell occupation becomes quite rare and the dispersed farmstead constitutes the predominant settlement unit (Bognár-Kutzian 1972; Sherratt 1982b, 1983).

The shift to farmsteads away from tells has three implications for social reproduction: (1) the dominance of the household as the primary economic unit, in contrast to the densely packed overlapping social networks on the tells; (2) the importance of extensive local networks linking perhaps as many as 100 dispersed farmsteads into an exogamous breeding unit; and (3) the predominance of a competitive ideology of prestige goods accumulation over the overtly traditional, egalitarian values of the tell village. Thus it is no surprise to find a wide range of rich grave goods in the inhumation graves of complete, articulated skeletons that characterize the mortuary population of Early Copper Age cemeteries such as Tiszapolgár-Basatanya (Bognár-Kutzian 1963). These cemeteries are often partitioned into lines or rows of graves, which may represent household groups from particular farms. Barrett (1990) has shown the significance of placement for individual burials in barrow cemeteries of the Bronze Age of southern Britain; the Copper Age cemeteries show the emergence of complex cemetery topography without a monumental burial form. The denial of monumentality is perhaps a symbolic distancing from the ancestral tell monuments, standing unoccupied, if not unused, in the landscape.

The Copper Age cemeteries tend to be located some distance not only from tells but also from contemporary farms, giving them a liminal status between the farmland of the living and the world of the ancestors—the locus of transition of states of being. The removal of the newly-dead from direct association with the houses of the ancestors (on the tells) and those of the living (the dispersed farms) suggests a different conception of ancestral landscape, more in harmony with the dispersed social relations of an exogamous network than the place-based values of the tell communities. The spatial linearity of the cemeteries is matched by their linear concept of time, with the once-and-for-all insertion of a sequence of dead bodies until dissolution of the lineage leads to abandonment of the cemetery.

What of those few communities who lived on tells in the Early Copper Age? Although different sequences occur at each excavated site, less intensive occupations occur, with lower densities of artifacts and less solid structures, with more interruptions in the sequence and, consequently, a less active contribution to tell-building. At Herpály, an arrangement of loosely spaced houses in early phase 5 is replaced by an occupation defined only by hearths, both associated with pottery transitional between the Late Neolithic and the Early Copper Age (Raczky 1987: 111). At Gorzsa, a similar assemblage was found mostly in graves on the tell but settlement areas are to be excavated (Horváth 1987: 36-37). The tell at Vésztő was abandoned at the end of the Late Neolithic for several centuries, only to be reoccupied in the Copper Age (Hegedűs and Makkay 1987: 89). At present, it is the only tell with occupation and mortuary remains in the Middle as well as the Early Copper Age. Although the main mortuary rite consisted of inhumation burial in coffins, an exceptional act was the burial of seven children inside the burnt debris of a house (Hegedűs and Makkay 1987: 91). Unfortunately, the excavators do not clarify whether the burials are under the burnt remains (a primary burial inside a house that was subsequently burnt) or in them (a secondary burial, as the beginning of another cycle of life and death on tells). In either case, the Vésztő burial is the sign of a renewed concern for the extended social group and its social reproduction, in contrast to the individual households of the coeval farmsteads.

Middle Copper Age (3700–3200 cal BC)
This continued occupation of tells in the midst of an ideological landscape developed in opposition to tell values indicates a lengthy period of tensions between two incompatible modes of social reproduction and two contrasting conceptions of time and space. In the succeeding Middle Copper Age, tell occupation is even rarer than in the Early Copper Age and flat communal cemeteries continue to receive the newly-dead from surrounding small farmsteads (for example, the cemetery of 54 graves at Tiszavalk-Kenderföld: Patay 1978). Another new feature is the creation of separate ritual enclosures, such as the ring-ditch (or *Rondel*) at Szarvas 38 (Makkay 1980–81); the new possibilities of aerial photography will doubtless transform our knowledge of such cropmark sites. At the same time, wealth indices make a quantum leap upwards, with rich hoards such as the Tiszaszőlős gold treasure (Makkay 1989) and wealthy cemeteries such as Tibava (Šiška 1968). Sherratt (1982a) has documented a shift in settlement concentration to the edge of the plain, so as to control access to important rocks and minerals in the hills north of the plain. The increasing dominance of household units and strategies of prestige goods accumulation ensures that the tell has little place in the more flexible, opportunistic social landscape of this period. In the Early and Middle Copper Age, the mortuary arena of social power has overtaken the domestic arena in importance, not least as the key spatial context for social reproduction.

Late Copper Age (3200–2400 cal BC)

The first half of the late Copper Age is a period of maximum dispersion of settlement into the small farms of the Baden group (Banner 1956), with their small cemeteries distinct from the farms. In the middle phase of the late Copper Age, c. 2800 cal BC, this pattern changes abruptly with the creation of a new monumental burial class, the barrow (or 'kurgan', as in Russian). Most commentators view the kurgan as the outward sign of an invasion or migration of north Pontic nomadic pastoralists into an ecological zone of rich pastureland not dissimilar to their steppic homeland (Ecsedy 1979; Gimbutas 1978, 1979; Sherratt 1982a; Anthony 1990: cf. reply by Chapman and Dolukhanov 1992). The distribution of burial mounds is indeed strikingly broader than the typical site clusters occupied since the start of the Neolithic, dispersed far out into the interfluves (Sherratt 1983: Fig. 16). Ecsedy calculates a total of 3000 barrows in eastern Hungary, found occasionally in twos and threes but mostly in extensive, dispersed barrow cemeteries with hundreds of metres separating pairs of barrows (Ecsedy 1979: 14).

The kurgans cover individual inhumation burials of articulated, complete male skeletons (Figure 5), furnished with a narrow range of specific grave goods (lumps of red ochre, the remains of blankets, caprine astragali, perforated dogs' teeth, rare silver earrings and copper beads). All of these undisputed facts would seem to be sufficient to convince readers that we are in the presence of that rare prehistoric specimen, a well-attested migration.

The alternative view of kurgans is that most of the elements defining the phenomenon have already occurred, singly or jointly, in the earlier Copper Age and that the kurgan 'package' is a strikingly novel arrangement of local forms legitimated by symbolic associations with the past.

We should begin with the kurgan itself, since it is the visual embodiment of the new monumental burial. All archaeologists who have participated in field survey on the Alföld plain will agree that it is very difficult to distinguish visually between a kurgan and a tell. This will have been the case in the Late Copper Age, when the appearance of few tells was emphasized by building houses on the top (for a rare exception, see Gorzsa: Horváth 1987: 33). The visual similarity in size and shape leads one to the hypothesis that kurgans were built to imitate tells or, more accurately, to reincorporate the ancestral place-values of tells and their ancestors into the mortuary domain. The impetus for this imitation was local—those abandoned mounds so rich in oral tradition and folk memory, the locus of the tribal ancestors whose ways were not necessarily followed by the acquisitive Copper Age households. The burial form of the kurgans was also not novel: individual inhumations of complete skeletons were the standard rites for the newly-dead of the earlier Copper Age (Bognár-Kutzian 1963), often oriented west–east (Bognár-Kutzian 1972: 153), although extended inhumations were rare (Tiszapolgár-Basatanya and Srpski Krstur: Bognár-Kutzian 1972: 153).

The grave goods of the barrow graves also find some parallels in earlier Copper Age graves: red ochre at Tibava (Bognár-Kutzian 1972: 155), copper beads at Deszk A and Hódmezővásárhely-Népkert (p. 138), perforated animal teeth at Lebő A (p. 136), while long blades are clearly paralleled at many earlier Copper Age sites. It can thus be demonstrated that many of the elements of the kurgan 'package' were available for combination and recombination in the mortuary arena of the earlier Copper Age of eastern Hungary. It is therefore difficult to test the two opposing hypotheses: whether 'outsiders' moved into the Alföld plain and marked their dominance with monumental barrows, or 'local' elites exploited traditional and well-understood mortuary symbols in order to underscore their success in regional alliance and breeding networks. After all, the more dispersed the farmsteads of this period, the more widespread the requisite breeding network needed to be.

The other aspect of the Late Copper Age is that the decline of the domestic arena coincided with the rise of the monumental mortuary arena. Field survey results are unanimous that settlement debris from this period is closer to invisibility than site sherds from any other period in Hungarian prehistory (Sherratt 1983: 37). The region marked by kurgan burial may be contrasted with other parts of Hungary, where large

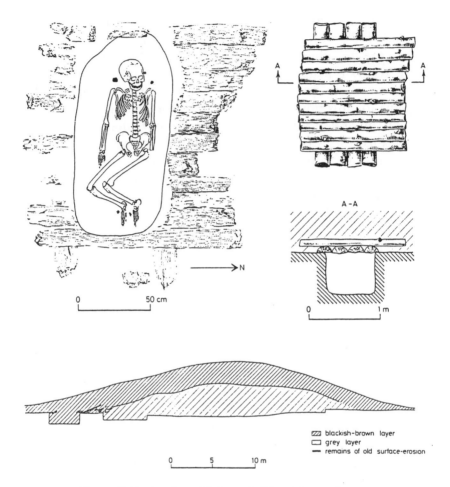

Figure 5. *Section through kurgan 3, Kétegyháza, with plan and section of primary burial (after Ecsedy 1979: Figs. 12 and 13).*

communal cemeteries dominated the mortuary arena (for example, the Baden cemeteries in the Danube Valley: Banner 1956) but, here too, the domestic arena was attenuated. How did these changes affect social reproduction in the kurgan lands?

Barrett has argued persuasively that burial under barrows forms the focal point for the redefinition of genealogical status; only after burial could mourners return to the wider community (Barrett 1990). Certainly he is right to stress that, unlike partial burials after exhumation in the Hungarian Neolithic, barrow burial represented the end of burial rites, whether it concerns a primary or a secondary burial. However, some excavated kurgans reveal successive burials, with the height of the barrow increasing with each burial, after the fashion of the growth of tells (Ecsedy 1979). There is, however, a paradox here: the full, open, public burial rites in front of the grave of a prominent male, set against the concealment of the body so deep in a 'communal' individual monument as to deny his death. Another reading of kurgan burial concerns the reintegration of the body with the earth, so as to produce fertile offspring—a transformation marked by the swelling of the barrow. However, this transformation may also be read as a denial of death, since the proof of this is the fertility of the mound itself (I am indebted to Colm O'Brien for this reading). An alternative is that barrows were conceived of as the primeval land rising out of the waters of Chaos, often literally in the frequently flooded Alföld plain (thanks to Jon Davies for this suggestion). Here, the cyclical process of life–death–new life is dramatically symbolized by burial under barrows that imitated the ancestral homes of the Neolithic tells. By the same token, the extension of the landscape 'settled' by the kurgans is an extension of ancestral land, a legitimation of settlement expansion in a period of agronomic change, the full implementation of the secondary products revolution after its initial fifth-millennium impact on eastern European communities (Sherratt 1979).

In summary, barrow burial represents yet one more solution to the problem of the polluting bodies of the newly-dead: abolition of the pollution–purity problem. Denial of the importance of the body leads to a focus on the fertility recreated through use and reuse of the barrow itself, with its primary and secondary burials set in linear time. While the body may be unimportant, the identity of the deceased is memorialized in the barrow, that visual symbol of tell living.

Early–Middle Bronze Age (2400–1600 cal BC)
The final stage (for consideration here) of this long-term alternation of the domestic and mortuary arenas as nodal domains

for social reproduction concerns the return to tell occupation in the Early–Middle Bronze Ages (Meier-Arendt 1992). The Bronze Age communities followed various strategies for inserting their new sites into an ancestral landscape already resonant with the symbolism of both domestic and mortuary mounds: resettlement of Neolithic tells (for example, Herpály: Kalicz and Raczky 1987b: 106); occupation of land previously reserved for burial (for example, Berettyóújfalu-Szilhalom: Sz. Máthé 1992: 169); or, more rarely, tell construction on virgin soil (for example, Tószeg: Bóna 1992). The obvious act of tell-formation so that one's village resembled an ancestral tell was, of course, a long-term strategy not available to those building new tells.

While Bronze Age and Neolithic tells showed general similarities in the elaboration of house construction, domestic artifacts and ritual paraphernalia, there was a fundamental difference between tells of the two periods. The standard Neolithic ritual practice of incorporating the ancestors into their living space through on-tell burial was rarely, if ever, renewed in the Bronze Age. This suggests a fundamental difference in social reproduction, based on the more equal development of both mortuary and domestic arenas within a tradition of strict spatial separation (or as we might say, following Heraclitus, one can never walk through the same tell twice).

The mortuary domain in eastern Hungary shows significant regional variation, with Nagyrév and Hatvan communities tending to bury the newly-dead in small clusters near their tell, while Füzesabony groups created large, bounded cemeteries, some of them near tells (for example, Tiszafüred-Ásotthalom: Kovács 1992: 96) but mostly at some distance from the domestic domain. The most remarkable combination of domestic and mortuary arenas occurs outside the Alföld plain at Dunaújváros, where a very large cemetery was planned to form a semi-circular space around one of the very few tells in the Vatya landscape (Bóna 1992b; Vicze 1992). The cemeteries contain a variety of inhumations and/or cremations, with an emphasis on the newly-dead within some form of community grouping. The implication of the total absence of mortuary remains on the tells is that funeral processions led mourners to the graveside or to the cremation pyre, sometimes found within the cemetery. The development of mortuary rituals distinctly different from the Neolithic rites may explain why relatively few Bronze Age houses on tells were destroyed by fire in comparison with those of the Late Neolithic. Linear time is symbolized in the cemeteries, in contrast to the cyclical time of the tell settlements.

In summary, Bronze Age communities of eastern Hungary thus participated in, and continued, the tradition of monumental tells and barrows by stressing the domestic use of ancestral monuments but also linking up to the earlier Copper Age practice of the bounded flat cemetery. Social reproduction was thus based on the successful integration of prestige goods accumulation into corporate tell group ideology, with the ancestors still omnipresent in the fabric of the tells while their bodily remains were deposited in communal cemeteries.

Summary

This long-term sequence of the later prehistory of eastern Hungary can be read as a suite of alternating arenas of social power, in which domestic and mortuary domains vie for control of the key practices through which social reproduction is validated. The existence of prior uses of similar monuments in the sequence, at least from the Middle Neolithic onwards, leads to a contrast between place-centred, ancestor-based ideologies and ideologies of competitive prestige goods accumulation and alliance building. This contrast is matched in the mortuary sphere: the dead body can be dangerously polluting or relatively innocuous, and may be buried in containers symbolic of cyclical or linear time. The earlier Bronze Age appears to represent a period in which tensions arising out of the two contrasting ideologies of time and space led to the use of elaborate material culture to stress social boundedness, as in the Late Neolithic.

Discussion

This study of the long-term social aspects of time and space
from the later prehistory of eastern Hungary has attempted to
indicate the main strategies which communities used for social
reproduction. While it is accepted that a detailed understanding of past communities' concepts of time and space is beyond
the reach of prehistory, some significant regularities emerge in
the material record which allow us some insights into this
intractable problem.

We may start with the scale of social action. The long-term
sequences that we have studied were neither necessary nor
inevitable but relied on small-scale, often cumulative changes in
short-term social action as well as the structural constraints of
the medium term and long term. These short-term changes are
particularly significant in the creation of new arenas of social
power. For example, the first burial which made use of novel
mortuary rites would always have been a critical step in the
sequence of subsequent events, though only with hindsight
could it be seen as the start of a tradition which has survived
for recognition in the archaeological record. The most optimistic principle of interpretation is that only those innovations
which gain lasting social significance survive in the archaeological record at all; we must not delude ourselves that this is
always the case.

The presence of the newly-dead and the ancestors in the
domestic space of the living is a regularity among all the early
farming groups under study. The recurrent pattern of intramural burial of part or whole of the skeleton of the newly-dead
is a strong indication of the importance of ancestral remains to
the living community. In most cases, intramural burial refers to
social space within the settlement. In some cases, the end of the
household cycle coincides with the burial of a significant
individual as the last act before deliberate destruction of the
house. The *pars pro toto* principle of only a small percentage
of the dead being reincorporated into the settlement is
ubiquitous. It is a sign of the removal of the body in order to
clear away the pollution before reincorporation of pure

ancestral remains into the domestic domain.

Length of site occupation and form of settlement are critical determinants in the contribution of the mortuary sphere to social reproduction. In long-lasting tells or forager communities, ancestral values and memories permeate the settlement and there is a ready home for the return of the ancestors. In less long-term sites such as some Hungarian Neolithic flat sites, burial of complete skeletons may represent a strategy for the establishment of closer ties between ancestors and the living, and indicate that the bodies of the newly-dead are deemed less polluting than before. While the domestic arena of power remains the principal, if not the only, resting place for the newly-dead, the cyclical principle of social reproduction of small-scale social units (village, lineage, household) remains dominant.

Two main causes have been identified for the differentiation of arenas of social power. Colonization of new landscapes, such as the interfluves of eastern Hungary in the Late Copper Age, led to novel opportunities for the exercise of social power. In this case, the legitimation of such settlement expansions was based on the insertion of symbols of the traditional occupied areas into the newly settled landscape—that is, barrows which imitated tells. In this case of settlement expansion (as with others in prehistoric Dalmatia: Chapman and Shiel 1993) the predominance of a linear conception of time may be noted.

The contradictions between traditional community values and new opportunities consequent upon the expansion of exchange and alliance structures into interregional networks is a common theme in later prehistory and forms the strongest patterning in this exploration of mortuary change. For the tell communities in Hungary, the introduction of new prestige goods of copper and gold brought opportunities for accumulation by individuals, households or lineages which ran counter to traditional values of communal ownership and tenure.

There is widespread evidence for long and strenuous resistance to change by the guardians of the traditional ideologies. Ancestral values on tells were maintained in opposition to the new spirit of competitive accumulation for centuries if not a millennium in eastern Hungary.

It is in the period of sharpest conflict between competitive prestige goods accumulation and the traditional ideologies that mortuary arenas become the solution to structural contradictions. The creation of new spatial contexts for prestige goods display permitted the development of change through the interstices of the old order. It is in this interstitial change that we find the clearest instances of the use of the mortuary domain for the ideological aims of different groups, stimulated by the adoption of new attitudes to bodies, linear irreversible time and the linearity of space. It is also in times of greatest social conflict that there is the most obvious overlap of the life cycles of persons and artifacts through deposition of grave goods with individual burials. The cemeteries of the Early and Middle Copper Age are the most extreme example of the death of a considerable diversity and quantity of prestige metalwork to provide a clear mortuary message about the struggle for social power among the living.

In other contexts, the metaphor of the human life cycle is found to be only partially successful in explaining settlement or cemetery patterning in the archaeological record. The fullest coincidence of the end of the life cycle of persons, artifacts and households is found among the first farmers of eastern Hungary, where burial of a significant individual in a house full of symbolic artifacts preceded its deliberate destruction—a sign of the belief in the extreme polluting powers of the bodies of the newly-dead. While such concentrated juxtapositions were expected in the Late Neolithic tells, there is as yet no evidence for such events, though it is possible that houses full of their furniture, fittings and artifacts were ritually burnt down. A less specific insight from life cycles is the notion of the occupation and abandonment of a former settlement followed by incorporation of some of the site's cultural remains into a new settlement. This is found in Hungary at the household level, with the incorporation of old house debris into the floors of new houses. Similar practices can be identified in the insertion of the fertile chernozoem soil into Hungarian barrows.

Conclusion

In conclusion, I would suggest that this study has demonstrated the utility of the concept of arenas of social power in the conceptualization of social change in the landscape. The alternation of emphasis on mortuary and domestic arenas is a characteristic of the long-term sequence in eastern Hungary. The creation of social power in small-scale communities rested on differential use of the economic and ritual possibilities inherent in the domestic landscape and the wildwood, as well as very different classifications of the natural and cultural world in which all the communities were embedded. The increasing scale of social interaction in exchange and alliance networks led to the creation of novel opportunities for social change in the context of an often hostile traditional ideology. In this sense, the linkage of internal and external sources of social change is inevitable if we are to develop an integrated approach to the study of the mortuary domain in European prehistory.

Acknowledgments

I am happy to acknowledge the financial support for the *Upper Tisza Project* from the following: the National Geographic Society, the British Academy, the University of Newcastle upon Tyne and the Society of Antiquaries of London, the Research Committee of the University of Newcastle upon Tyne and the Prehistoric Society. It has been a source of great strength to have received support for these bodies from Colin Renfrew, David Harris, John D. Evans, Geoffrey Dimbleby, Rosemary Cramp, Anthony Harding, Jimmy Griffin, Bernard Wailes and Greg Johnson. I am more than grateful to all my co-workers on these two projects for discussing and criticizing these ideas, especially Robert Shiel, Sándor Bökönyi, Istvan Bóna, Pál Raczky and József Laszlovszky. I received invaluable comments on the problems of purity and pollution, on linear and cyclical time and on many aspects of the interpretation of the data sets from Mike Rowlands. Helpful comments on earlier drafts of this research have also been made by Bob Layton, János Makkay, John Bintliff, Paul Halstead, John Barrett, Chris Smith, Marek Zvelebil, Diane Whaley, Colm O'Brien and Jon Davies. What is left that does not convince is my problem.

Bibliography

Anthony, D.W.
1990   'Migration in Archaeology: The Baby and the Bathwater', *American Anthropologist* 92: 895-914.
Atkinson, R.J.C.
1968   'Old Mortality: Some Aspects of Burial and Population in Neolithic Britain', in J. Coles and D.D.A. Simpson (eds.), *Studies in Ancient Europe* (Leicester: Leicester University Press): 83-94.
Bailey, D.W.
1990   'The Living House', in R. Samson (ed.), *The Social Archaeology of Houses* (Edinburgh: Edinburgh University Press): 19-48.
Banner, J.
1956   *Die Péceler Kultur* (Archaeologia Hungarica, 35; Budapest: Akadémiai Kiadó).
Barrett, J.C.
1990   'The Monumentality of Death', *World Archaeology* 22.2: 179-89
Bartel, B.
1982   'A Historical Review of Ethnological and Archaeological Analyses of Mortuary Practice', *Journal of Anthropological Archaeology* 1: 32-58.
Berger, J.
1984   *And our Faces, My Heart, Brief as Photos* (London: Granta).
Bernardi, B.
1985   *Age Class Systems: Social Institutions and Polities Based on Age* (Cambridge: Cambridge University Press).
Bloch, M.
1985   'Almost Eating the Ancestors', *Man* NS 20: 631-46.
Bognár-Kutzian, I.
1963   *The Copper Age Cemetery of Tiszapolgár-Basatanya* (Archaeologia Hungarica, 42; Budapest: Akadémiai Kiadó).
Bognár-Kutzian, I.
1972   *The Early Copper Age Tiszapolgár Culture in the Carpathian Basin* (Budapest: Akadémiai Kiadó).
Bohannan, L.
1958   'Political Aspects of Tiv Social Organisation', in J. Middleton and D. Tait (eds.), *Tribes Without Rulers* (London: Routledge): 33-66.

Bökönyi, S. (ed.)
1992   *Cultural and Landscape Changes in South East Hungary*. I. *Reports on the Gyomaendrőd Project* (Archaeolingua, 1; Budapest: MTA Institute of Archaeology).

Bökönyi, S.
1992   'The Early Neolithic Vertebrate Fauna of Endrőd 119', in Bökönyi (ed.) 1992: 95-300.

Bóna, I.
1992a   'Bronzezeitliche Tell-Kulturen in Ungarn', in Meier-Arendt (ed.) 1992: 9-39.
1992b   'Dunapentele-Dunaújváros-Kosziderpadlás', in Meier-Arendt (ed.) 1992: 149-52.

Bourdieu, P.
1977   *Outline of a Theory of Practice* (Cambridge: Cambridge University Press).

Bradley, R.
1989a   'Comments on Cannon 1989', *Current Anthropology* 30.4: 448-49.
1989b   'Deaths and Entrances: A Contextual Analysis of Megalithic Art', *Current Anthropology* 30.1: 68-75.

Bradley, R.
1990   *The Passage of Arms: An Archaeological Analysis of Prehistoric Hoards and Votive Deposits* (Cambridge: Cambridge University Press).

Cannon, A.
1989   'The Historical Dimension in Mortuary Expressions of Status and Sentiment', *Current Anthropology* 30.4: 437-58.

Chapman, J.C.
1981   'Clusters of Sites or Sites of Clusters? The Békés II Survey in Eastern Hungary' (unpublished paper read to Northern Universities Archaeological Research Seminar, Bradford).
1983   'Meaning and Illusion in the Study of Burial in Balkan Prehistory', in A. Poulter (ed.), *Ancient Bulgaria Volume 1* (Nottingham: University of Nottingham Press): 1-45.
1988   'From "Space" to "Place": A Model of Dispersed Settlement and Neolithic Society', in C. Burgess, P. Topping and D. Mordant (eds.), *Enclosures and Defences in the Neolithic of Western Europe* (International Series, 403; Oxford: British Archaeological Reports): 21-46.
1989   'The Early Balkan Village', *Varia Archaeologica Hungarica* 2: 33-53.
1991a   'The Creation of Social Arenas in the Neolithic and Copper Age of South East Europe: The Case of Varna', in P. Garwood, P. Jennings, R. Skeates and J. Toms (eds.), *Sacred and Profane* (Oxford Committee for Archaeology Monograph, 32; Oxford: Oxbow).
1991b   'The Early Balkan Village', in O. Grøn, E. Engelstad and I. Lindblom (eds.), *Social Space: Human Spatial Behaviour in Dwellings and Settlements* (Odense: Odense University Press): 79-99.

1992   'The Creation of Arenas of Social Power in Serbian Prehistory', *Zbornik Narodnog Muzeja (Beograd)* 14 (Festschrift for D. Garašanin): 305-17.

1993   'Social Power in the Iron Gates Mesolithic', in J.C. Chapman and P. Dolukhanov (eds.), *Cultural Transformations and Interactions in Eastern Europe* (Worldwide Archaeology Series, 5; Aldershot: Avebury): 71-121.

in press   'Froth Flotation Results from the Hungarian Neolithic'.

Chapman, J.C., and P. Dolukhanov

1992   'The Baby and the Bathwater: Pulling the Plug on Migrations', *American Anthropologist* 94: 169-74.

Chapman, J.C., and R. Shiel

1993   'Social Change and Land Use in Prehistoric Dalmatia', *Proceedings of the Prehistoric Society* 59: 61-104.

Chapman, R., I. Kinnes and K. Randsborg (eds.)

1981   *The Archaeology of Death* (Cambridge: Cambridge University Press).

Chayanov, A.V.

1966   *The Theory of Peasant Economy* (Homewood, IL: Richard D. Irwin for the American Economic Association).

Criado Boado, F.

1989   'We, the Post-Megalithic People', in I. Hodder (ed.), *The Meaning of Things* (London: Unwin Hyman): 79-89.

Ecsedy, I.

1972   'Neolitische Siedlung in Dévávanya, Katonafőldek', *Mitteilungen des Archäologischen Instituts der Ungarischen Akademie der Wissenschaften* 3 (1972): 59-63.

1979   *The People of the Pit-Grave Kurgans in Eastern Hungary* (Fontes Archaeologici Hungariae; Budapest: Akadémiai Kiadó).

Eliade, M.

1960   *Myths, Dreams and Realities* (London: Fontana).

Evans-Pritchard, E.E.

1940   *The Nuer* (Oxford: Oxford University Press).

Fitzpatrick, A.P.

1992   *Westhampnett from the Ice Age to the Romans* (Salisbury: Trust for Wessex Archaeology, 1992).

Fortes, M.

1949   'Time and Social Structure: An Ashanti Case Study', in M. Fortes (ed.), *Social Structure: Essays Presented to A.R. Radcliffe-Brown* (Oxford: Clarendon Press): 54-85.

Foucault, M.

1984   'Interviews', in P. Rabinow (ed.), *The Foucault Reader* (London: Penguin Books, 1984).

Gimbutas, M.

1978   'The First Wave of Steppe Pastoralists into Copper Age Europe', *Journal of Indo-European Studies* 5.4: 277-338.

1979 'The Three Waves of the Kurgan People into Old Europe, 4500–2500 BC', *Archives suisses d'anthropologie générale* 43.2: 113-37.

Glazier, J.
1984 'Mbeere Ancestors and the Domestication of Death', *Man* NS 19: 133-48.

Goldstein, L.
1981 'One-Dimensional Archaeology and Multi-Dimensional People: Spatial Organisation and Mortuary Analysis', in R. Chapman, Kinnes and Randsborg (eds.) 1981: 53-69.

Graslund, B.
1993 'The Archaeology of Death: Prehistoric Concepts of Soul' (Europa Lecture to the Prehistoric Society, London).

Greene, K.
1983 *Archaeology: An Introduction* (London: Batsford).
1987 'Gothic Material Culture', in I. Hodder (ed.), *Archaeology as Long-Term History* (Cambridge: Cambridge University Press): 117-30.

Harrison, S.
1982–83 'Yams and the Symbolic Representation of Time in a Sepik River Village', *Oceania* 53 (1982–83): 141-62.

Hazan, H.
1984 'Continuity and Transformation amongst the Aged: A Study in the Anthropology of Time', *Current Anthropology* 25.5: 567-78.

Hegedűs, K., and J. Makkay
1987 'Vésztő-magor: A Settlement of the Tisza Culture', in Raczky (ed.) 1987: 85-104.

Horváth, F.
1987 'Hódmezővásárhely-Gorzsa: A Settlement of the Tisza Culture', in Raczky (ed.) 1987: 31-46.

Howell, S.
1989 'Of Persons and Things: Exchange and Valuables amongst the Li of Eastern Indonesia', *Man* NS 24: 419-38.

Jankovich, B.D., J. Makkay and B.M. Szőke
1989 *Békés megye régészeti topográfiája* (Magyarország Régészeti Topográfiája, 8; Budapest: Akadémiai Kiadó).

Kalicz, N., and J. Makkay
1977 *Die Linienbandkeramik in der Grossen Ungarischen Tiefebene* (Budapest: Akadémiai Kiadó).

Kalicz, N., and P. Raczky
1987a 'The Late Neolithic of the Tisza Region: A Survey of Recent Archaeological Research', in Raczky (ed.) 1987: 11-30.
1987b 'Berettyóújfalu-Herpály: A Settlement of the Herpály Culture', in Raczky (ed.) 1987: 105-25.

Kopytoff, I.
1986 'The Cultural Biography of Things: Commoditization as Process', in A. Appadurai (eds.), *The Social World of Things* (Cambridge: Cambridge University Press): 64-91.

Kovács, T.
1992   'Tiszafüred-Ásotthalom', in Meier-Arendt (ed.) 1992: 131-33.

Lambek, M.
1990   'Exchange, Time, and Person in Mayotte: The Structure and
            De-Structuring of a Cultural System', *American Anthropologist* 92:
            647-69.

Layton, R.L.
1989   'Introduction', in *idem* (ed.), *Who Needs the Past? Indigenous Values
            and Archaeology* (London: Unwin Hyman): 1-20.

Leach, E.R.
1961   'Two Essays concerning the Symbolic Representation of Time',
            in *idem*, *Rethinking Anthropology* (London School of Economics
            Monographs on Social Anthropology, 22; London: Athlone): 124-
            43.

Makkay, J.
1980–81   'Eine Kultstatte der Bodrogkeresztur-Kultur in Szarvas und Fragen
            der sakralen Hugel', *Mitteilungen des Archäologischen Instituts der
            Ungarischen Akademie der Wissenschaften* 10, 11: 45-57.

Makkay, J.
1982   'Some Comments on the Settlement Patterns of the Alföld Linear
            Pottery', in B. Chropovsky and H. Friesinger (eds.), *Siedlungen der
            Kultur mit Linearkeramik in Europa* (Internationales Kolloquium,
            Nove Vozokány, 17–20/XI.1981; Nitra: Archäologisches Institut
            der Slowakischen Akademie der Wissenschaften): 157-66.

1989   *The Tiszaszőlős Treasure* (Budapest: Akadémiai Kiadó).
1992   'Excavations at the Körös Culture Settlement of Endrőd-Oregszőlők
            119', in Bökönyi (ed.) 1992: 121-94.

Mann, M.
1986   *The Sources of Social Power*. I. *A History of Power from the Beginning to
            AD 1760* (Cambridge: Cambridge University Press).

Mauss, M.
1974   *The Gift* (London: Routledge & Kegan Paul, 1974).

Meier-Arendt, W. (ed.)
1992   *Bronzezeit in Ungarn: Forschungen in Tell-Siedlungen an Donau
            und Theiss* (Frankfurt-am-Main: Museum für Vor- und
            Frühgeschichte).

Mellaart, J.
1975   *The Neolithic of the Near East* (London: Thames & Hudson).

Mosko, M.
1989   'The Developmental Cycle among Public Groups', *Man* NS 24: 470-
            84.

O'Shea, J.M.
1981   'Social Configurations and the Archaeological Study of Mortuary
            Practices: A Case Study', in R. Chapman, Kinnes and Randsborg
            (eds.) 1981: 39-52.

Patay, P.
1978 *Das kupferzeitliche Gräberfeld von Tiszavalk-Kenderföld* (Fontes Archaeologici Hungariae; Budapest: Akadémiai Kiadó).

Poole, F.J.P.
1984 'Symbols of Substance: Bimin-Kuskusmin Models of Procreation, Death, and Personhood', *Mankind* 14.3: 191-216.

Raczky, P.
1982–83 'Origins of the Custom of Burying the Dead inside Houses in South-East Europe', *Szolnok Megyei Múzeumi Evkönyv* 1: 5-10.

Raczky, P. (ed.)
1987 *The Late Neolithic in the Tisza Region* (Budapest–Szolnok: Szolnok County Museums).

Ray, K.
1987 'Material Metaphor, Social Interaction and Historical Reconstructions: Exploring Patterns of Association and Symbolism in the Igbo-Ukwu Corpus', in I. Hodder (ed.), *The Archaeology of Contextual Meanings* (Cambridge: Cambridge University Press): 66-78.

Riesman, P.
1986 'The Person and the Life Cycle in African Social Life and Thought', *African Studies Review* 29.2 (1986): 71-138.

Riley, R.
1987 *Aerial Photography in Archaeology* (London: Duckworth).

Rothschild, N.A.
1989 'Comment on Cannon', *Current Anthropology* 30.4: 453-54.

Rowlands, M.R.
1993 Review of *The Passage of Arms: An Archaeological Analysis of Prehistoric Hoards and Votive Deposits*, by R. Bradley, *European Journal of Archaeology* 1 (1993): 205-207.

Ruoff, U.
1992 'The *Pfahlbauland* Exhibition, Zürich 1990', in B. Coles (ed.), *The Wetland Revolution in Prehistory* (Exeter: Prehistoric Society and Wetlands Archaeology Research Project): 135-46.

Sahlins, M.D.
1972 *Stone Age Economics* (Chicago: Aldine).

Samson, R., (ed.)
1990 *The Social Archaeology of Houses* (Edinburgh: Edinburgh University Press).

Saxe, A.A.
1970 'Social Dimensions of Mortuary Practices' (PhD thesis, University of Michigan).

Shanks, M., and C. Tilley
1982 'Ideology, Symbolic Power and Ritual Communication: A Reinterpretation of Neolithic Mortuary Practices', in I. Hodder (ed.), *Structural and Symbolic Archaeology* (Cambridge: Cambridge University Press): 129-54.

Sherratt, A

1979 'Plough and Pastoralism: Aspects of the Secondary Products Revolution', in I. Hodder, N. Hammond and G. Isaac (eds.), *Patterns in the Past* (Cambridge: Cambridge University Press): 261-305.

1982a 'Mobile Resources: Settlement and Exchange in Early Agricultural Europe', in C. Renfrew and S.J. Shennan (eds.), *Ranking, Resources and Exchange* (Cambridge: Cambridge University Press): 13-26.

1982b 'The Development of Neolithic and Copper Age Settlement in the Great Hungarian Plain: Part 1: The Regional Setting', *Oxford Journal of Archaeology* 1.3: 287-316.

1983 'The Development of Neolithic and Copper Age Settlement in the Great Hungarian Plain: Part 2: Site Surveys and Settlement Dynamics', *Oxford Journal of Archaeology* 2.1: 13-41.

1984 'Early Agrarian Settlement in the Körös Region of the Great Hungarian Plain', *Acta Archaeologica Hungarica* 35: 155-69.

Siška, S.

1968 'Tiszapolgárska kulture na Slovensku', *Slovenska Archaeologia* 16: 61-171.

Strathern, A.

1980 'Death as Exchange: Two Melanesian Cases', in S.C. Humphreys and H. King (eds.), *Mortality and Immortality: The Anthropology and the Archaeology of Death* (London: Academic Press): 205-24.

Sz. Máthé, M.

1992 'Bakonszeg-Kádárdomb; Berettyóújfalu-Szilhalom; Berettyóújfalu-Herpály-Földvár', in Meier-Arendt (ed.) 1992: 166-74.

Todorova, H., S. Ivanov, V. Vassilev, M. Hopf, N. Quitta and G. Kohl

1975 *Selisnata mogila pri Goljamo Delčevo* (Sofia: Bulgarska Akademia Nauk).

Tringham, R., and D. Krstić (eds.)

1991 *Selevac—A Neolithic Village in Yugoslavia* (Monumenta Archaeologica, 15; Los Angeles: University of California Press).

Trinkhaus, K.M.

1984 'Mortuary Ritual and Mortuary Remains', *Current Anthropology* 25.5: 674-78.

Trogmayer, O.

1969 'Die Bestattungen der Körös-Gruppe', *A Móra Ferenc Múzeum Evkönyve* 2: 5-15.

Velde, P. van der

1979 'The Social Anthropology of a Neolithic Cemetery in the Netherlands', *Current Anthropology* 20.1: 37-47.

Vicze, M.

1992 'The Bronze Age Site of Dunaújváros-Kosziderpadlás' (paper presented to University of Newcastle Department of Archaeology).

Wilk, R.W., and W.L. Rathje
  1982   'Household Archaeology', *American Behavioral Scientist* 25.6: 617-39.
Woodburn, J.
  1982   'Social Dimensions of Death in Four African Hunting and
             Gathering Societies', in M. Bloch and J. Parry (eds.), *Death and the
             Regeneration of Life* (Cambridge: Cambridge University Press): 187-
             210.
Worsley, P.M.
  1956   'The Kinship System of the Tallensi: A Revaluation', *Journal of the
             Royal Anthropological Institute* 86: 37-75.

Isaiah as a Source Book for Scriptural Texts about Death and Mourning

John F.A. Sawyer

The book of Isaiah, known to Christians as the 'Fifth Gospel', has played a unique role in the development of doctrine and liturgy. A glance at the pages of quotations from Isaiah listed in the *Oxford Dictionary of Quotations* (1953) will illustrate the extent of Isaiah's influence on English literature and on Western European culture in general: 'swords into ploughshares', 'the wolf dwelling with the lamb', 'the desert blossoming like the rose', 'a voice crying in the wilderness', 'a light to the nations', 'a man of sorrows', 'good news to the poor' and 'a new heaven and a new earth' are only a few of the best known. Isaiah's contribution to the language and imagery of the cult of the Virgin Mary, late mediaeval passion iconography and anti-Semitism (Sawyer forthcoming a), as well as in more recent times to Christian feminism and liberation theology, has been studied elsewhere (Sawyer forthcoming b). Isaiah has had a significant role to play in the history of Judaism as well, not least in the history of Zionism.

It is the aim of this paper to consider what texts and images from Isaiah have been important in the context of Christian and Jewish beliefs and practices associated with death and mourning. I shall begin with images of death and life after death, and then look at some of the texts that have been used by mourners in funeral services, epitaphs and elsewhere. The list is not exhaustive by any means, but will serve to illustrate, in general, how successfully sacred texts can be used to express the hopes and beliefs of a community living in a world very different from that of the texts' original authors, and in particular, how rich a source Isaiah has been in this context as in others.

Images of Death in the Book of Isaiah

The death of kings gives the first part of the book (chs. 1–39) its overall structure. It is striking that, instead of a phrase like 'in the year when King Ahaz came to the throne' (cf. 2 Kgs 15.1; 16.1; 18.1; 21.1; 22.1), a more ominous formula referring to the death of the previous king is chosen twice; this is unique to Isaiah and must be significant. The first occasion is the date of Isaiah's famous vision in 6.1: 'In the year that King Uzziah died I saw the Lord sitting on a throne, high and lifted up...' The death of a king is here cited both as a watershed in the history of Jerusalem and as a turning point in the life of the prophet. The reign of King Uzziah (787–736 BCE) had been long, peaceful and prosperous, but marred by a widening gap between rich and poor and countless instances of social injustice and oppression such as those described and denounced in chs. 1–5:

> How the faithful city has become a harlot,
> she that was full of justice! (1.21)

> What do you mean by crushing my people,
> by grinding the face of the poor? (3.15)

> Woe to those who join house to house,
> who add field to field...
> who acquit the guilty for a bribe,
> and deprive the innocent of their rights! (5.8, 23)

Uzziah's death marks the beginning of a period of instability, during which repeated invasions by Assyrian armies led ultimately to the complete destruction of almost every city in the region (cf. Isa. 36.1). Scenes of death and destruction abound:

> cities lie waste without inhabitant,
> and houses without people, and the land is utterly desolate (6.11)

'The year that King Uzziah died' was also the year in which the prophet had his vision of the heavenly court and heard the

seraphim singing the *Sanctus* ('Holy, Holy, Holy'; 6.3). It was
then that he received his commission to preach divine
judgment to his people, interpreting the disintegration of the
proud hierarchies of Israel and Judah under King Ahaz (736–725
BCE) as the punishment they deserved:

> Through the wrath of the Lord of hosts
> the land is burned,
> and the people are like fuel for the fire (9.19).

He described Assyria as the rod used by Yahweh to beat his
godless people (10.5; cf. Prov. 13.24; 26.3).

The other occurrence of the 'royal death' formula is in 14.28,
where it again symbolizes a significant change, this time from
the reign of the wicked Ahaz who 'did not do what was right
in the eyes of the Lord' (cf. 2 Kgs 16.2) to what turned out to
be the more glorious reign of King Hezekiah (725–699 BCE) who
'did what was right in the eyes of the Lord' (2 Kgs 18.3).

Near the end of the first part of the book, however, there are
two other, more spectacular images of death, which have made
a deep impression on Christian tradition and which prepare
the way for the 'chapters of consolation' beginning 'Comfort,
comfort my people, says your God' (40.1). The first comes in
the story of Sennacherib's invasion of Judah in 701 BCE. It is
told three times in the Bible (2 Kgs 18.13–19.37; 2 Chron. 32; Isa.
36–37), and immortalized in Byron's poem *The Destruction of
Semnacherib*, beginning

> The Assyrian came down like the wolf on the fold,
> And his cohorts were gleaming with purple and gold

It is the story of Jerusalem's miraculous escape, alone of all the
cities of Judah, and of the total destruction of the Assyrian
army. The prophet Isaiah, summoned to assist the king as he
confronted the Assyrian army, had compared Jerusalem to a
young woman bravely dismissing a suitor with a toss of her
head (36.22), and, in language reminiscent of earlier Zion faith
(cf. 2.3; 7.3), had prophesied that 'a band of survivors' would
escape from the besieged city (37–32). In the event the focus is
not on the escape of Jerusalem, but on the dramatic end of
Sennacherib and his army. The biblical account, in typically

economic style, tells of two spectacular scenes of horror. The first is one verse long:

> And the angel of the Lord went forth, and slew a hundred and eighty-five thousand in the camp of the Assyrians; and when morning came, they were all corpses (37.36).

The implication is that the whole army died in their sleep without a blow being struck. Byron fills in the details:

> Like the leaves of the forest when autumn has blown,
> That host on the morrow lay withered and strown...
> And the eyes of the sleepers wax'd deadly and chill,
> And their hearts but once heaved and forever grew still...
>
> And there lay the rider, distorted and pale,
> With the dew on his brow and the rust on his mail,
> And the tents were all silent, the banners alone,
> The lances unlifted, the trumpet unblown...
>
> And the might of the Gentile, unsmote by the sword,
> Hath melted like snow in the glance of the Lord!

The second scene is almost as gruesome, although again the biblical account leaves almost everything to the imagination (37.38). It tells how Sennacherib himself, having presumably escaped the fate of his army, returned home to Nineveh. There he was assassinated at the hands of his two sons while he was worshipping in the temple of his god:

> And it came to pass, as he was worshipping in the house of Nisroch his god, that Adrammelech and Sharezer his sons smote him with the sword; and they escaped into the land of Armenia: and Esarhaddon his son reigned in his stead.

The 'angel of the Lord' is reminiscent of the 'destroyer' in the exodus story (Exod. 12.23), and ancient tradition such as Herodotus, Josephus and Jerome tried to explain the fate of the Assyrian army by reference to a plague. Modern scholarship questions whether the event has any basis in history at all (Clements 1980). As it happens we have Sennacherib's own version of the siege of Jerusalem in 701 BCE, and he makes no mention of it (Pritchard 1969: 288).

Whatever happened, the fact is that Jerusalem, alone of all the cities of Judah, survived the Assyrian invasions, and the story of its survival, embellished with such gruesome images of death, is recounted at this point in the book of Isaiah to round off the catastrophic story of eighth-century crime and punishment. In subsequent chapters Jerusalem is told that 'her warfare is ended, her iniquity pardoned' (40.2), and exhorted to 'awake' (52.1), 'break forth into singing' (54.1), 'fear not' (54.4), 'arise, shine for your light is come' (60.1) (cf. Sawyer 1989).

No doubt readers of Byron's poem, which is dated 19th February 1815, used these dramatic images to celebrate the end of Napoleonic power at Waterloo later that year (McGann [ed.] 1981: 472). There is also a painting by Rubens of the subject in the Alte Pinakotek in Munich, painted in about 1616. But in his version of the story, very similar to his *Conversion of St Paul* painted at about the same time, the Assyrians are still alive:

> a wild and raging tumult of flight caused by heavenly apparitions, with men, mostly mounted, fighting against an unearthly enemy; even the horses are beside themselves, and over the whole there pour streams of light and night (Burckhardt 1950: 84).

It is noteworthy that these two paintings were produced before the beginning of the Thirty Years' War (1618–1648), and in striking contrast to his later and better-known comment on the horrors of war, *The Allegory of War* in the Pitti Palace in Florence, dated 1638 (Burckhardt 1950: 113).

The other image of death at the end of the first part of the book of Isaiah comes in the story of Hezekiah's 'near-death experience' or, to use the biblical phrase, 'sickness unto death' (Isa. 38). In a graphic poem Hezekiah celebrates his unexpected and miraculous recovery from illness as though he had returned from the dead. The poem, reminiscent of some of the Psalms (for instance 6, 13, 88), found its way into the Christian Psalter, where it is known as the 'Hezekiah Canticle', regularly sung, according to some liturgical traditions, both monastic and secular, at Lauds. It contains some interesting details picked out by preachers, manuscript illuminators and other commentators.

The first line, which gives the canticle its Latin title (*Ego dixi in dimidio dierum*) is about the youth of the king:

> I thought that, halfway through my life, I was going to the gates of hell: and that I had been deprived of the rest of my years.

Death at any age is tragic, but death 'halfway through life' is particularly sad. The Latin means literally 'at half my (allotted) days', reminiscent perhaps of the familiar words of Ps. 90.10, where our allotted years are 'threescore and ten'. In fact Hezekiah was miraculously cured and fifteen years added to his life (38.5). By contrast, the untimely death in battle of one of his successors, Josiah (640–609 BCE), at the age of 31 was interpreted as being due to God's mercy, in that it saved him from witnessing the disasters that were shortly to befall his country. We shall look later at a text from Isaiah (57.1-2) in which this view of death is expressed. Ben Sira's well-known comments on death have a similar ambivalence: death is a source of bitterness to someone who is 'at peace among his possessions', but welcomed by someone 'in need and failing in strength' (Ecclus 41.1-2).

Hezekiah's prayer also contains some vivid images of death, which inspired the illuminator of the St Alban's Psalter to show death as a monster lurking beside Hezekiah's feet (Plate 92a). He also singled out a reference to Hezekiah's failing eyesight ('my eyes are weary with looking upward', v. 14) as having some special significance in this context. The fear of death in terms of never 'seeing the Lord again' or 'looking upon another human being' comes at the beginning of the prayer (v. 11). This link between human life and sight occurs elsewhere in the Bible, as for example at the end of Psalm 17 and in Jonah's prayer from the bottom of the sea (Jon. 2.4).

But it is what Hezekiah says about Sheol, the biblical Hebrew name for the place where the dead lead a colourless and shadowy existence, that is most often quoted in discussions of biblical views of death. The nature and finality of death is expressed in two ways. First, the image of 'the gates of hell' (cf. Job 38.17; Ps. 9.13; Jon. 2.6) compares dying to being locked up in a prison. Some modern English versions of the text such as the Revised Standard Version and the New English Bible make a minor change in the punctuation of the Hebrew to heighten the effect: 'I am consigned to the gates of hell for the rest of my years'.

Secondly, Sheol is a place where there can be no communication with God, and therefore a place where there can be no hope:

> For Sheol cannot thank you,
> death cannot praise you;
> those who go down to the pit
> cannot hope for your faithfulness
> (Isa. 38.18).

Death according to this belief is less to do with physical decay and departing from this life than with being cut off from God. The mention of God's faithfulness suggests an allusion to the notion of a covenant between God and his faithful servants, although the term itself is not actually used here. Elsewhere in Isaiah there is talk of a 'covenant with death...an agreement with Sheol' by which God's enemies, by their lies and falsehood, were 'in league with death' and thought they could escape (28.15, 18). Wilfred Owen uses this image to devastating effect, taken up by Britten in the *War Requiem* (see Eric Cross's paper in this volume):

> Out there, we've walked quite friendly up to Death;
>   Sat down and eaten with him, cool and bland...
> We whistled while he shaved us with his scythe.
>
> Oh, Death was never enemy of ours!
>   We laughed at him, we leagued with him, old chum.

But the two covenants or 'leagues', one with God and the other with Death, are mutually exclusive.

Another celebrated Isaianic description of Sheol appears in ch. 14. In a taunting, ironic lament the author portrays the king of Babylon arriving in Sheol, in images more reminiscent of Homer or Virgil or Dante than of any biblical parallel. His arrival stirs up some excitement amongst the inhabitants of Sheol. The ghosts of former world leaders, some apparently still on their thrones, stand up to greet him:

> You too have become as weak as we are,
>   you have become like us!

Their insubstantial, shadowy, colourless existence in Sheol is set against their former power and regal splendour. It was from this chapter that Milton derived some of his inspiration for the description of the fall of Satan, 'hurl'd headlong flaming from th' ethereal sky', at the beginning of *Paradise Lost* (Book II, l. 45):

> How you are fallen from heaven,
> O Day Star [Latin *lucifer*], son of Dawn!
> ...you said in your heart, I will ascend to heaven;
> ...I will make myself like the Most High,
> But you have been brought down to Sheol,
> to the depths of the pit (Isa. 14.12-15).

The second part of the lament focuses on this world and the fate of the dead body of the king of Babylon, not placed in a royal tomb like all the other kings of the nations, but lying with other corpses, unburied, 'trodden under foot', on 'a bed of maggots...with worms as a coverlet' (v. 11). This brings us to one final example of Isaiah's contribution to Jewish and Christian eschatology, which comes in the very last verse of the book:

> And they shall go out and look at the corpses of the people that have rebelled against me: their worm shall not die, their fire shall not go out, and all humankind will be sickened at the sight of them (*erunt usque ad satietatem visonis*) (Isa. 66.24).

According to the Jewish liturgical tradition, when Isa. 66.24 is read at public worship, the immediately preceding verses (22, 23), with their reference to 'the new heavens and the new earth', are repeated so as to avoid ending on such an ugly and frightening note.

The specific mention of unquenchable fire makes this passage a much-used scriptural prooftext for the notion of hellfire, elaborately developed in Christian (and also, incidentally, Islamic) tradition. It is alluded to in the Greek and Latin versions of Ecclesiasticus (Sirach): 'Cultivate great humility, since the punishment of the ungodly is fire and worms' (7.17). According to Mark's Gospel, it was used by Jesus in a

description of hell (Greek *gehenna*) (Mk 9.47-48), and the book
of Revelation, which is heavily dependent on Isaiah, describes
the fate of the wicked in terms of a 'lake burning with fire and
sulphur' (21.8; cf. 1.20; 20.10). The verse is quoted frequently in
patristic and mediaeval discussions of hell. St Ambrose, on the
other hand, in an entirely different use of the text, quotes it to
comfort the bereaved with the hope of the resurrection of the
body: if the worm of sinners does not die, he argues, how shall
the flesh of the just perish (*Fathers of the Church* 22.235)? This
brings us to the second part of our survey.

Isaiah and Mourning

Isaiah 25 and 26 (part of what is commonly known today as the
'Isaiah Apocalypse') have always been a particularly rich
source for epitaphs and texts for funeral orations. Martin
Luther, for example, lists four passages from Isaiah among his
'biblical texts suitable for epitaphs' (in Pelikan [ed.] 1965: 328-
29); all but one are from these chapters. The first focuses on
victory over death: 'He will swallow up death for ever' (25.7-
9), a passage quoted by Paul in his discourse on resurrection in
1 Corinthians 15. From there it found its way (via the Anglican
Order for the Burial of the Dead) into Handel's *Messiah*. It also
appears in Brahms's *German Requiem*.

Isaiah was a particular favourite of St Ambrose (c. 339–397;
Bishop of Milan), as mentioned above. According to Augustine,
when he asked the Bishop for advice on vacation reading, the
Bishop prescribed Isaiah (*Confessions*, 9.5). A number of funeral
orations delivered by Ambrose in Milan Cathedral at the end
of the fourth century provide us with a useful case-study. He
used Luther's first Isaianic epitaph from Isaiah 25 to good effect
on the occasion of the funeral of his brother Satyrus in 378. In
particular, by stressing the second verse, he turns the listeners'
attention to the faith that survives death: 'It will be said on that
day, "Lo, this is our God; we have waited for him that he
might save us..."' (*Fathers of the Church* 22.224-25). The passage
is still widely used as one of the readings at masses for the dead
according to the *New Sunday Missal* (p. 985), the *Lectionary*
(pp. 942, 960, 964, 1001) and the *Alternative Service Book* (pp. 331-

32), and it provides the last words in the Jewish 'prayer in the house of mourning', which I shall discuss later.

Luther's other two Isaianic epitaphs both come from Isaiah 26. One refers to the resurrection of the dead ('Thy dead shall live...', 26.19), and the other to hiding from the wrath of God (26.20). Ambrose also uses these verses in the funeral address just referred to (*Fathers of the Church* 2.226-27). The first speaks of the divine dew that makes our bodies grow again after we die:

> Awake and sing for joy, you who dwell in the dust!
> Your dew is the dew of light...

The second verse provides him with scriptural authority for his belief that there are hidden chambers where the redeemed can hide safely until the Judgment is past—a notion expressed more graphically elsewhere in Isaiah:

> People shall go into caves in the rocks
>   and holes in the ground
> to escape the terror of the Lord
>   and the glory of his majesty
>   when he rises to terrify the earth (2.19).

Another verse from ch. 26, containing the word 'peace' repeated twice and traditionally translated into English 'peace, perfect peace' (Isa. 26.3), provided the only text from Isaiah included in a collection of recommended epitaphs published in 1897 by J. Braithwaite & Son, a firm of undertakers, in Derby. It was also the inspiration for a hymn once popular at funerals: 'Peace, perfect peace, in this dark world of sin'. The author, Dr Edward Bickersteth (1825–1906), is said to have written it in a few minutes as he sat at the bedside of a dying friend, and then recited it to him. It was also sung at the funeral of the Scottish theologian and orientalist, William Robertson Smith, in 1894 (Moffat 1935: 152).

Isa. 26.3 was not one of Luther's four Isaianic epitaphs, but his fourth does express a similar view of death:

> The righteous perish...they are taken away from the evil to come.
> They shall enter into peace; they shall rest in their beds (57.1-2).

The Latin of this passage contains the words *justus perit, pax* and *requiescat*, all very common in funerary inscriptions.

The rest of Isa. 26.3 appears as an epitaph in a fresco by Raphael (1483–1520). This was commissioned by the papal protonotary and humanist Johannes Goritz in 1510 to overlook his tomb in the Church of Sant'Agostino in Rome (Ettlinger and Ettlinger 1987: 121-23, Plates 117, 118). It shows Isaiah displaying a scroll with the first part of 26.2-3: 'Open the gates that a righteous nation which keeps faith may enter'. Allusions to the themes discussed above in connection with the Hezekiah Canticle are obvious, although the papal official's self-righteousness gives the text a different slant. The inscription, which is in Hebrew letters, surprisingly stops just before the twice-repeated word *shalom*, 'peace, perfect peace', which as we have just seen figures elsewhere in funeral traditions.

On a lighter note, it is reported that a gravestone in memory of one Obadiah Wilkinson and his wife Ruth bears the epitaph (cf. Isa. 40.2) 'Their warfare is ended' (Simpson 1986: 59). The word 'warfare' (RSV 'service') was no doubt intended to refer, as in the original Hebrew, to this life as time spent in the service of God. Rather thoughtlessly applied to the way a couple had spent their married life together, it cannot help suggesting something rather different!

Isaiah was as much 'prophet of the Passion' as of the nativity, especially in late mediaeval iconography, and various texts and images are regularly cited in association with the death of Christ. Chapter 53 provides some of the most common. The statue of Isaiah by the French sculptor Claus Sluter, completed between 1380 and 1400, is a famous example. On the hexagonal base of what was probably once a large crucifix over a fountain in Dijon visited by pilgrims are represented six prophets, each holding a scroll with a verse about Christ's suffering. Isaiah's is:

> Like a sheep that before its shearers is dumb,
> he opened not his mouth (53.7).

Other 'epitaphs' for Jesus from the same chapter in Isaiah include the following:

they made his grave with the wicked
and with a rich man in his death (53.9)

he poured out his soul to death (53.12).

One of the most strikingly original features of feminist exegete Phyllis Trible's *Texts of Terror* is her appropriation of two passages from the same chapter as epitaphs for women. To Hagar, the rejected Egyptian slave woman, she gives the epitaph 'She was wounded for our transgressions; she was bruised for our iniquities' (Isa. 53.5; Trible 1984: 8); to Tamar, princess of Judah and victim of rape, 'A woman of sorrows and acquainted with grief' (Isa. 53.3; Trible 1984: 36).

Another messianic text used in this way comes from Isa. 11.10, a passage celebrating the final victory of 'the root of Jesse'. It ends with the words 'And his resting place [Latin *sepulcrum*] will be glorious'. This is later applied, like 53.9, to the tomb of the wealthy Joseph of Arimathaea, where Christ was buried, and probably to the later veneration of the Holy Sepulchre as a shrine (Henry 1987: 102).

The apocryphal legend of the martyrdom of Isaiah, which links his death, in various grisly ways, with a tree, is also cited in mediaeval literature and iconography as a type of Christ's death on the 'tree' of the cross (Bernheimer 1952: 19-37). The wine-press in Isaiah 63, with the 'epitaph' *torcular calcavi solus* ('I trod the wine press alone'), is another frequent image of Christ's saving death, the woodwork of the press echoing the wood of the cross, and the sacramental juice of the grapes the blood of Christ, flowing into a chalice beneath (Marrow 1979: 83; Schiller 1972: 228ff.).

Even the wood of the 'tree of Jesse' (cf. 11.1), originally intended to celebrate the Davidic ancestry of Christ, often turns into a cross, or has a cross built out of it (Schiller 1972: 133ff.). Victor Hugo employs this imagery beautifully in his poem *Booz endormi*. This tells how Boaz, grandfather of Jesse, with Ruth the Moabite lying at this feet (cf. Ruth 3), dreamed a dream. In the dream he saw an oak tree coming out of his belly reaching up to the sky, and on it a long line of people with David at one end and Christ at the other:

> Et ce songe était tel, que Booz vit un chêne
> Qui, sorti de son ventre, allait jusqu'au ciel bleu;
> Une race y montait comme une longue chaine;
> Un roi chantait en bas, en haut mourait un dieu.

The frequent messianic references in Isaiah are occasionally used to dramatic effect in the context of death as well as in reference to messianism. Ambrose uses one such text to prove to mourners that there is nothing wrong with weeping and grief (*Fathers of the Church* 22.166). He argues that Jesus wept and experienced real grief, because he was human as well as divine. This he proves by reference to Isa. 9.6 ('For unto us a child is born, unto us a son is given'), interpreting the two halves of the verse as referring to the two natures of Christ. He was both 'born' (of the Father and therefore divine), and 'given' (by the Virgin and therefore human). Without commenting on this highly patriarchal view of childbirth, it is to be noted that the use of Isa. 9.6 in this context is not to make a theological point concerning the true humanity of Christ. It was to apply what we must suppose was, both for the congregation and the preacher, familiar and much loved language, in such a way as to bring comfort to the bereaved—a use of Isaiah not so different from the way the same verse is used in Handel's *Messiah*.

An intriguing example of the use of another messianic text from one of Isaiah's visions of a messianic age appears, as a kind of epitaph, in the mausoleum built by Queen Victoria for herself and her consort. Four statues surround the central sarcophagus on which the queen and consort lie. Isaiah is one of the four, the others being David, Solomon and Daniel. The statue of Isaiah is by Herman Hultzsch, of Dresden, working in Rome from a fresco by Raphael (Prince Albert's favourite artist) in Santa Maria della Pace.

The texts on the statues of David (2 Sam. 23.4), Solomon (1 Kgs 3.11), and Daniel (Dan. 12.3) are unproblematic. These deal with sunrise, royal wisdom and the resurrection of the dead, respectively, and are entirely appropriate. The Isaiah text is:

> But the liberal deviseth liberal things,
> and by liberal things shall he stand (32.8).

The application of messianic language from Isaiah to the monarch is not without parallel; the coronation service, for example, cites 11.2 at the anointing with oil: 'the spirit of the Lord shall rest upon him, the spirit of wisdom...'. But the choice of the Isaiah text at Frogmore, removed from its messianic context, is certainly odd. The queen, it is known, supervised every detail: could it be a reference to her favourite prime minister? Or did she know of a sermon preached on this text by John Donne in the presence of King Charles I in 1628: 'the very forme of the office of a king is Liberality, that is Providence, and Protection and Possession and Peace and Justice shed upon all' (Simpson and Potter 1956: 243).

Other Isaiah texts appear in Brahms's strikingly original *German Requiem.* This contains settings of three more texts from Isaiah in addition to one of the passages already mentioned (25.8). The first is his magnificent choral setting of the words of 1 Pet. 1.24, citing Isa. 40.6-8. The gentle, wistful acceptance of human transitoriness ('All flesh is as grass...'), repeated twice, with Jas 5.7 ('Be patient therefore...') inserted between the two choruses, is answered by the triumphant statement of faith: 'But the word of the Lord stands forever'.

By contrast, a deeply pessimistic novel by the distinguished Argentinian novelist Eduardo Mallea (b. 1903) takes its title *Todo Verdor Perecerá* ('all the verdure will perish) from Isa. 15.6. The allusion to the more familiar words of 40.8 which I have just mentioned is unmistakeable, but in the text so poignantly used by Mallea, there is no trace of the hope expressed in the second half of the verse.

Brahms follows the 'word of God' chorus from 40.8 with Isa. 35.10 ('...sorrow and sighing shall flee away'). This was a passage familiar to Brahms from its popularity as an Advent or Christmas reading, and it provides a beautiful gloss on the impersonal theological statement preceding it. The fourth text from Isaiah set to music by Brahms in his *Requiem* is one of the few biblical passages in which God is compared to a mother (66.13). This brings us to our final three examples, all of them from Jewish tradition.

The first comes from the concluding paragraph of the

'Prayer in the house of mourning' (in the *Authorised Daily Prayer Book* [1892]):

> As those who are comforted by their mother, so will I comfort you: in Jerusalem you will be comforted [66.13]. Your sun shall not set again, and your moon shall not be withdrawn: the Lord shall be your everlasting light and your time of mourning shall be over [60.20]. He will swallow up death for ever. The Lord God will wipe away tears from all faces; and the reproach of his people he shall remove from the whole earth. The Lord has spoken [25.8].

It is entirely composed of passages from Isaiah. Only the 'God as mother' passage, just mentioned, requires comment. It is one of the few passages in Scripture in which female imagery is applied to God (Gen. 1.2, 26-27; Deut. 32.11, 18; Ps. 131.2; Isa. 31.5; 42.14; 45.10, 46.3; 49.14; 66.13; cf. Trible 1978: 50-56; Ackerman 1992: 166-68). Of these a significant proportion are in the book of Isaiah. The concentration of female images of Zion and her children alongside those of God as mother (Sawyer 1989: 89-90) is a striking feature of these chapters of Isaiah and introduces a most effective additional dimension to language designed to bring comfort to the bereaved.

Secondly, comfort for a community mourning the destruction of the Temple at Jerusalem is offered in seven *haftarot* (readings from the Prophets) from Isaiah 40–66: 40.1-26; 49.14–51.4; 54.11–55.6; 51.12–52.13; 54.1-10; 60.1-22. These are known as the 'Haftarot of Consolation' or 'Comfort' (Hebrew *neḥāmâ*) from the first words of ch. 40: 'Comfort ye, comfort ye my people'. They are prescribed to be read at public worship on the seven sabbaths after the Fast on the Ninth of Ab (late summer), and are among the best-known and best-loved portions of Hebrew Scripture.

Finally, it is appropriate that it should be from Isaiah that the name given to the Holocaust memorial established on the outskirts of Jerusalem in 1953, *Yad VaShem* ('a monument and a name'), is derived. In its original context (Isa. 55.5) the recipients of this memorial were actually eunuchs, and the promise was that it would be 'better than sons and daughters... an everlasting name which shall never be destroyed'.

There is an almost uncanny poignancy in the application of the phrase, first, to efforts in general to ensure the survival of the Jewish people, and then finally to the massive international operation to collect and preserve archival material about the six million victims of Nazi persecution.

Bibliography

Ackerman, S.
1992   'Isaiah', in C.A. Newsom and S.H. Ringe (eds.), *The Women's Bible Commentary* (London: SPCK; Louisville, KY: John Knox): 161-68.
Bernheimer, R.
1952   'The Martyrdom of Isaiah', *Art Bulletin* 34.1: 19-37.
Burckhardt, J.
1950   *Recollections of Rubens* (London: Phaidon).
Clements, R.E.
1980   *Isaiah and the Deliverance of Jerusalem: A Study of the Interpretation of Prophecy in the Old Testament* (JSOTSup, 13; Sheffield: JSOT Press).
Ettlinger, L.D., and H.S. Ettlinger
1987   *Raphael* (Oxford: Phaidon).
Gombrich, E.H.
1972   *The Story of Art* (Oxford: Phaidon).
Henry, A. (ed.)
1987   *Biblia Pauperum: A Facsimile and Edition* (London: Scolar Press).
McGann, J.J. (ed.)
1981   *Lord Byron: The Complete Works* (Oxford: Oxford University Press), III.
Mallea, E.
1968   *Todo Verdor Perecerá* (ed. D.L. Shaw; Oxford: Pergamon Press).
Marrow, J.H.
1979   *Passion Iconography in Northern European Art: A Study of the Transformation of Sacred Metaphor into Descriptive Narrative* (Brussels: Van Ghemmert).
Moffat, J.
1935   *A Handbook to the Church Hymnary* (Oxford: Oxford University Press).
Pelikan, J. (ed.)
1965   *Luther's Works* (Philadelphia: Fortress Press), LIII.
Pritchard, J.B. (ed.)
1969   *Ancient Near Eastern Texts relating to the Old Testament* (Princeton, NJ: Harvard University Press, 3rd edn, 1969).

Sawyer, J.F.A.

1989   'Daughter of Zion and Servant of the Lord in Isaiah: A Comparison', *JSOT* 44: 89-107.

forthcoming a 'The Ethics of Comparative Interpretation', *Currents in Research: Biblical Studies* 2.

forthcoming b *The Fifth Gospel: Isaiah in the History of Christianity* (Cambridge: Cambridge University Press).

Schiller, G.

1972   *Iconography of Christian Art* (London: Lund Humphries), II.

Simpson, E.M., and G.R. Potter (eds.)

1956   *The Sermons of John Donne* (Berkeley and Los Angeles), VIII.

Simpson, J.A.

1986   *Holy Wit* (Edinburgh: Gordon Wright).

Trible, P.

1978   *God and the Rhetoric of Sexuality* (Philadelphia: Fortress Press).

1984   *Texts of Terror: Literary Feminist Readings of Biblical Narratives* (Philadelphia: Fortress Press).

Death and Remembrance in Modern Paganism

Graham Harvey

Introduction

Alexander the Great, compliment-seeking, asked some Celts what they were most afraid of. 'That the sky might fall on our heads', they replied (Arria, *Anabasis of Alexander* 1.4.6-8).

Julius Caesar said that Gallic warriors were 'recklessly fearless' because they believed that 'souls do not die but after death pass from one to another' (Caesar, *Gallic Wars* 6.14).

Modern Paganism is an increasingly significant part of the spiritual life of Britain. It is growing numerically, in coherence and in its self-confidence about its relationship with other faith communities and its place in society. While it is hard to be sure how many people name themselves Pagan an estimate of twenty thousand seems conservative and half a million possible. Its significance may also be measured by the number of books available in 'all good bookshops' by, for and about Witches, Druids, Shamans and Magicians. Christian bookshops stock a not inconsiderable number of books against Paganism and 'the occult'. Although the New Age movement is a discrete phenomenon there is both debate and some cross-fertilization between it and Paganism.

The self-designation 'Pagan' draws on earlier usages of the name although it is by no means bound by any one of them. Most Pagans take the name to refer to those who honour Nature or the Earth. They draw on the name's Latin association with 'countryside' which they apply more widely to the whole earth. They are often aware of its derogatory connotation, 'peasant', 'country bumpkin', but see this as just another way of saying 'alternative' and therefore no great insult.

Christian uses of the name are not forgotten. Here 'Pagans' could mean 'those who live in the countryside and therefore have not yet been enlightened by our predominantly urban faith'. Soon, however, the country versus city connotation became less important than the 'non-Christian' one. Pagans were those 'not enlisted in the army of God' and sometimes those 'in hostile forces'. Everyone but Christians became 'pagan' (and perhaps 'uncivilized'). Recently Christians have recognized some other faith communities as having at least some validity and have ceased referring to them as Pagan. A new label, 'World Religions', has been invented to categorize such traditions. Numerical strength and global distribution seem to be key factors in this trend, which frequently leaves Primal Religions, tribal traditions, popular religion and that other new category 'New Religious Movements' outside its consideration. Only rarely are such traditions considered worthy of dialogue. 'Pagan' is now frequently used to mean 'not religious', 'uncultured' or 'hedonistic'.

The previous paragraph is intended not merely as a linguistic and historical parenthesis but as an introduction to some of the themes important to an understanding of Pagan dealings with death. Pagans honour Nature particularly in the countryside and draw on both ancient traditions and on other spiritual traditions, primarily non-monotheistic ones. They are frequently misunderstood, misrepresented, opposed or ignored. Pagans are now able to be somewhat more open about their activities. This openness might be due to a more general pluralism in modern Britain or to two specific factors: the repeal of the Witchcraft Act of 1735 in 1951 and to the widespread popularity of being 'Green' or 'ecologically friendly'.

My intention here is to discuss Ancient Understandings and Nature in more detail and then look at the ways these themes are understood by modern Pagans in Britain. I intend only to suggest some of the roots of modern Pagan approaches to death and the dead.

Ancient Understandings

Artefacts

It seems fitting in a discussion of death to pay attention first to what the dead, now become 'ancestors', have left behind. As Jon Davies has noted (see his papers in this volume), the death of these ancestors is itself a great gift to the living.

Artefacts recovered by archaeologists are also great gifts, despite (or perhaps because of) the fact that only some of these artefacts were produced to be given, to be passed on. The ancestors have left us unintended gifts of life-associated objects such as cooking pots, old boots, pickaxes and rubbish tips. They also more deliberately left stone circles, fields, hillforts, cathedrals and castles. Some of their offerings (to divinities, ancestors or places) have survived, including jewellery, weapons, ornaments, pots and inscriptions. Perhaps our descendants will wonder whether supermarket trolleys in streams were our votive offerings or whether, as is the case, we used such places as rubbish tips. Of course, most of us lack a concept of votive offerings altogether. Objects which are merely 'fossilised lumps of human labour' do not have the eloquence and fluidity of our ancestors' 'overlapping and poly-semous system of classification' (Thomas 1991: 184) which made their artefacts ideal for gifting to descendants, places or divinities.

Our ancestors also left death-associated artefacts such as burial mounds and, sometimes, grave goods. Things handed down directly to immediate descendants are unlikely to have survived to become deliberate bequests to remote descendants like ourselves. Most of what the ancestors have left behind tells us more about their lives than the few things they placed in tombs. They supposed these entombed things to have been removed from circulation and are unlikely to have intended them as messages to any descendants. The tombs themselves might have been the only intentional message of any sort. Death- and life-associated things are our ancestors' greatest gifts to us, after the gift of life itself, of course.

Beliefs and rituals leave only ambiguous evidence behind in

the form of artefacts which can and have been interpreted in different ways. We cannot be certain (in most cases) what those things associated with death and dealings with the dead really meant to the ancestors. Too often the heritage industry presents the past with little imagination and without interest in visions alternative to its own (Bender 1993).

While (burial) mounds are often taken to be eloquent statements addressed to the living and the yet-to-be-born about life after death, some might have been intended to function only as large notices warning neighbours against trespass. John Chapman (1989: 39) suggests that, in some areas at least, burial mounds might have been signs to neighbours that 'our ancestors lived here and we still live here'. To people who lived above the debris of their ancestors' homes and remains, that is on 'tells' (see John Chapman in this volume), there was no problem. It was obvious that they lived in a place with antiquity and could claim that their ancestors gave them the right to live here (even if the 'ancestors' were not in fact theirs at all). At the very least, 'the megalithic builders employed the presence of the ancestors as a medium for the transformation of space' (Thomas 1991: 182). To others it seems to have been necessary to build some sort of large permanent structure (with or without burials) indicative of ancestral authority to carry on living in this place.

However, it seems likely that those mounds containing human remains were connected to a belief in some sort of continuing life beyond the grave. Burials in foetal position might be evidence of a belief in rebirth (Gadon 1990: 50), although it might have been merely the typical 'rest' position (Hutton 1991: 2). Even if barrows were primarily territorial signs their human contents can be assumed to have some sort of postmortem relationship with their descendants. Possessions deposited with a body might only be treasured belongings of the recently dead rather than things they might require in some life after burial. In some cases, however, objects deposited suggest that the ancestors needed similar things to the living. Food placed with the dead probably means that the ancestors would need to eat. The burial of the dead in prominent mounds means that they had become 'ancestors' (the non-Christian equivalent of saints?), they had a continuing life, albeit vicariously in the lives of those who constructed the mounds, buried the remains and continued living in the area.

We have no way of telling what principle of belief or ideology directed the choice of who or what would be buried. That is to say, only a select few were placed in the tombs so elaborately built at times. Some burials are only of a few select parts of those chosen few. We do not know what happened to the last remains of the vast majority of the dead. Although I have concentrated here on burial, our ancestors used many different ways of dealing with dead bodies, cremation, burial and excarnation being only three popular ones. Evidence for these still does not account for the vast numbers of missing remains.

Not all the dead became 'ancestors', although all who died are in a general sense our ancestors. Perhaps we should posit two sorts of ancestor: those who are significant for the life-associated things (including life itself) which they passed on and those who are significant because their significant burial by the wider mass of ancestors immortalized them. But we still do not know why the second group were chosen and whether they were supposed to live beyond the grave, or what the category 'ancestor' meant to our ancestors.

Nor can we know what these burials might have meant to all intervening generations. Some mounds appear to have been deliberately blocked up and their previously open and accessible chambers filled in. This is probably evidence of a major change of belief. Thomas (1991: 185) sees it as part of a wider '"distancing" of the ancestors from the living'. It is certainly a clear change of practice and it would be a mistake to see the past as changeless, undifferentiated and monocultural.

A final note on death-related things left behind by our ancestors concerns violence. There is evidence of violence by humans against humans from a very early period (Hutton 1991: 18). If there has ever been a period of peace and harmony between people—and particularly between the genders—it must have been at a very early period of human development. (None of this, of course, invalidates the attempt to bring about such a period of peace). Among those buried in ancient barrows were some who died violently and some who were probably not there by their own choice. Among excavated settlements, otherwise life-associated places, are many fortified places from periods previously thought peaceful.

Literature

In addition to artefacts inherited from our ancestors we have also received literature (inscriptions, mythology, sagas, stories and histories) which tells us something of their approaches to death and the dead. I do not intend to list the entire corpus nor to provide examples of each type of literature. Rather, I intend to suggest some of the themes from this literature which are of significance in modern Pagan understandings.

Among the inscriptions there are gravestones expressing continuity of affection and family relationship between the deceased and those who erected the stones. Such inscriptions are evidence of widespread beliefs about life beyond the grave. Our more recent ancestors have left explicit literature about where they thought that life continued—heaven, hell or purgatory. Most modern Pagans are not particularly interested in their Christian ancestors, or in the Christianity of these ancestors at least. They are more interested in pre- or non-Christian tomb inscriptions which indicate some belief in life beyond the grave. However, these inscriptions require a context in wider ancient beliefs to be of much value and such a context has not been given to us.

More fruitful for modern Pagan thinking about death and life after death are classical and early mediaeval writings about pre-Christian Paganism. The Celts who failed to flatter Alexander and those who seem to have impressed Caesar did not consider death a cause for concern. The possible breaking of the natural boundaries between Sky and Earth, the collapse of Order into Chaos, was more frightening. The belief in continuity beyond death meant that even violent death was less fearful than Caesar evidently thought it should be. The classical authors describe Celtic and Gallic belief in transmigration of souls. When people died their souls (or some separable continuing essential part of them) took up residence in another already existing physical form. This is different to belief in reincarnation, which normally involves the soul taking on a new physical form. Transmigration also means that a body (of a person, an animal, a tree, a rock or any other physical form) could be inhabited by more than one 'soul'.

Even more popular literary sources for modern Pagans are the surviving mediaeval literatures of Wales and Ireland. Some other literature is also significant, particularly Arthurian epics from whatever place of origin. I shall briefly note three of the themes most often drawn from this literature today.

First, there is the 'Matter of Arthur'. There are innumerable versions of who Arthur was, what he did, when, where and why. I have no intention of adding to this speculation. The theme of Arthur's present whereabouts is, however, of significance here. After receiving a mortal wound Arthur is said to have been taken away to a mysterious location where he is said to be awaiting 'the hour of Britain's greatest need'. Glastonbury is only one claimed site of Arthur's resting place; there are many hills from Cornwall to Scotland where Arthur is said to rest (and there are more of these in the north than anywhere else). What is significant here is the belief that there is such a place of seeming immortality. Death is not always final, the Otherworld of the ancestors can be reached and its inhabitants are interested in the affairs of their descendants.

Another popular story is that of Taliesin, primary bard of Britain. The tale of his origins is significant for its linking of death with initiation. Having gained wisdom from a cauldron he was meant to be merely watching over, the hero realizes his danger and flees. He transforms himself into various animals and eventually into grain only to be swallowed by his pursuer, Ceridwen. She then gives birth to him only to tie him in a bag and hurl him into the sea, which he survives to be 'born from the bag' with all his wisdom and the ability to speak and prophesy. Later in life he is alleged to have travelled to the Otherworld on a fearful quest from which he was one of a very few to return. Death in these tales is not necessarily final, at least not for the heroic or the initiated. Death is itself an initiation leading to rebirth, a mythic restatement of the unbreakable ties between the living and the dead. There is an

Otherworld where there is both great danger and much to be gained.

Thirdly, this literature associates the burial mounds with the feast-halls and regal courts of the Otherworld. On occasions the barrows open and their inhabitants can enter this world and the brave or foolish from this world can enter the Otherworld. Two particular times when this can happen are identified, the beginning of winter feast and the beginning of summer feast. The ancestors continue to live in a realm that is intimately linked with the realm they have left to their descendants. Modern Pagans continue to attempt to make this perilous journey.

While some Pagans sincerely believe in direct lines of descent from ancient Paganism through mediaeval traditions to their own belief and practice it is certainly true that the clearest continuities exist in folk-traditions. Here too we meet the theme that death is not a final end, a full stop. The slaying of the Turkish Knight by the George of Mummers plays is rapidly followed by the call for the Doctor who raises the Knight to fight again. The song about John Barleycorn deliberately confuses the human with the grain. These folk-traditions can be seen as an attempt to link human mortality to the continuous cycle of Nature in which death is often merely apparent: grains buried in the soil soon produce shoots and then a vast return of further grains. In the normal scheme of things a dead person remains dead and gone, removed from the living and not productive of further human life. These folk-celebrations, however, often imply a linking of death with rebirth, the end with a new beginning. They stress continuity against the painful (apparent) finality of that greatest fact of life: death.

Nature

Paganism is an ecological spirituality. It celebrates or venerates Nature. Where many other religions denigrate the body, physical experience, Nature and the Earth, Paganism celebrates these things. The physical is the manifestation, sometimes the only manifestation of the divine. That is, divinity is so immanent that it might not exist in completely disincarnate forms.

Paganism therefore involves learning from Nature. One of the most common shared experiences of Paganism (and one thing that enables us to speak of Paganism as a movement) is the celebration of eight annual solar festivals. These, in addition to the lunar celebrations, are marked by the physical relationship between Earth, Sun and Moon. I shall comment later on one of these festivals which is centred on honouring the dead. Here I merely note the cyclical nature of these celebrations. The Sun and the Moon regularly return to the same places along the eastern horizon in their rising and the western horizon in their setting. If the Sun appears to die in the west every evening it is soon reborn in the east each morning.

Death in nature is not, however, usually a mere metaphor. There is certainly as much death as there is birth, but there is also considerably more death than there is growing to healthy maturity (Dillard 1976). Somehow this has to be taken account of, lived with, honoured. Paganism claims to honour both that which benefits humanity and that which harms us, that which is giving birth and that which is taking life. This is not an easy thing and no Pagan says that it is, but it is part of honouring Nature or the Earth as the primary manifestation of the Goddess or Life.

I shall now turn to modern Pagan ways of dealing with death and remembrance of the dead.

Modern Paganism

No Pagan group has a written text comparable in authority or centrality to the Bible in Judaism or Christianity, or to the Quran in Islam. Yet there is a considerable homogeneity among Pagans. Perhaps the unifying role of a 'Scripture' is fulfilled among Pagans by the shared experience of the celebration of the eight festivals in the cycle of the year. This is not to say that all Pagans do the same thing on any one of these festivals, but they do form a focal point through which a range of experiences and understandings can be related. Briefly stated, the festivals provide a context in which everything in life, from conception to death and beyond, is related. They are a humanly conceptualized echo of the radically interconnected universe. They portray the Web of Life with the simplicity of a web of eight threads.

Samhain

A particular focus for death-related celebrations is the feast which modern Pagans usually name *Samhain*. This is a combination of a beginning of winter feast with a New Year feast. In the cycle of the years any such beginning also means an end of a previous cycle. *Samhain* is the main point in the Pagan calendar when the dead (ancient and recent) are honoured and death acknowledged as part of the cycle.

Traditionally 'the whole day of 1 November was regarded as exciting and perilous' (Hutton 1991: 177). Now most Pagans celebrate *Samhain* with a bonfire on the night before and often treat the 1st as a normal day. This is comparable with popular celebrations of Hallowe'en. Traditionally the Christian feast of All Hallows was more significant than its 'eve', Hallowe'en. Now, however, it is probably only a minority of clergy who would attempt to insist on the old balance.

If All Hallows and the following feast of All Souls celebrate Christian Otherworld beings (holy ones, saints and souls) so the Pagan festival honours Pagan ancestors and Otherworld beings. Typically, stories are told based on traditional stories, myths and legends of those ancestors with whom the group or individual most identifies. The dead may be named and something said about them, especially if their death is recent. At the end of this article I append three examples of the way that some Pagans deal with death (Harvey forthcoming). Two of them note *Samhain* as a context for remembrance.

It is said that at *Samhain* the veil separating this world from the Otherworld is drawn aside and it is possible to journey between the two. So rituals at *Samhain* often include some sort of invitation to the inhabitants of the Otherworld, be they ancestors, faery or divinities, to join the celebration taking place around the fire. The effects of their presence might be experienced in all manner of ways, the simplest being in the practice of some sort of divination. Rune casting, tarot reading and scrying in water can take place at any time of year, but it is claimed that they are particularly effective at *Samhain* and at *Beltain* (the beginning of summer feast on 1st May).

Another connection between these two feasts and between them and death is suggested in Terry Pratchett's novel *Reaper Man*, in which the May Day morris dance has a lesser known but equally important counterpart in a dance at the beginning of winter (Pratchett 1992). Both should be danced to honour the whole cycle including birth and death, growth and decline, beginnings and endings, summer and winter. Given the popularity of Terry Pratchett's 'Discworld' series, this idea, based on a valid intuition of the significance of both these times of year, will probably gain popularity in the coming years.

Initiation

Terry Pratchett's Death (who always speaks in capital letters) has another important offering to make when he says, 'IF PEOPLE KNEW WHEN THEY WERE GOING TO DIE, I THINK THEY PROBABLY WOULDN'T LIVE AT ALL' (Pratchett 1992: 210). Death may be the last experience of all living beings, but knowledge of when it is going to happen is not something most people have or want. However, many esoteric or initiatory systems include the theme 'die before you die'. The initiate is introduced to some experience which is said to be analogous with or a foretaste of the experience of death. Initiation is not solely intended for the purpose of helping people deal with death; it is much more eloquent than that. Initiation takes people through a breaking and an ending into a new beginning, a new birth. The initiate, having died, is reborn into a fuller participation in his or her chosen world-view. Facing death is intended precisely to help people to live in a new and richer way.

For Pagans, death is ritualized, at *Samhain* in particular, as a journey to the Otherworld, or is encountered in the form of a participant acting the role of the Lord of Death (Starhawk 1989: 193-96, 248; Luhrmann 1989: 258-60). Death can then be seen as something ordinary (Lurhmann 1989: 260) whereas the pervasive taboo against talking about it suggests some sort of unusual, unlikely or esoteric idea. Those participating in these rituals are, then, theoretically at least, better able to appreciate the whole life cycle which includes death. One thing that might be understood better is the nature of divinity.

Thealogy and Theoilogy

Pagans who acknowledge only one divinity refer to her as Goddess, since all life-givers in Nature are birth-givers, i.e. mothers. Other Pagans speak of plural divinities, hence the terms 'theaology' and 'theoilogy'.

Pagans following these two approaches are not in conflict, since Paganism is not a religion with a creed or dogma. Some Pagans quite happily talk of 'the Goddess' in one breath and 'the Goddesses and Gods' in the next. A Pagan who acknowledges one divine origin mediated through the polarity of a female and a male divinity will have little difficulty celebrating with someone who names many Goddesses and Gods.

Underlying the diversity is a unity in which most Pagans would assert that divinity (whatever its number) is immanent rather than transcendent. Starhawk rejects the idea that Witches 'believe' in the Goddess, saying that nor do they '*believe* in rocks'. Instead, she says,

> we connect with Her, through the moon, the stars, the ocean, through trees, animals, through other human beings, through ourselves. She is within us all. She is the full circle: earth, air, fire, water, and essence—body, mind, spirit, emotions, change... Birth, death, and decay are equally sacred parts of the cycle (Starhawk 1989: 91-92).

The Goddess includes the dark as well as the light. Starhawk encourages us to face the dark which is 'all that we are afraid of, all that we don't want to see—fear, anger, sex, grief, death, the unknown' (Starhawk 1982: xiv). This all-inclusive Goddess embraces all our actions, intentions and desires as well as our regrets and fears. At the end of this paper I comment on views about what happens, or might happen, after death. A Goddess like the one most Pagans talk about is unlikely to be any sort of judge or punisher.

Clearly, then, Pagan views of divinity predispose people to

deal with death. Paganism sees the cycles of nature as revelatory of the divine and aims both to celebrate such cycles and to attune the individual's life to them. Death is a major part of those cycles.

Death

At Death

At the moment there is little distinctive about the way that Pagans deal with the immediate effects of the death of family or friends. Pagan funeral rituals are beginning to be produced and there is some debate as to what to do with the 'mortal remains' (bury, cremate, donate to medicine or science). Ancient remains and literature evidence a wide range of alternatives.

The Pagan Hospice and Funeral Trust publishes a newsletter and occasional information leaflets relevant to its interests. It is concerned with caring for the sick and making sure they get sympathetic treatment, as well as with death itself. These publications express a diversity of views of death and do not advocate either cremation or burial as the preferred option. Their fourth *Newsletter* (November 1992) enthusiastically reports the use of fireworks to take one man's ashes high into the atmosphere.

Philip Carr-Gomm describes a Parting Ceremony for Lucie, the daughter of friends and members of the Order of Bards, Ovates and Druids of which he is Chosen Chief (Carr-Gomm 1993: 114-21, 149-51). This is a funeral service which took place at a crematorium and was intended 'to wish [Lucie] well as she left our world', 'to celebrate the new life that the soul has been born into and a celebration of their time on earth'. It also expresses the sorrow of the mourners and aims to enable them to 'say farewell' to the one now travelling towards the Otherworld, here envisaged as 'the Summer Isles, the Isles of the Blessed'. It is deeply moving and will probably inspire others to craft similar Parting Ceremonies.

The Odinic Rite, one of several organizations which seek to continue the Norse Heathen tradition in Britain, includes a funeral ceremony or 'Bael' in its *Book of Blots* (sacred ceremonies, rituals and invocations) (Stubba 1991: 114-17). It includes instructions for sea or earth burial and for cremation and the scattering of ashes. Only once does the officiating Gothi (priest) address the deceased, saying, 'when to strife the warriors go through silver portals, as they ride we'll gaze on you [name], a trusty comrade and sit rejoicing by your side'. Elsewhere the ceremony speaks to 'friends and comrades' about the meaning of life and death, about Valhalla (home of dead heroes) and about the deceased's current life. I shall return to this in the following section.

Before I look at what Pagans think happens after death, I want to introduce the three appended narrations of how three Pagans have dealt with death. These are drawn from responses to my continuing research into Paganism in modern Britain and are quoted by permission. The first exemplifies the widespread shock at the death of Wally Hope (founder of Stonehenge Peoples Free Festival). His ashes were eventually scattered within the circle of stones at Stonehenge. Secondly, I include the narration of the resolution of twenty-eight years' mourning by a woman who found in Paganism a way of doing what she had felt unable to do within Christianity. Having had no satisfactory role in her dead baby's funeral she was able to create a 'ritualistic re-carrying of Barry to the Earth'. Thirdly, there is an example of the honouring of a teacher at *Samhain*. In this example the one honoured was a Christian and the funeral one in which the narrator was one of the congregation. I include it here as an example of the way some Pagans deal with the death of friends of other traditions.

Beyond Death

In this final section I want to ask: what happens to a dead Pagan? What happens beyond the moment of death?

Paganism is not centrally concerned with beliefs so much as with experiences. Obviously, however, there are beliefs underpinning the experiences, especially the belief that experience is to be celebrated rather than repressed. Death is a common experience but no one returns to describe it or what happens next. Life beyond death, therefore, has to be a area for theorizing or belief. However much Pagans assert that initiation is like death, they cannot be sure until it happens. It is only certain that beyond death is something different, just as beyond initiation things are meant to be different.

As with every other issue there are a range of beliefs about death held by different Pagans. I can only summarize them here. First, there is the belief that when one is dead one is dead and gone, and nothing survives but memories held by other people. This has its earliest recorded expression in the Epic of Gilgamesh (Sanders 1972) in which the only immortality is the survival of the great deeds done while living. The city walls survive even beyond the memory of the builders' names and that is their only real life beyond death. In a Nature-venerating tradition the return of Nature-given nutrients to the Earth by the dead body is worth celebrating.

Secondly, some Pagans believe in a form of reincarnation. This is expressed in Lucie's Parting Ceremony. Initially, Lucie is incorporated into a community of Otherworld inhabitants who are asked to journey with her. At the end of the journey Lucie is expected to be at the heart of all things and therefore always nearby. Her parents are told that Lucie is 'always with you in Spirit' and 'lives in your hearts as you live in hers'. Near the end of the ceremony Lucie is told that she will 'be born again on earth—when it is right, in your own time'. Here Lucie remains in relationship with her parents and friends, communicating her own farewells in a dream, joins the ancestors and rests until she is ready to reincarnate (Carr-Gomm 1993: 116, 120-21).

Thirdly, some Pagans still believe in transmigration. This is reflected in the remembering of Wally Hope. It might explain the flashes of insight some Pagans claim to have when they visit ancient sacred places if some sort of ancestral spirit is waiting there to act as tour-guide from the Otherworld (T. Sebastian, personal communication 1993).

There are, then, basically two options (each with nuances): an end of conscious existence or some continuity in another form. I have not yet heard of any Pagan who believes in an after-death state analogous to the Christian heaven or hell. Even those Asatru (the chosen name of those who honour Norse divinities) who talk about Valhalla do not see this as a permanent state, first because Valhalla itself will be destroyed in flames when the Giants attack and secondly because all things will be ground down to become the basic material or building blocks of the succeeding universe (Titchenell 1985: 46-51, 90). Immortality is itself conditional. However, it is not conditional on good or bad deeds. If once upon a time *only* warriors killed in battle could make it to Valhalla now the Odinic Rite seems to have democratized the afterlife.

The Bael (memorial ceremony) of the Odinic Rite, rather confusingly, tells the gathering both that the deceased is now 'born again into this world elsewhere' and that they have 'passed through the silvery gates into the Valhalla of renown' (Stubba 1991: 115, 116). There is no hint that the ancestors envisaged any final destination other than Valhalla for all who died. This is especially significant for women. Once the only female inhabitants of Valhalla were Valkyries (apart from the occasional visiting Goddess perhaps and Heidrun 'the goat in Hostfather's Hall' who provides mead for the warriors to drink). The Odinic Rite has not only opened the gates for those who have not died heroically on the battlefield but also allows entry to women. Here, at least, women are not invisible as they are in other sacred (and not so sacred) literature (see Manucha Lisboa's article in this volume).

In my research so far no Pagan has yet expressed a belief in any sort of judgment after death, and especially not in a rewarding and punishing divinity. As Death's apprentice Mort says of his master in another of Terry Pratchett's novels, 'he doesn't care if people are good or bad, so long as they're punctual. And kind to cats' (Pratchett 1987: 83). As noted above, Pagan divinities are immanent and are experienced within rather than in opposition to everyday life. When another of Terry Pratchett's characters dies Death tells him that at the end of the desert that all the dead face is Judgment, he responds '*which* end?'. It is intimated that this is an appreciation of the truth (Pratchett 1992: 380). Those Pagans who believe in a life beyond the grave (whether among the ancestors or back in this world by reincarnation or transmigration) believe that each individual is the only judge of his or her own actions.

Appendix

Wally Hope

'On the third of September 1975, Phil Russell, alias Phil Hope, alias Wally Hope, alias Wally, choked to death on his own vomit' (Crass 1982: 1).

The name 'Phil Russell' is almost unknown. The name 'Wally' is frequently heard at festivals and gatherings. Perhaps not everyone knows why they repeat the cry 'WALLY', but the sense of veneration in which Wally Hope is held is infectious. The following is extracted from an interview with a would-be Stonehenge Festival-goer who wishes to be known only as 'Flidais of Pen Bal Crag'.

'Wally Hope is the ancestor and guiding spirit behind Stonehenge People's Free Festival. He established the Festival around the time of Summer Solstice, June 1974. Wally was the Son of the Sun and the people gathered around him, though it rained, for two months and more, in his camp in the ancient and modern Temple of Stonehenge. You can read in the Crass book what happened to him, what is known anyway. He was arrested and sectioned, forced to take mind-destroying drugs. When he was released, thrown out of the 'hospital', just after the Festival of 1975, he was destroyed. No longer the confident Sun God, happy drumming dancing hero that he had been, now a frightened, incoherent wreck.

'He died and some say it was suicide. Some say differently. If it was suicide it was inspired by those who'd destroyed him. His ashes were scattered inside the Temple of Stonehenge. I wasn't there at the scattering but I was there when Syd Rawles [a leading and colourful figure in the continuing community of those who wish to celebrate at Stonehenge] told the story of how it happened. He carried the urn of Wally's ashes past the barbed wire barriers into the Stones. Others followed. He scattered Wally's ashes where many other ancestors had been buried or scattered. Wally joined that other tribe. Syd passed the Urn to others and they all scattered some ashes. Then a child took the Urn and dipped her finger into the ashes and tasted them. Everyone else joined her in the tasting. Wally became part of his people in a different way.

'Wally is still alive. Some say his soul joined with Syd. That's like what the ancient Druids believed in. Not exactly like reincarnation that they believe in in India. But something of him moved in to join in Syd's life. Others say his life goes on in the many gatherings that take place now and especially when they laugh and dance and try to go to Stonehenge. The urn that contained Wally's ashes is now carried by another of his old companions and is often seen at festivals and at the meetings we're still holding to try to get access to our Temple again. 'WALLY!'

Saying Goodbye to Barry

The following is the record of one woman's relationship with her lost son.

'My son Barry was born to me on January 23rd. On February 28th he died. In deep mourning and bewilderment I was forced to stand by while others, mainly men, 'took care' of everything. I watched his small coffin being lowered into the ground. Without having said goodbye to him he took his place in the earth. And that was all that was to happen. I was expected to leave that place of the dead and my dead son and get on with the living.

'For the following twenty-eight years my January and February were troubled. I dreamed of him. Neither of us were contented. There had been no ritual for me at his going. I was denied access to him. I was sent away from him at his dying. At his baptism strange arms held him. Not mine.

'At the end of this tormented twenty-eight years I felt as a woman who'd left Christianity and all its strictures behind. I could now do something about what happened. I had kept cards of sympathy and wreath ribbons carefully folded and together all that time. How often I read my own words of goodbye over and over again. But the words weren't enough. I needed to carry out an act—a ritualistic re-carrying of Barry to the Earth but this time it would be me, his mother.

'It was the summer of '92. My partner and I went out to our favourite wood. Near to an oak tree and beneath an ancient stone, the charred remains of cards and ribbons were buried. Incense smouldered sweetly while my tears and quiet words left me. I had said goodbye to Barry wrapped up in my solitude in the company of my partner.

'Six months later at Samhain we took a gift to the place. We lit a fire and honoured the arrival of my baby grandson James'.

Lee at Samhain

This piece is extracted from an interview with another Pagan who wishes to remain anonymous.

'I had a teacher at school who I had a lot of respect for. His idea was that education wasn't about exams and bits of paper but about life. He loved travelling and encouraged us to travel.

'Some years after I'd left school and been travelling for a while, I heard Lee had died. Not in bed of course. He was out in Darjeeling delivering aid (and leading dancing and laughing no doubt) when he set off up a mountain and had a massive heart-attack. He was buried somewhere there and his family and friends had a memorial service in his home town. Being Welsh and Methodists you can imagine the power of the singing. It was a real celebration of Lee's life. Sad that he'd gone, but glorying in his life and his influence.

'Every year at Samhain, Hallowe'en, I name Lee among the ancestors. The Christians may have tried to abandon their ancestors and their feast of Hallowe'en in their obsession about Paganism but we still honour them.

'Lee has gone back to the Earth and she cares for him. Maybe he's even taken on a new life, a hill or a tiger probably. He lives not just in our memories and not just in the way we continue to do what he encouraged us to do. He is among the ancestors.'

Bibliography

Bender, B.
  1993   'Stonehenge—Contested Landscapes (Medieval to Present-Day)', in *idem* (ed.), *Landscape, Politics and Perspectives* (Oxford: Berg).
Carr-Gomm, P.
  1993   *The Druid Way* (Shaftesbury: Elements).
Chapman, J.
  1989   'The Early Balkan Village', in *Neolithic of Southern Europe and its Near Eastern Connections: Varia Archaeologica Hungarica II*.
Crass
  1982   *A Series of Shock Slogans and Mindless Token Tantrums* (London: Existential Press).
Dillard, A.
  1976   *Pilgrim at Tinker Creek* (London: Picador).
Gadon, E.W.
  1990   *The Once and Future Goddess* (Wellingborough: Aquarian).
Harvey, G.
  forthcoming *Pagans in Modern Britain: An Empirical Overview.*
Hutton, R.
  1991   *The Pagan Religions of the Ancient British Isles* (Oxford: Basil Blackwell).
Luhrmann, T.
  1989   *Persuasions of the Witch's Craft* (Oxford: Basil Blackwell).
Pratchett, T.
  1987   *Mort* (London: Corgi).
  1992   *Reaper Man* (London: Corgi).
Sanders, N.K.
  1972   *The Epic of Gilgamesh* (London: Penguin).
Starhawk
  1982   *Dreaming the Dark* (Boston: Beacon Press).
  1989   *Spiral Dance* (San Francisco: Harper & Row).

Stubba
   1991   *The Book of Blots* (London: The Odinic Rite).
Thomas, J.
   1991   *Rethinking the Neolithic* (Cambridge: Cambridge University Press).
Titchenell, E.-B.
   1985   *The Masks of Odin* (Pasadena: Theosophical University).

Part II

Death in War

Death in War: Britten and the *War Requiem*

Eric Cross

Benjamin Britten's *War Requiem* was commissioned to celebrate the consecration of the new Coventry Cathedral, built to replace the old mediaeval building which was destroyed in the Second World War. It was first performed on 30 May 1962 and had an immediate and profound impact on the audience. Indeed, the stir caused by its early performances was greater than that of any Britten work since *Peter Grimes*, and its popularity has remained undiminished over the last thirty years.

That Britten chose to set the traditional Requiem text for this important event is unsurprising, but his idea of juxtaposing the Latin liturgy with the war poems of Wilfred Owen was highly original. Through this combination the *War Requiem* links those killed in the bombing of Coventry with both the victims of the trenches who died alongside Owen in the Great War and with the dead across the ages who are remembered in the timeless Latin text. The work also prompts various questions about the nature of Requiem settings in general. It was not, of course, the first work by Britten in which death is a central concern, nor was it the last, for from the early pacifist protests of the 1930s to his final opera *Death in Venice* the individual and collective mortality of humankind was of crucial concern to the composer. This essay will explore some of these different strands in turn—the tradition of the Requiem Mass, the view of violent death portrayed in the poetry of Wilfred Owen and in other contemporary works, and the importance of death in Britten's compositions—before examining their relationship to the *War Requiem* itself.

The Requiem Mass

Evidence for the celebration of the Eucharist for departed church members in Africa and Syria goes back to the end of the second and the early third centuries.[1] The Roman Sacramentaries indicate masses for the dead to be celebrated on the third, seventh and thirtieth days, plus the annual anniversary. Their function was to maintain the link between the living and the dead, the continuing fellowship through the Eucharist ensuring that death was not a barrier. Thus these services can be viewed in part as the liturgical equivalent of the announcements common in today's newspapers which commemorate the anniversary of the death of a family member or friend.[2]

Soon one of the important reasons for celebrating masses for the dead, in addition to escaping damnation to hell, became the idea that they could win remission from sin, thereby shortening the period spent in purgatory before judgment. The concept of purgatory is also, of course, a sociable concept, as Jon Davies discusses elsewhere;[3] it centres around the communion of the living and the dead—a kind of spiritual waiting-room. By the beginning of the second millennium, funeral rites placed increasing emphasis on sin and judgment, with important penitential psalms such as the Miserere. In the fourteenth century the commemoration of the faithful departed became focused on 2 November (All Souls' Day),[4] thereby increasing even more the communal and public nature of the celebrations.

Musical settings of the Requiem Mass—or rather of parts of the service—to polyphony as opposed to plainchant were rare

---

1. For a brief history of burial services see A.S. Duncan-Jones, 'The Burial of the Dead', in W.K. Lowther Clarke and C. Harris (eds.), *Liturgy and Worship: A Companion to the Prayer Books of the Anglican Communion* (London: SPCK, 1932), pp. 616-25; also pp. 365-70.

2. These are discussed by Jon Davies in his essay 'One Hundred Billion Dead: A General Theology of Death' in this volume.

3. Davies, 'One Hundred Billion Dead'.

4. J. Harper, *The Forms and Orders of Western Liturgy from the Tenth to the Eighteenth Century* (Oxford: Clarendon Press, 1991), p. 125.

before 1500.[1] Ockeghem's setting of parts of the text survives, while Dufay directed that his Requiem, 'newly composed' in 1470–71 though now lost, should be sung by twelve good adult singers on the day after his death.[2] Thus Dufay began a long tradition of composers writing music for their own funeral services, which in the seventeenth century was to include Heinrich Schütz and Jean Gilles, the latter's *Messe des morts* not only being used frequently at funerals but also being performed regularly as a concert work. Gilles's work reflects both the great increase in Requiem settings during the seventeenth century (along with separate settings of the Dies Irae and the Libera Me, both highly emotive texts) and the importance of works written for special occasions, whether for the death of leading composers such as Josquin or Mozart or in memory of distinguished figures such as politicians (for instance, Gilles's work was performed in memory of Jean-Philippe Rameau and Louis XV, Cherubini's Requiem in C minor of 1817 was sung to commemorate the execution of Louis XVI, and Verdi's setting was written for Alessandro Manzoni). James W. Pruett gives the following figures for Requiem settings up to c. 1975:[3]

Polyphonic Requiem Settings

Date	Approximate Number of Works
up to 1620	70
1620–1750	325
1750–1825	250
1825–1910	620
1910–c. 1975	335

The approaches of different composers vary enormously. Some are overtly dramatic, as in the case of Verdi, whose most memorable passage must surely be the pounding orchestral

1. For a short history of musical settings of the Requiem see J.W. Pruett, 'Requiem Mass', in S. Sadie (ed.), *The New Grove Dictionary of Music and Musicians* (London: Macmillan, 1980), XV, pp. 751-55.

2. D. Fallows, *Dufay* (London: Dent, 1982), p. 78, suggests that the work was a setting of the Propers of the Requiem.

3. 'Requiem Mass', p. 754.

chords and terrifying shouts of the Dies Irae. Berlioz's *Grand messe des morts* is monumental in every sense of the word, with its demands for huge forces including four separate brass bands, while Fauré's setting provides a well-known example of a more intimate approach, particularly when performed with the composer's original lighter scoring. Here it is the more contemplative movements, such as the Pie Jesu and In Paradisum, which linger in the memory. Not all Requiem settings were intended for liturgical use; Brahms's *German Requiem* is probably the most famous example in the non-liturgical category, which also includes Britten's *War Requiem*. Many of these works can also be regarded as *public* works: memorials on a grand scale, aural mausoleums which fill the listener with a sense of awe.

The Great War, Monuments and the Arts

Death in war is also in some senses a public event. In the first few months of the First World War 3000 men per day died on the Western Front, and the official US War Department figures for the whole war give $8\frac{1}{2}$ million military deaths and around 1 million civilian fatalities, making a total of c. 10 million.[1] Death on this scale inevitably led to a degree of dehumanization; for the servicemen it resulted in a feeling of alienation, both from ordinary emotions—they became simply killing machines—and from their leaders, whom they believed to be totally out of touch with reality (a feeling exacerbated by the class system).[2]

As the dead became statistics, recording death became vitally important in order to provide a focus for grief and a sense of dignity.[3] In 1918 there were over 500,000 unmarked British

1.   These statistics are discussed in G. Elliot, *Twentieth Century Book of the Dead* (London: Allen Lane and Penguin, 1972), pp. 218ff., a book which examines various aspects of death in war.

2.   Wilfred Owen dwells on these disturbing feelings in both his letters and his poetry.

3.   Shirley Park Lowry discusses the urge to forestall oblivion by recording names and genealogies, from the sealed tombs of ancient Egypt to the vast underground vaults of Utah, in *Familiar Mysteries: The Truth in Myth* (Oxford: Oxford University Press, 1982), pp. 216-17.

graves in the war zones, and many of the dead had no graves
at all, so that the Roll of Honour—the lists of dead and
wounded published regularly in newspapers—served as a kind
of surrogate headstone. Other forms of monument included
war memorials such as the Cenotaph, often commemorating
the unknown dead as opposed to the recorded names on the
Roll of Honour. A temporary structure was erected for Peace
Day 1919, but Lutyens's permanent Cenotaph was unveiled by
the king on Armistice Day the following year. Its simple all-
embracing inscription, 'The Glorious Dead', paralleled the
ceremony held the same day at Westminster Abbey, the burial
of the Unknown Warrior, in an attempt to provide some sense
of dignity and peace to the millions who had suffered an
undignified, violent death.[1]

There were also musical monuments from this period.
Patriotic songs such as Ivor Novello's 'Tipperary' and 'Keep the
Home Fires Burning' were, of course, very popular, as were
national anthems, while composers like Elgar were encouraged
to cultivate a heroic style. John Foulds's *A World Requiem*,
written between 1918 and 1921, was first performed on
Armistice Night 1923 in a British Legion commemorative
service in the Albert Hall. This work was monumental in
several ways. It lasted around two hours, was in 20 movements
and required 1200 singers and instrumentalists, thereby out-
doing even Mahler's Eighth Symphony. Its text is eclectic,
drawing on the Bible, Bunyan's *Pilgrim's Progress*, Hindu poetry
and free verse. The score announces it as 'a tribute to the
memory of the Dead—a message of consolation to the
bereaved of all countries'; a musical cenotaph. According to
the *Times*'s critic, 'it was received by a very large number of
listeners, who...found perhaps in the communal note of that
choir of 1,200 the sympathy of which they stood in need'.[2]
Later critics, however, have been less understanding. Eric Blom

1.   Much of the discussion here on memorials from the period around
the Great War is based on material from Samuel Hynes's excellent book *A
War Imagined: The First World War and English Culture* (London: Bodley Head,
1990).

2.   Quoted in Hynes, *A War Imagined*, p. 276.

describes the work as 'a rather tawdrily sentimental commem-oration of the World War I dead',[1] and although it was performed annually for a few years, the British Legion withdrew its support after 1926.

One of the problems for all artists at this time was whether art should be viewed as a commemorative monument or as a protest. According to Middleton Murry, worried by some of the gruesome war paintings, 'Art is not a protest, but the art that deals with war must be a protest. There is the dilemma.'[2] The function of art as a medium for protest led to the concept of the 'anti-monument'.

William Orpen was appointed an official artist with the army in France early in 1917. He was commissioned to depict the peace ceremonies at Versailles in 1919, but by then his admiration for the fighting soldiers was coupled with a disgust for the statesmen or 'frocks' as he termed them. A formal group of delegates in the Hall of Peace involved 36 individual portraits and, although he worked for nine months on the picture, in the end he found himself unable to complete it. Eventually he painted out the delegates entirely, substituting a coffin draped with the Union Jack, guarded by two half-naked soldiers with two cherubs hovering above (see Figure 1).[3] Shown at the Royal Academy's summer exhibition of 1923 under the title *To the Unknown British Soldier in France*, it was voted picture of the year by the public. Five years later, however, following negotiations with the Imperial War Museum, Orpen submitted a revised version as a memorial to Field Marshal Earl Haig, in which the soldiers and cupids were painted out, leaving just the coffin and an eerie emptiness.[4]

1.   E. Blom, 'Foulds, John', in Sadie (ed.), *The New Grove Dictionary of Music and Musicians*, VI, p. 733.

2.   Hynes, *A War Imagined*, p. 275.

3.   For details of Orpen's career as a war artist see M. Harries and S. Harries, *The War Artists: British Official War Art of the Twentieth Century* (London: Michael Joseph, 1983). *To the Unknown British Soldier in France* is discussed on pp. 146ff.

4.   Hynes, *A War Imagined*, p. 460. The tunnel-like passage behind the coffin evokes images of the underworld; see below in relation to Owen's *Strange Meeting*.

Figure 1. *William Orpen,* To the Unknown British Soldier in France, *first version (reproduced by permission of the Trustees of the Imperial War Museum, London).*

Paul Nash was another painter sent to the Western Front as an Official War Artist. (He was also commissioned as an Artist to the Royal Air Force in 1940.) He was stationed at Ypres Salient in 1917, and although he spent only a few months in France, and just a few weeks in the front line, the effect on his painting was profound.[1] The graceful pre-war elms of the Home Counties became mutilated, shattered trunks amid the desolate waste and stinking mud of no-man's-land. *We are Making a New World* (Figure 2) dates from 1918 and vividly captures the sense of annihilation at the Front with its mutilated trees and ravaged landscape. Also from the same period, *The Menin Road* has many similarities (see Figure 3). In this 'large memorial painting', the diminutive figures are overshadowed by the powerful geometrical diagonals and verticals: all sense of honour or glory has gone, to be replaced with a stark, impersonal realism. The size of this canvas, 6' × 10'5", is almost identical to that of Wyndham Lewis's *A Battery Shelled*, a similarly monumental painting in which the figures are unemotional, dominated by the devastated landscape in which they find themselves.[2]

Figure 2. *Paul Nash,* We are Making a New World (*reproduced by permission of the Trustees of the Imperial War Museum, London*).

1. See Harries and Harries, *The War Artists,* and J. Rothenstein, *Paul Nash* (Norwich: Purnell, 1967).
2. This painting is reproduced in Hynes, *A War Imagined.*

Figure 3. Paul Nash, *The Menin Road* (reproduced by permission of the Trustees of the Imperial War Museum, London).

The best known anti-war art from the time of the Great War, however, is poetry. War has always inspired poets, from Homer to Kipling and beyond, and this continuous tradition, as Hynes points out,[1] serves to link the current generation of living soldiers with the military dead of past ages. The majority of the First World War poets were, in fact, not in uniform; Rupert Brooke, for example, despite his popularity at the time, was never at the Front. Wilfred Owen, however, did write from direct experience, even if, like Nash, he was only in the trenches for a few weeks.

In many ways Owen is symbolic, returning to the trenches after a period of hospitalization out of love for the men under his command and being killed at the age of 25 on 4 November 1918, just seven days before the Armistice was signed. Under the strong influence of Siegfried Sassoon, Owen developed a powerful and personal language drawing directly on his own disturbing experiences of war, and his poetry, though initially little known, rapidly grew in popularity after his death. His approach is perhaps best summed up in the famous Preface, drafted for the planned publication of a volume of poems. This was heavily revised by Owen and includes the lines taken by Benjamin Britten as his preface to the *War Requiem*:[2]

> My subject is War, and the pity of War.
> The Poetry is in the pity...
> All a poet can do today is warn.

Britten, War and Death

Britten's aim in the *War Requiem* was to make a *public* statement: a monumental yet accessible work, 'calculated...for a big reverberant acoustic'.[3] This acoustic was provided by

1. *A War Imagined*, pp. 29ff.
2. Owen's Preface is reproduced as the frontispiece of J. Stallworthy (ed.), *Wilfred Owen: The Complete Poems and Fragments* (London: Chatto & Windus, Hogarth Press and Oxford University Press, 1983), I, and in D. Hibberd, *Wilfred Owen: The Last Year 1917–1918* (London: Constable, 1992), p. 122. The third line is actually misquoted in the 1962 edition of Britten's full score, although it is correct in the vocal score.
3. B. Britten, *On Receiving the First Aspen Award* (London: Faber & Faber,

St Michael's Cathedral, Coventry, designed by Sir Basil Spence. The new building was a potent symbol, rising from the ashes of war in the shadow of its ruined mediaeval predecessor. The contrasts between old and new were deliberately exploited, Spence's architecture being viewed against the skeleton of the fifteenth-century spire and original east end (see Figure 4). Among the other artists involved were Graham Sutherland (designer of the famous tapestry), John Hutton, Jacob Epstein (who produced the massive sculpture of St Michael and Lucifer) and John Piper, who also collaborated as designer on stage works with Britten.

Figure 4. *The new Coventry Cathedral, designed by Sir Basil Spence, beside the ruins of the fifteenth-century building (reproduced by permission of A.F. Kersting).*

The consecration of the new cathedral was celebrated with a special arts festival, and Britten's *War Requiem* was given its first performance on 30 May 1962. Although Britten saw it as a public work, it also carried a more private aspect: the score

1964), p. 11, quoted in M. Kennedy, *Britten* (London: Dent, 1981), p. 78.

bears a dedication to four friends, three servicemen killed in action during the Second World War and a fourth who later committed suicide. The original choice of soloists was also highly significant. Britten wanted an international trio which could represent opposing wartime factions; the tenor soloist was to be Peter Pears, and on 16 February 1961 the composer wrote to the German baritone Dietrich Fischer-Dieskau inviting him to take part in the premiere.[1] In this letter he describes Owen's poems as 'a kind of commentary on the Mass'—a commentary which was made all the more poignant in the final *Strange Meeting* by its setting for English tenor and German baritone. The soprano soloist was to have been the Russian Galina Vishnevskaya, for whom the Latin Mass text would have been easier than English words, but in the end she was not granted permission to leave Russia and her place was taken at the last minute by Heather Harper.[2] In November 1962 the *War Requiem* was also performed in Berlin, again reflecting Anglo–German symbolism. Michael Tippett described the piece as 'the one musical masterwork we possess with overt pacifist meanings',[3] and clearly the whole concept of a *War Requiem* had a powerful appeal to a lifelong committed pacifist like Britten.

Britten's pacifist leanings started early on. As Head Boy at South Lodge Preparatory School, Lowestoft, he had helped to stamp out bullying, and during his final term at the school he produced a highly controversial anti-hunting essay on 'Animals'.[4] At Gresham's School, Holt, he refused to join the OTC, and in the 1930s he became deeply affected by the European political scene. Among the works from this period are a *Pacifist March* for the Peace Pledge Union, incidental music for the anti-war propaganda film *Peace of Britain*, a motet *Advance Democracy* for the Co-operative Movement, setting

1. H. Carpenter, *Benjamin Britten: A Biography* (London: Faber & Faber, 1992), p. 404.

2. Carpenter, *Benjamin Britten*, p. 405. Vishnevskaya did eventually take part in a performance of the work in the Royal Albert Hall on 9 January 1963.

3. Quoted in Carpenter, *Benjamin Britten*, p. 410.

4. Kennedy, *Britten*, p. 7.

words by the editor of *Left Review*, and the *Ballad of Heroes*, written in 1939 to honour the men of the British Battalion of the International Brigade killed in the Spanish Civil War.

But perhaps the most unlikely political episode involved the *Sinfonia da Requiem*. The Japanese Embassy had approached the British Council about commissioning an English composer to write a large orchestral work for the 2600th Anniversary Celebration of the Japanese Empire. Britten's immediate reaction was that there should be 'no jingo', and in an interview with the *New York Sun* on 27 April he said:

> I'm making it just as anti-war as possible... I'm dedicating this symphony to the memory of my parents, and, since it is a kind of requiem, I'm quoting from the Dies Irae of the Requiem Mass. One's apt to get muddled discussing such things—all I'm sure of is my own anti-war conviction as I write it.[1]

The titles for the three movements were all taken from the Requiem, although Britten himself noted[2] that the connection was more emotional than liturgical: (1) Lacrymosa; (2) Dies Irae—a Dance of Death, something also found in *Our Hunting Fathers* and the *Ballad of Heroes*; (3) Requiem Aeternam. Not surprisingly, the work was rejected by the President of the Japanese Committee:

> Mr Benjamin Britten's composition is so very different from the anticipation of the Committee which had hoped to receive from a friendly nation felicitations expressed in musical form on the 2,600th anniversary of the founding of the Japanese Empire... Besides being purely a religious music of Christian nature, it has melancholy tone both in its melodic pattern and rhythm making it unsuitable for performance on such an occasion as our national ceremony. We are puzzled...[3]

1.   D. Mitchell and P. Reed (eds.), *Letters from a Life: The Selected Letters and Diaries of Benjamin Britten, 1913–1976* (Berkeley and Los Angeles: University of California Press, 1991), II, p. 705. Other composers commissioned by the Japanese included Richard Strauss from Germany, Jacques Ibert from France, Ildebrando Pizzetti from Italy and Sandor Veress from Hungary.

2.   In an additional paragraph to his programme note for the first performance; see Mitchell and Reed (eds.), *Letters from a Life*, II, p. 997.

3.   Mitchell and Reed (eds.), *Letters from a Life*, II, p. 881.

Britten's most overt pacifist statement, however, came in May 1942, when he appeared before the Local Tribunal for the Registration of Conscientious Objectors:

> Since I believe that there is in every man the spirit of God, I cannot destroy, and feel it my duty to avoid helping to destroy as far as I am able, human life, however strongly I may disapprove of the individual's actions or thoughts. The whole of my life has been devoted to acts of creation (being by profession a composer) and I cannot take part in acts of destruction.[1]

In June Britten was granted unconditional exemption, a more fortunate fate than that which befell his fellow conscientious objector and composer Michael Tippett. He, like Britten, also used his art to advertise his pacifist principles, most notably in his moving oratorio *A Child of our Time* (written at the beginning of the war but not performed until 1944), but his appeal was unsuccessful and in June 1943 he was sentenced to three months in Wormwood Scrubs.

Britten continued his firm belief in pacifism throughout his life, and his anti-military convictions reappear in the television opera *Owen Wingrave*, recorded in 1970. Like *The Turn of the Screw*, this work is based on a short story by Henry James. Owen is destined to follow the family tradition of a military career, but he rebels and is disinherited by his furious grandfather General Sir Philip Wingrave. Taunted by his fiancée Kate, Owen attempts to prove his courage by spending the night in a haunted room in which two of his ancestors died. Kate later relents, but it is too late: Owen is already dead.

In Act II, before his last fatal gesture of defiance, Owen rejects his family with a passionate hymn to peace: 'In peace I have found my image, I have found myself. In peace I rejoice amongst men and yet walk alone'.[2] This idea of self-discovery is crucial, though Arnold Whittall suggests that here, unlike the *War Requiem*, there is 'no evidence that Wingrave's self-sacrifice has achieved more than his own personal and brief moment of truth'.[3] Nevertheless, the work contains resonances with many

1. Mitchell and Reed (eds.), *Letters from a Life*, II, p. 1046.
2. Vocal score (London: Faber Music Ltd, 1973), pp. 175-76.
3. A. Whittall, *The Music of Britten and Tippett* (Cambridge: Cambridge

of Britten's earlier works. The bullying and eventual killing of a young boy by an older man recalls Peter Grimes and his apprentices, Claggart and Billy Budd, and Quint and Miles in *The Turn of the Screw*, while the figure of a lonely individual, unable to fit into the society in which he is forced to live, appears in many works from *Peter Grimes* to *Death in Venice*. Humphrey Carpenter also points out that Sir Philip's final words to the dead Owen, 'My boy!', were suggested to the librettist Myfanwy Piper by the role's creator Peter Pears, this being a phrase with which Pears had frequently addressed Britten in his early letters.[1]

Alongside pacifism, death is a constant thread running through much of Britten's output, especially his later works. The pre-ordained victim, for whom death is the inevitable outcome, is at the centre of many of his operas, including *Peter Grimes*, *The Rape of Lucretia*, *The Turn of the Screw*, *Billy Budd*, *Owen Wingrave* and *Death in Venice*.[2] Often the individual is rejected and ultimately defeated by society, something which reflects Britten's own underlying insecurity and paranoia resulting from both his pacifist leanings and his homosexuality. In *The Rape of Lucretia* and *Billy Budd* the story is also set against the background of war, Captain Vere's indecision over how to save Billy in the latter work also reflecting his own internal psychological warfare between the opposing forces of duty and conscience.[3]

University Press, 1982), p. 250. Self-discovery is also at the heart of many of Tippett's works, for example *A Child of our Time*, whose final General Ensemble begins 'I would know my shadow and my light'.

1.   Carpenter, *Benjamin Britten*, p. 513.

2.   Death is also central to one of Britten's very last works, the cantata *Phaedra*, in which Phaedra's calm, philosophical approach to death is summed up in Racine's lines: 'Death will give me freedom; oh it's nothing not to live; death to the unhappy's no catastrophe!'

3.   Similarly, in the Storm Interlude of *Peter Grimes*, the physical turmoil of the sea parallels the psychological conflicts in the mind of the protagonist. *The Rape of Lucretia* also offers the analogy between rape and warfare.

In many of Britten's works, death is the direct result of the defiance of a 'dark side'—an attempt to prevent the corruption of innocence by evil. Sometimes this has clear homosexual overtones, as in the relationships between Peter Quint and the boy Miles in *The Turn of the Screw* or between Claggart and Billy Budd, and often other 'good' characters are at least partly responsible. In *The Turn of the Screw* it is the Governess who fails to comprehend the danger to Miles, while in *Billy Budd* it is Captain Vere who has been unable to restrain Claggart's sadistic tendencies and who himself sentences Billy to death. In the *War Requiem* this sense of responsibility is widened to a communal level: we are all responsible for the hatred and destruction of war, even when we believe that we are in the right, and the impotent fury at the futility of war is directed not at the past dead but at the *living*.

The significance of death for Britten is, of course, most obvious in his final great autobiographical opera *Death in Venice*. Here the emphasis is on the links between love and death: in the words of Aschenbach's Act II Hymn to Phaedrus, 'And senses lead to passion, Phaedrus / And passion to the abyss'.[1] Ambiguous Venice reflects the Janus-like combination of beauty and corruption (musically depicted by the false relation between first E natural and E flat and then F natural and F sharp to which this phrase is set), while a ubiquitous motive based around the ambiguity between the minor and major third links both the cries of 'Serenissima' (i.e. Venice) and the plague which ultimately kills Aschenbach:[2]

---

1.   *Death in Venice* vocal score (London: Faber Music Ltd, 1975), p. 252.
2.   *Death in Venice* vocal score, pp. 38-39, 19, 167. The conflict of the major/minor third is a familiar one in Britten's music; it can be seen, for example, in the setting of 'O rose, thou art sick' from Blake's 'Elegy' in the *Serenade* of 1943.

Aschenbach's death as he gazes at the beautiful young boy Tadzio walking out to sea is really a *Liebestod*, the final luminous orchestral epilogue, with its searing string lines, as powerful in its own way as that of Wagner's *Tristan*.[1]

The autobiographical resonances of Britten's final opera, written while struggling against illness and with a plot centring on the protagonist's realization and ultimate acceptance of his homosexual nature, are clearly very strong, although Gary Schmidgall believes that 'the crux of the story is not sublimation of homosexual instincts, but more generally the sublimation of vital instincts—the instincts of life—which is a danger courted by the superior intellect—an intellect like Mann's own'.[2]

1.   The treatment of the sea as a symbol of death and a return to nature (again with strong Wagnerian overtones) is also found in *Peter Grimes* and *Billy Budd*.

2.   G. Schmidgall, *Literature as Opera* (New York: Oxford University Press, 1977), p. 330.

Britten's War Requiem

If for Thomas Mann 'the principle of beauty and form does not spring from the sphere of life... [What conditions this world] is the idea of beauty and death...',[1] Wilfred Owen's view of death certainly has little to do with beauty. In a letter of 4 February 1917 to his mother Susan he writes:

> I suppose I can endure cold, and fatigue, and the face-to-face death, as well as another; but extra for me there is the universal pervasion of *Ugliness*. Hideous landscapes, vile noises, foul language and nothing but foul, even from one's own mouth (for all are devil ridden), everything unnatural, broken, blasted; the distortion of the dead, whose unburiable bodies sit outside the dugouts all day, all night, the most execrable sights on earth. In poetry we call them the most glorious.[2]

By adopting the disturbing and powerful images of Owen's poetry into the traditional context of the Latin Mass, Britten was seeking to find a 'new' language and symbols appropriate to a modern secular age, a language in keeping with the historical and cultural context of a society which had largely rejected traditional religious doctrine. Thus the *War Requiem* is a non-liturgical work in which the interplay of language and symbols works on different levels, the relationship between the traditional Requiem Mass (sung in the 'dead' language of Latin) and the contemporary soldiers of Owen's poems (sung in English) reflecting the communion between the living and the

---

1. From *Essays of Three Decades* (trans. H.T. Lowe-Porter; London: Secker & Warburg, 1947), p. 261, quoted in C. Palmer, 'Towards a Genealogy of "Death in Venice"', in *idem* (ed.), *The Britten Companion* (London: Faber & Faber, 1984), p. 253. This essay is on the poet August Graf von Platen-Hallermünde, also a homosexual with a particular fascination for the ambiguous city of Venice who was one of the models for Aschenbach. Palmer quotes a couplet from Platen's most famous poem 'Tristan': 'Wer die Schönheit angeschaut mit Augen / Ist dem Tode schon anheimgegeben' ('He who once has looked on Beauty has lost himself irretrievably to Death').

2. Cited in D. Hibberd (ed.), *Wilfred Owen: War Poems and Others* (London: Chatto & Windus, 1973), p. 64.

dead. These different levels are in turn reflected by three different musical planes:

1. The tenor and baritone soloists who portray Owen's soldiers, the innocent victims of war, accompanied by a twelve-piece chamber orchestra. On a personal level they can also be seen to represent the four servicemen to whom the work is dedicated.

2. A 'monumental' or 'public' level represented by the full orchestra, chorus and soprano soloist singing the Latin Mass text: a symbol of humanity and the Christian concept of salvation.[1]

3. A distant boys' choir and organ, also singing in Latin: an angelic sound-world (already explored in 1959 with the *Missa brevis*) of purity and innocence beyond the grave.

The use of these three largely independent planes highlights the contrasts between the liturgy and the stark realism of Owen's poetry, but it also carries with it the danger of excessive fragmentation. This is skilfully avoided by a complex web of textual and musical cross-references. The most obvious musical element which permeates the whole work is the interval of the tritone. The two bells, heard at the outset of the work, first separately and then together, are tuned to C and F sharp; these notes are taken up by the chorus, whose Verdian liturgical mutterings are restricted entirely to these pitches for the whole of the opening movement until the last nine bars. The bells are, of course, the tolling funeral bells of the church, which, along with the tritone interval itself, cast the shadow of death across the whole work, liturgy and poems alike. In Owen's 'Anthem for Doomed Youth', enclosed within the Requiem Aeternam, the same interval (now spelt enharmonically C–G flat) is outlined by the phrase 'What passing bells for those who die as cattle?', and it reappears at the further mention of bells: 'No mockeries for them from prayers or bells':

1. This overtly Christian concept is particularly important in *The Rape of Lucretia* and *Billy Budd*, which latter Philip Brett views as a 'parable of redemption'; see P. Brett, 'Salvation at Sea: "Billy Budd"', in Palmer (ed.), *The Britten Companion*, pp. 133-43.

The tritone also forms both the melodic and the harmonic framework for the first entry of the boys' choir at 'Te decet hymnus'. The opening vocal phrase, built out of eleven of the possible twelve pitches (G natural is omitted) moves from C to F sharp and is promptly inverted, while the accompanying harmonies consist of triads on all twelve notes, also emphasizing the tritone relationship (the opening chords of each phrase are F major and F sharp major, while the closing ones are B minor and C major).

Even the Sanctus bells, represented by vibraphone, glockenspiel, antique cymbals and tubular bells, shimmer to the deathly C–F sharp interval. Here the ritual element of the Mass comes to the fore: not just in the Sanctus bells, but in the free chanting of the chorus at 'Pleni sunt coeli' and the organum-like parallel fifths and octaves of the Benedictus. The movement ends not with the blazing triumph of the D major Hosanna, but with the bleak pessimism of Owen and a distortion, low down on bassoon, cello, harp, horn and double bass, of the Dies Irae's fanfares, moving from C to a bottom F sharp on the bass.

The ensuing Agnus Dei is the shortest and in many ways the simplest movement. It presents the Latin Mass and Owen's poetry in unusually close juxtaposition.[1] Owen was involved in fighting near the River Ancre in January 1917, and 'At a Calvary near the Ancre' is like a parable in which the biblical images are adapted to fit the setting of war.[2] The tension between Christianity and patriotism is the theme of one of the poet's letters to his mother, in which he ridicules contemporary religious leaders for ignoring Christ's principle of 'passivity at any price' and goes on to describe himself as a conscientious objector:

> And am I not myself a conscientious objector with a very seared conscience?
> ...Christ is literally in no man's land. There men often hear His voice: Greater love hath no man than this, that a man lay down his life—for a friend.

1.   The only other passage with such rapid alternation comes at the end of the Dies Irae sequence. Here Owen's 'Futility' is split into four sections and interspersed between phrases of the Lacrymosa for soprano and chorus, the two planes being emphasized by contrasting tonal centres. These are, typically for Britten, a semitone apart, the tenor being centred around A major compared with the Lacrymosa's B flat minor. At each cadence point, however, the tenor is drawn towards both the key and the melodic shape of the soprano's line, until in the end tenor and chorus meet on the inevitable C–F sharp tritone.

2.   See Hibberd, *War Poems*, p. 116, and Stallworthy, *The Complete Poems*, I, p. 134. The new perspective on biblical material is similar to that in 'The Parable of the Old Man and the Young'.

Is it spoken in English only and French?
I do not believe so.
Thus you see how pure Christianity will not fit in with pure patriotism.[1]

The three stanzas of Owen's poem are divided in Britten's work by the three statements of the Agnus Dei, thus alternating tenor solo and chamber orchestra with full orchestra and chorus. Here Owen's lines are not used to end the movement: there is an extra final Latin phrase, 'Dona nobis pacem'. This is sung not by the chorus, to whom the previous Latin text has been given, but by the tenor soloist over a soft held chord. The words are the final response from the Mass for the *living*, not the Requiem Mass, and Britten has clearly chosen the tenor here to address the living, not the dead. The strings have a relentless scalic ostinato figure built around the C–F sharp tritone, an interval which also provides the framework for the tenor's vocal line. Although the chorus and orchestra eventually settle on an F sharp major chord, the soloist's moving plea is set to the ostinato figure and its retrograde inversion, exploiting the exact division of the octave into two tritones:

---

1.   Letter of 16(?) May 1917, quoted in Hibberd, *War Poems*, p. 68. Owen used the phrase 'Greater Love' as a title for a separate poem, and the arguments in his letter reappear in the final couplet of 'At a Calvary': 'But they who love the greater love / Lay down their life; they do not hate.' The poet's view of himself as a conscientious objector would naturally have found sympathy with Britten. So, too, would his latent homosexuality, something underplayed by most discussions of the poet, as Andrew Motion points out in his review of Dominic Hibberd's new biography *Wilfred Owen: The Last Year 1917–1918* in the *Times Literary Supplement* of 6 November 1992, p. 10.

If the deathly shadow of the tritone is the most significant feature of Britten's music for the *War Requiem*, fanfares also play a very important and equally symbolic role. Bugles are a recurrent image in Owen's poetry, not surprisingly considering their military connotations. They also carry with them echoes of old-fashioned country life and the hunt.[1] For Britten, the bugle fanfare may also have recalled his schooldays and the OTC. The musical potential of this imagery is obvious (Britten had already exploited it at the line 'Blow, bugle, blow' from Tennyson's 'Nocturne' in the *Serenade*), and it appears in the first two of the nine poems chosen for the *War Requiem*—the 'Anthem for Doomed Youth' and the opening seven lines of the fragment 'Bugles Sang'. In the latter case the fanfares permeate the wind writing, their triadic flutterings bringing to mind the nocturnal area of that other doomed youth—Billy Budd—as he awaits his execution.[2]

These fanfares may be muted, but there are more powerful ones elsewhere in the work. The concept of the Day of Judgment and the Last Trumpet of the Tuba Mirum are traditionally linked with brass fanfares, most memorably in the Requiem settings of Berlioz and Verdi, and Britten follows this lead from the very beginning of the Dies Irae. Verdi, indeed, is an important influence throughout the work, from the *sotto voce* liturgical mutterings of the Requiem Aeternam to the choice of B flat minor for the Lacrymosa and G minor for the Tuba Mirum and the cataclysmic climax of the Libera Me.

All three levels of the *War Requiem* interact in the Offertorium. The mention of Abraham in 'Quam olim Abrahae' creates a direct link with Owen's 'The Parable of the Old Man and the Young'. This is a parody of Genesis 22, telling the story of Abraham and Isaac; but instead of offering the 'Ram of

1.   A way of life which affected not only Owen but also his friend Siegfried Sassoon, author of *Memoirs of a Fox-hunting Man* and *The Old Huntsman*.

2.   Billy sings this aria while half asleep, and it is perhaps no coincidence that the fourth line of Owen's poem begins 'Sleep mothered them', while Britten chooses to end his setting by isolating the word 'slept', anticipating the significance of the sleep and death parallel of 'Let us sleep now' in the work's final pages.

Pride', Abraham kills his son, 'And half the seed of Europe, one by one'. In the Table of Contents to his projected book of poems, Owen gives under the heading 'Motive': 'Willingness of old to sacrifice young', something of which the young soldiers in the trenches were acutely conscious.[1]

Chorus

Sed signifer sanctus Michael	But may the holy standard-bearer,
repraesentet eas in lucem sanctam:	Michael, lead them into the holy light;
quam olim Abrahae promisisti, et semini ejus.	which once Thou promised to Abraham and to his seed.

Baritone and Tenor Solos

So Abram rose, and clave the wood, and went,
And took fire with him, and a knife.
And as they sojourned both of them together,
Isaac the first-born spake and said, My Father,
Behold the preparations, fire and iron,
But where the lamb for this burnt-offering?
Then Abram bound the youth with belts and straps,
and builded parapets and trenches there,
And stretchèd forth the knife to slay his son.
When lo! an angel called him out of heaven,
Saying, Lay not thy hand upon the lad,
Neither do anything to him. Behold,
A ram, caught in a thicket by its horns;
Offer the Ram of Pride instead of him.
But the old man would not do so, but slew his son,—
And half the seed of Europe, one by one.

1.   The lack of concern on the part of the elderly generals for the young soldiers dying at the front was a recurrent theme in letters from the trenches, and one on which Owen also dwelt in the final lines of 'Inspection' (in Stallworthy, *The Complete Poems*, I, p. 95):

> 'The world is washing out its stains,' he said.
> 'It doesn't like our cheeks so red:
> Young blood's its great objection.
> But when we're duly white-washed, being dead,
> The race will bear Field Marshal God's inspection.'

Owen's Table of Contents is reproduced in Hibberd, *Wilfred Owen: The Last Year*, p. 123, and transcribed in Stallworthy, *The Complete Poems*, II, p. 538-40.

Boys' Choir and Chorus

Hostias et preces tibi, Domine, laudis offerimus; tu suscipe pro animabus illis, quarum hodie memoriam facimus: fac eas, Domine, de morte transire ad vitam: quam olim Abrahae promisisti, et semini ejus.	We offer sacrifices and prayers to Thee, Lord, with praises: receive them for those souls whom we commemorate this day: let them, Lord, pass from death to life; which once Thou promised to Abraham and to his seed.

Britten follows tradition in setting 'Quam olim Abrahae' as a fugue, taking his fugue subject from *Canticle II, Abraham and Isaac* written ten years earlier.[1] The rich war imagery of the 'Parable' is strengthened musically by Britten's recollections of the Dies Irae fanfares and the wailing shells from the first Owen setting at the words 'And builded parapets and trenches there'. The poem's crucial final line is understated in an almost casual fashion, aptly reflecting the matter-of-fact approach of the generals so despised by Owen. The line is sung over and over again to the fugue subject, the vocal phrases becoming gradually softer and more and more fragmented. This is overlaid by the entry of the distant organ and boys' choir singing the Hostias, the final organ notes overlapping with the return of the choral fugue, this time marked 'ppp' and including an inversion of the subject. The reference to sacrifices in the opening line of the Hostias provides a link with the Owen poem, while the boys' singing of the 'Quam olim Abrahae' refrain means that here all three of the work's different levels are carefully integrated.

The Libera Me is part of the Burial Service rather than the Requiem Mass, and its text stresses the ideas of eternal death and judgment. Britten's setting starts with distant drumbeats: an ominous funeral march, full of tortuous chromatic lines, which gradually gathers momentum, working itself up into a frenzy. As the pace quickens, the brass fanfares from the Dies Irae return in readiness for the Day of Judgment, and the tension finally explodes into a thunderous G minor chord with

---

1. Here it sets the text 'Father, I am all ready' (perhaps a reason for Britten's choice of this particular subject for the fugue?) and is in straightforward 6/8 time, lacking the hemiolas of the *War Requiem*. Material from the Canticle is also reused to depict the ethereal voice of the angel.

the addition of full organ, the ultimate and inevitable resolution of the dominant seventh implications of the F sharp– C interval (perhaps signalling the inevitable consequences of war?). As the terrifying chord fades away, accompanied by the 'broken cries [which] reach us from the pit that has swallowed them', an eerie silence envelops everything—'the terrible calm of Hades'.[1]

Following such a monumental climax, the soft sustained G minor chord produces an uneasy, almost post-nuclear sense of calm and timelessness as a background to the last and most famous of Owen's poems, 'Strange Meeting'. This is a work full of resonances, from the Bible, through Dante, Shelley and Keats to Sassoon,[2] and Britten's setting is similarly eclectic, the melodic fragments in the instruments which punctuate the vocal phrases resembling ideas from earlier in the work.[3] Owen's opening lines, 'It seemed that out of battle I escaped / Down some profound dull tunnel...', present a traditional image of hell and the underworld, as well as bringing to mind the horror of the trenches.[4] The dialogue between the 'Strange friends', one of whom identifies himself as 'the enemy you killed, my friend', presents the enemy/friend paradox with which the poet, and many of his colleagues at the front, had constantly to come to terms: his job as a soldier required him to fight and kill, while his instincts as a poet were to call for

1.   P. Evans, *The Music of Benjamin Britten* (London: Dent, 1989), p. 463.

2.   See Stallworthy, *The Complete Poems*, I, pp. 149-50.

3.   This is a technique used somewhat more explicitly in the mad scene from *Peter Grimes*, in which many of the opera's most important motives are recalled in a distorted fashion as Grimes's deranged thoughts flit from one memory to another. Here, too, a sustained chord provides a backdrop; this time it is a dominant seventh chord on D, played by the horns in the orchestral interlude and then taken up by the off-stage chorus for their cries of 'Grimes!'—an aural symbol of both the physical fog of the Suffolk marshes and the fog in Grimes's mind. In one of his last letters to his mother of 4–5 October 1918, Owen describes the unreality of his experiences: 'I lost all my earthly faculties, and fought like an angel'; see Hibberd, *War Poems*, p. 107.

4.   For a discussion of the tunnel in the imagery of the underworld see Lowry, *Familiar Mysteries*, p. 65.

peace.[1] The reconciliation between the former enemies can be seen as representing that between humanity and God sought in the Libera Me, but Owen's poem is inconclusive. The manuscripts suggest that the final line, 'Let us sleep now...', may only have been intended as a temporary ending. It was originally added in pencil as an afterthought, although it was later inked in.[2]

Whatever the poet's intention, Britten seizes on this phrase as the basis for the peroration of the whole work, drawing the parallel between the soldiers' sleep and the eternal rest of the Requiem, something underlined by his inclusion of the Dismissal 'Requiescant in pace' ('may they rest in peace').[3] The tenor and baritone soloists repeat the poem's final line over and over again, the music occupying a gentle modal no-man's-land between D and A major. Now, for the first time in the work, all three planes overlap, the boys' choir being integrated thematically as they sing 'In paradisum' alongside the main choir and soprano solo. The music builds to an incandescent climax as the soprano soloist soars up to a top b″, before slowly fading. The bells return, drawing first the boys' choir and then finally the chorus back to the inevitable C–F sharp tritone. Death is never far away, and the work ends with the same quiet, unaccompanied choral passage which closed the Requiem Aeternam and the Dies Irae.

Hibberd regards the sleep after death described in 'Strange Meeting' as the passivity which Owen always dreaded, and talks of his deep, unshakeable pessimism.[4] Certainly the poem leaves a question mark hanging over the ultimate destiny of the Unknown Warrior: is it heaven, or is it merely burial under the mud of France? Britten, too, ends in ambiguity. It is a

1. See Hibberd, *War Poems*, pp. 45-50 for an illuminating discussion of 'Strange Meeting'.

2. Hibberd, *War Poems*, p. 132; the second surviving draft is reproduced in Hibberd, *Wilfred Owen: The Last Year*, pp. 110-11.

3. The idea of sleep also comes near the end of the *Cantata misericordium* of 1963. Here the setting of the phrase 'Dormi nunc, amice' ('sleep now, my friend') again uses the harp as part of the instrumental accompaniment.

4. Hibberd, *War Poems*, p. 46.

'mundane' ending in that it is understated—it is 'of this world' and has already been heard twice before. The boys' choir is left, as the whole work began, with the ominous tritone—a far cry from Fauré's angelic In Paradisum—and the final F major chord in no sense provides a resolution for the ubiquitous tritone. But there is an inescapable warmth and possibly even optimism about these final pages of the *War Requiem.*

Perhaps the ambiguity simply reflects Britten's own view of religion. Rita Thompson thought that 'Ben wanted to have religion when he was dying, but he could never really quite come to it', while according to Peter Pears, 'I don't think he really had any particular conviction as to what was going to happen after death, but he was certainly not afraid of dying'.[1] This ambivalent view of death and religion is clearly apparent in the *War Requiem*, hovering as it does between the sacred liturgy and Owen's secular poetry; and yet is there an underlying, almost illogical sense of hope as the music fades into the distance?

1. Carpenter, *Benjamin Britten*, p. 583.

The Martial Uses of the Mass:
War Remembrance as an Elementary Form of Religious Life

Jon Davies

Introduction

Archaeological, anthropological and historical records show that the societies of the last ten thousand years have at least two things in common. They all have religious systems, and they all experience war—and death in war. As a society comes to terms with war and its consequences, it creates forms of war remembrance which are explicitly religious in nature. An alien visitor to, for example, Winchester Cathedral could quite reasonably believe that England's religion was centred on war remembrance. Sixty per cent of the memorial tablets in that cathedral are dedicated to the war dead.

The same visitor, on a journey around Europe, would find his or her opinion on the mutual coexistence and covariance of war and religion substantially reinforced by the hundreds of thousands of war memorials which cover our continent. In war, and in the sacralization of war, is to be found the most common articulation of European religion. No European could fail to understand the following three symbols:

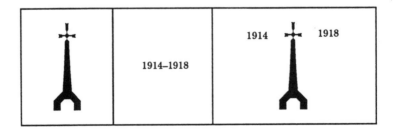

War memorials are the most common form of British and European public, vernacular, sacralized statuary. They are probably the art form most readily understood by the population at large, partly because the huge war-mobilizations of this century have given the majority of European households a direct experience of war, and partly because each new European experience of war both reinvests the existing memorials with symbolic power and adds to their numbers. As religious objects, war memorials draw upon a grim and potent pedigree, rooted in a long and complex iconic ancestry, reaching deep into the archaeology of European religious identity.

In this essay I will concentrate on one expression of this religio-military identity, the Christian version of the dying king-god, as told in the Passion story of Jesus. When seen through twentieth-century war memorials, this version is of course both 'merely' European and 'merely' modern, but even a perfunctory analysis of the iconography and epigraphy of such memorials shows the ways in which they transcend the immediate and draw on a trans-European, classical, pagan and mythic inheritance. It is primarily from war memorials of one kind or another, as well as from funerary artefacts, that we are able to construct a sense of the moral culture of the past and of our connection to it. Our own war memorials are windows on that past, as well as paradigms of our own moral culture and history. They symbolize our ancestry.

The war memorials of particular interest to me are not the major national constructions in monument and ritual which clearly involve the great and powerful leaders of the state, although in Britain at least these leaders were, in commissioning monuments of war, responding at least as much to popular pressure as to their own personal motivations. Nor am I in this essay concerned with war cemeteries, which have a rather similar 'official' stamp upon them, as indeed do the great musical and dramatistic set-pieces such as the one analysed by Eric Cross in this volume. Nor am I directly concerned with war poets, in whose case choices relating to style and acceptability for anthologies also create an official or semi-official form of poetic war remembrance. There is, of course, a very high degree of overlap between the attitudes and emotions of the 'official' and the 'ordinary' producers of war memorials. It would be both silly and factually incorrect to claim that there was a kind of class war being waged about such matters: there is a shared religio-military view of the world. However, I am primarily interested in the ordinary village and small town vernacular war memorials, inspired by the deaths of ordinary young men, commissioned, located, paid for and looked after by the equally ordinary people and communities from which they came.

At every level, of course, these memorials celebrate the lives and deaths of *men*, indeed of violent men. Army Arms Manuals tell you that weapons are given to you to kill the enemy. A very great problem arises for every society when it faces the task of integrating or reintegrating into day-to-day, law-bound life men whose violation of the great taboo against killing creates not merely a problem for them individually—a *psychological* problem—but a problem for the entire society which required them to break the taboo in the first place, and whose security and prosperity is guaranteed precisely by that killing. The fact that soldiers kill, and do so on the instructions of, and with the support of, and for the benefit of, everyone else in society who does not kill, always makes war a collective or social problem, laden with guilt and a range of other, very deep emotions. The invocation of the Passion story of Christ is the way our own society has been able to deal with this recurring societal problem.

The Passion Story and War Memorial Calvaries

The Order for the Administration of the Lord's Supper, or Holy Communion,[1] is unusual in that it contains, as part of the liturgy, a story. This is the story of the voluntary, violent death of a young celibate male, who goes to his death in the company of a band of other young men, some of whom are also to die in violent circumstances. There are several distinct

1. In *The Book of Common Prayer of the Church of England* (Oxford: Oxford University Press, n.d.).

themes in the Passion story. The death is *voluntary*, as is made clear by 'The body of our Lord Jesus Christ...was *given* for thee' (my emphasis); and 'given' or 'gave' are the verb forms most commonly found on war memorials. The presentation of the death as voluntary deals to a large extent with another aspect of the recurrent social problem referred to above, that of reintegrating the dead into the society of those for whom they died. If they *gave* their lives, then no one made them do it, and no one has to feel guilty. Gratitude can replace guilt. The image of 'laying down one's life' makes it possible to ignore the fact that soldiers kill; that is, it reinforces the image of a young man being the passive (but courageous) victim of other people's violence. This in turn ties in with the fact that the European day of war remembrance is Armistice Day, not a Victory Day, and that the word 'fallen' appears on war memorials much more often than the word 'conquered'. The Enemy appear very rarely indeed on war memorials, and this makes it much easier to avoid having to mention or think about killing.

Both on war memorials and in the liturgy of the Passion, death is seen as *sacrificial*: 'a full, perfect and sufficient sacrifice', and many war memorials are sculpted as calvaries. The death is painful, involving mutilation of the body, and is surrounded with violence and productive of blood. The suffering is prolonged, and is preceded by a long and arduous journey into hostile territory. The death is *redemptive*, as well as sacrificial: it 'taketh away the sins of the world'. It is redemptive both for those making (or actually constituting) the sacrifice, and for those on whose behalf the sacrifice is made.

For these latter, however, the redemptiveness is associated with and even made conditional upon proper acts of remembrance—otherwise, the sacrifice is in vain and the redemption foregone. Implicit in the word 'remembrance' is the expectation that the example be followed and emulated. This insistence on active remembrance has as its mirror opposite the theme of *betrayal*, either directly through acts of treachery or cowardice, or indirectly through a failure to remember and to follow. Betrayal is also attributed to the rejecting or indifferent leaders of the community of which the dying martyrs are part. The Passion story ends, of course (inasmuch as it has an ending) in the story of the Cenotaph, the empty tomb, a version of which is at the centre of our annual Remembrance Day national war-ritual.

These various themes can be read in and on our war memorials in such inscriptions as 'When you go home, tell them of us and say: for your tomorrow we gave our today'. This particular inscription, echoing the message expressed after the Battle of Marathon, appears on several British war memorials, and was reproduced on a new memorial erected in 1991 in Newcastle-upon-Tyne. The general sentiment, that is the hortatory and even minatory insistence on gratitude and remembrance, occurs very frequently. Such sentiments are ritually witnessed to in, for example, the regular meetings of the Fellowship of the Services, which owes its origins to a fraternity of all those soldiers of the Great War who had volunteered before 1916 (when conscription was introduced in the UK). In the UK, not a night goes by without a group of old soldiers, somewhere, standing in remembrance of Absent Comrades; there are more days of remembrance in war remembrance diaries than there are days of obligation in the church year. Such gatherings, and indeed gatherings of ex-servicemen generally, are often characterized by a sense of being betrayed or forgotten by an ungrateful civil society.

In Ronald Blythe's *View in Winter* one of his respondents ('A Major') says: 'When I am at the Menin Gate, to me it is like Gethsemane and Calvary all over again'.[1] The following parallel texts, the left-hand column from the communion liturgy, the right-hand one from various village or small town war memorials, give clear evidence of the thematic interpenetration of these two styles of religious expression:

1.   R. Blythe, *The View in Winter* (London: Allen Lane, 1979), p. 194.

The Priest
Didst give thine only son
Jesus Christ to suffer death upon
the cross for our redemption...
who made there (by his one
oblation of himself once offered)
a full perfect and sufficient
sacrifice, oblation and satisfaction
for the sins of the
the whole world... and did
institute and in his Holy Gospel
command us to continue, a
perpetual memory of that his
precious death, until his coming
again. This is my body which
given for you... this is my blood
which is shed for you... do this
in remembrance of me.
Take this in remembrance that
Christ died for thee...

The People
We thy humble servants offer
and present unto thee O Lord,
ourselves, our souls and bodies,
to be a reasonable holy and lively
sacrifice unto thee... although
we be unworthy through our
manifold sins, to offer thee any
sacrifice, yet we beseech thee to
accept this our
bounden duty and service...

The body of our Lord Jesus Christ
which was given for thee
preserve thy body and soul unto
everlasting life.
Take eat this in remembrance
that Christ died for them.

War Memorials
They died that we might live.

Through the grave and gate of death
we pass to our joyful resurrection.

Be thou faithful unto death and I will
give you a crown of life.

This calvary was erected by their
friends.

They gave we have.
When you go home tell them of us
and say: for their tomorrow we gave
our today.

Greater love hath no man than this
that he lay down his life for his
friends.

These gave their lives that you who
live may reap a richer harvest ere
you fall asleep.
They shall not grow old as we that
are left grow old. At the going down
of the sun and in the morning we
shall remember them.

In loving memory and sure hope of
life eternal the King of
the World shall raise us up who
have died for his laws unto
everlasting life.

Les enfants de Château sur le
Loir morts pour la France

A Re-Catholicizing of the Mass?

Behold a table spread!
A battered corned-beef box, a length of twine,
An altar rail of twigs and shreds of string.
...For the unseen, divine,
Uncomprehended Thing
A hallowed space amid the holy dead.[1]

Ronald Blythe's Major (see above) would clearly not have agreed with Siegfried Sassoon, who described the Menin Gate (where the Major found Gethsemane) as a 'sepulchre of crime'.[2] Sassoon is in large measure giving expression to the idea that the ordinary soldiers had been betrayed by their military and political leaders—an old, often repeated theme in military writing, being perhaps another way of emphasizing the difficulty of the reintegration of soldiers into the civil community.

Both Sassoon and the Major would probably have identified in some measure at least with Enkidu, the comrade in arms of Gilgamesh, the subject of one of the oldest epic narratives. Enkidu felt that his manner of death was shameful because he had died, ill, in bed: 'Happy is the man who falls in the battle, for I must die in shame'.[3] Even war-hostile writers like Sassoon share this view of the particular tragedy and destiny of men who take part in and who die in battle, and in so doing participate in an evocatively constant theme of many cultures, as the *Epic of Gilgamesh* makes clear. The mythic forms of remembrance and moral evaluations of and for the death of young men in war transcend the immediately available repertoire of icons and epigraphies, and reach back into a shared human (male) experience.

This is perhaps particularly problematic for Protestant

1. W.H. Littlejohn, 'Holy Communion Service, Suvla Bay', in E.B. Osborn (ed.), *A Muse in Arms* (London: John Murray, 1917), p. 171.
2. S. Sassoon, 'On Passing the New Menin Gate', in *The War Poems of Siegfried Sassoon* (ed. R. Hart-Davis; London: Faber & Faber, 1983), p. 153.
3. N.K. Sanders (ed.), *The Epic of Gilgamesh* (Harmondsworth: Penguin, 1972), p. 93.

cultures, in which the rather meagre death aesthetic of that religion left twentieth-century people ill-prepared for the sudden massive irruption of war and mass death. Eamon Duffy's marvellous piece of anthropology—or theo-anthropology[1]—shows how important to late medieval laity was the complex set of ceremonies surrounding the burial and remembrance of the dead, and how actively participant in these practices the laity were. Central to this late medieval funerary activity was the idea of purgatory; that is that form of post-death imagining which retains an effective system of sympathy and empathy between the living and the dead.

The Reformation destroyed much of this communal and populist funerary tradition—or perhaps simply repressed it, pending its return. To a large extent British war memorials and war remembrance practices represent a reinvigoration or re-Catholicizing of this tradition, in the face of an Anglican funeral liturgy which commends God because 'thou with rebukes dost chasten man for sin, thou makest his beauty to consume away, like as it were a moth fretting a garment'.[2] Such a view of the dead is quite incompatible with that taken by war memorials and war remembrance practices, which invoke a much older tradition of the immortal male beauty of dead young soldiers. The most widely used poem or hymn on remembrance occasions is Laurence Binyon's 'For the Fallen', in which the young dead soldiers, like the young dead Christ, triumph over death:

> They shall grow not old, as we that are left grow old:
> Age shall not weary them, nor the years condemn.[3]

1. E. Duffy, *The Stripping of the Altars* (New Haven: Yale University Press, 1992).

2. The Anglican Order for the Burial of the Dead, in *The Book of Common Prayer*. For a more extended treatment of this theme, see my article 'One Hundred Billion Dead: A General Theology of Death' in this volume and my 'Lapidary Texts: A Liturgy Fit for Heroes', in J. Davies and I. Wollaston (eds.), *The Sociology of Sacred Texts* (Sheffield: Sheffield Academic Press, 1993), pp. 26-36.

3. L. Binyon, 'For the Fallen', in J. Benn (ed.), *Memorials* (London: Ravette, 1986), p. 98.

Very few memorials depict macerated or dismembered bodies, and most either imply (by use of the victor's laurel wreath or crown) or explicitly state in statue and words the transcendent and triumphant beauty of the young male warrior—a resurrection.

In the symbolism of our war memorials can be found a whole host of archetypal myths and symbols, refracted through medieval Catholicism perhaps, but relying for their didactic and emotive power on a much older and deeper array of death and war-death icons and resonances. At the Scottish National War Memorial in Edinburgh Castle can be found an extraordinary profusion of Christian, classical, pagan and primeval symbols. The Stone of Remembrance, located in the central shrine of the memorial, stands on the primal volcanic rock, which erupts out of and through the floor of the shrine to represent both the first Frame or Form emerging out of Chaos, and the earth, the first mother to whom, in Greek mythology, all dead soldiers belonged. Above the Stone, Saint Michael, the captain of the Heavenly Host, soars upwards towards angels trumpeting the victory over the powers of hell and death. Around the door of the shrine is the Tree of Life, another ancient pagan symbol. In another part of the memorial is to be found the Funeral Oration of Pericles, as unproblematically reused here as it had been decades earlier at the dedication of the battlefield cemetery at Gettysburg. Around the walls of the memorial are to be found a plethora of words and icons which together represent a summation of many thousands of years of mythic understanding of the meaning of the death of young men in war. The Passion story of Christ is a fully comprehensible part of this understanding, and is well articulated on our war memorials.

The Cross of Wood

God be with you and us who go our way
And leave you dead upon the ground you won.
For you at last the long fatigue is done,
The hard march ended: you have rest today.

For you no medals such as others wear—
A cross of bronze for those approvèd brave—
To you is given, above a shallow grave,
The Wooden Cross that marks you resting there.

Rest you content; more honourable far
Than all the Orders is the Cross of Wood,
The symbol of self-sacrifice that stood
Bearing the God whose brethren you are.[1]

Memorials are, obviously, designed and created by the living, be these survivors of the war or those who have little or no combat or even military experience. Cyril Winterbotham, the author of the poem above, was a soldier who was in fact killed in action on 27 August 1916, and he can clearly be assumed to have some direct understanding of what kind of religious feeling about the war was bound up in at least his own mind: the Cross marks the war.

In 1919 a rather worried Church of England commissioned an investigation into 'The Army and Religion: An Enquiry into its Bearing upon the Religious Life of the Nation'.[2] This was a commission composed almost entirely of clergymen, with a concern about the nature of the religion that they could expect to encounter in the postwar years, when the ten million British men who had at one time or another worn the uniform returned to civilian life. Their particular institutional focus need not concern us. The report is however very illuminating with regard to the kinds of religious *mentalités* which could be found in Kitchener's army. The commission was singularly unimpressed with the level of theological sophistication of the soldiers: 'a great preponderance were men who had no use for any of the Churches, [and were] under an extraordinary misunderstanding as to what the Christian religion really is'.[3] They felt that the army had religion, but not Christianity,

1. C. Winterbotham, 'The Cross of Wood', in Osborn (ed.), *A Muse in Arms*, p. 159.
2. 'The Army and Religion: An Enquiry and its Bearing upon the Religious Life of the Nation' (with a preface by the Bishop of Winchester; London: Macmillan, 1919).
3. 'The Army and Religion', p. xviii.

although they went on to comment that 'Surely there is a deep truth in the sentiment that has put a cross of wood on every grave'.[1] The crosses they were referring to were the wooden battlefield crosses spontaneously erected by soldiers when they temporarily buried their fallen comrades. Many of these crosses were later sent or taken back to Britain and were not infrequently preferred to more secular icons and symbols. There was also considerable popular objection when the Imperial War Graves Commission decided not to use the cross as the shape of the official war cemetery gravestone.

The authors of 'The Army and Religion' went on to state that troops at the actual war front and in combat did indeed experience a reawakening of religious feeling.[2] They quoted a Scottish officer's view that 'The religion of ninety per cent of the men at the front is not distinctively Christian, but a religion of patriotism and valour, tinged with chivalry and at the best merely coloured with sentiment and emotion borrowed from Christianity'.[3]

Time and again the authors note that most of the men got their Christianity through Sunday School and hymns, the source of 'the unconscious Christianity of our men'.[4] Charles Carrington, a serving soldier in the First World War and an officer in the Second, wrote about popular sing-songs which 'On Sunday evenings…just as easily turned to Hymns Ancient and Modern, a genuine part of our folk-lore'.[5] The clerical inquirers also noted how much religion was comprehended in very spontaneous cursing and swearing, but this they rather glossed over, preferring to say that 'It is the Cross they understand. Nearly all the serious questions about God come down in the end to the problem of suffering',[6] and 'The chaplain who can portray the Cross and the Resurrection in terms of the soldiers' own experience will find the soil crying

1.   'The Army and Religion', p. xviii.
2.   'The Army and Religion', p. 7.
3.   'The Army and Religion', p. 10.
4.   'The Army and Religion', p. 25.
5.   C. Carrington, *Soldier from the War Returning* (London: Hutchinson, 1965), p. 228.
6.   'The Army and Religion', p. 26.

for the seed'.[1] They quoted a Quarter Master Sergeant in the
Army Service Corps: 'There is certainly a great reverence for
Jesus and His teaching deep in the hearts of most of us, [as
shown by] the homage paid to the many shrines and the
wayside crucifixes'.[2] The commissioners comment that however 'antiquated and unintelligible [was the men's conception
of the Cross] suddenly it has crossed their path, and has won a
strange new meaning for them, a meaning thrilling with
memories of pain and honour and painful love'.[3] 'The appeal
of the cross is very strong, but not on its redemptive side. The
attraction of the cross is that in the main of a wounded hero, a
fellow-sufferer in a good cause... The thought of Christ's
wounds means a lot to a wounded man'.[4] The commission
concluded that 'The war seems to have revived something
ancestral in these men, something elementally religious'.[5]

All religions are syncretisms, and nowhere more so than
when dealing with war and death in war, one of the centrally
powerful myth-creating experiences of all societies. At whatever level one looks, at the Cross of Wood of ordinary soldiers
or at the 'high art' articulations of the war death/religious
theme, at simple wayside shrines, votive offerings or ancient
poems and older monuments, death in war unites cultures
across time and space to form a very large part of 'something
elementally religious'. This comes out very strongly in Eric
Cross's essay in this volume, and is at least implicit in several of
the other contributions. The theme—death in war—is, for
better or for worse, a large part of the reflexive construction of
what it is to be a man in a Euro-Christian culture: 'It is lawful
for Christian men...to wear arms and to serve in the wars',[6] as
the Anglican Article XXXVII has it. By contrast, this 'heroic'
form of death is not available for women, who have, as
Manucha Lisboa shows, to find other ways of dying.

1. 'The Army and Religion', p. 38.
2. 'The Army and Religion', p. 36.
3. 'The Army and Religion', p. 40.
4. 'The Army and Religion', p. 42.
5. 'The Army and Religion', p. 62.
6. In *The Book of Common Prayer*.

Historically, though, it is from the ancestral heroic dead that much of our sense of manliness is derived—for better or for worse—and it is by comparison with them that we construct the possibilities of a gentler world.

Heroic Death in the Early Nordic World

Diana Whaley

In or around AD 453 Attila, king of the Huns, died of a heavy
nose-bleed, on the night of his wedding to a woman whose
name, Ildico, suggests that she belonged to a hostile Germanic
tribe.[1] It was an ordinary, unheroic death, but one that was
transformed into a story of murder that migrated northwards
and eventually, in the imagination of Nordic[2] poets, was
absorbed into the great legendary cycle of the Volsungs and
Niebelungs which centres on Sigurðr[3] the dragon-slayer and his
ill-starred wife Guðrún (the Siegfried and Gutrune of Wagner's
Der Ring des Niebelungen).[4] Guðrún, after the death of Sigurðr, is

1. An account by the contemporary historian Priscus is preserved in
Jordanes's *De Origine Actibusque Getarum*. The relevant passage is printed,
and the development of the Attila legend discussed, in Dronke 1969: 32-33,
35-36.

2. 'Nordic' throughout this paper refers to the people and culture of
Scandinavia and its colonies, especially Iceland, and '(Old) Norse' to their
language and literature. The focus is especially on the poetry of Norway
and Iceland in the Viking Age (commonly taken as spanning the end of
the eighth century to the mid-eleventh) and on the Icelandic sagas of the
thirteenth century.

3. Names drawn from Old Norse texts are given in standard
normalized orthography. The symbols Ð, ð (upper and lower case 'eth')
and Þ, þ ('thorn') are pronounced like the initial sounds of English 'this'
and 'thick' respectively. The vowels spelt ø and ǫ are pronounced
similarly to that of Modern German *schön*. Translations from Old Norse,
Old English and Latin are my own, unless otherwise stated.

4. The most coherent Old Norse account of the Volsung–Niebelung
story, based partially on older poetry, is the thirteenth-century *Vǫlsunga saga*,
'The Saga of the Volsungs'.

married against her will as a peace pledge to Atli (the Norse form of Attila).[1] In the starkly brilliant *Atlakviða*, 'Lay of Attila', probably composed in Norway in the ninth century, Atli treacherously invites Guðrún's brothers Gunnarr and Hǫgni to his court, and puts them to death. Hǫgni's heart is cut from his living body:

> *Hló pá Hǫgni*
> *er til hiarta skáro*
> *kvikvan kumblasmið—*
> *kløkkva hann sízt hugði.*

> Hǫgni laughed then
> as they cut to the heart
> the living sculptor of scars—
> to cry out never entered his thoughts (*Atlakviða* 24; text and translation from Dronke [ed.] 1969: 8).[2]

It is taken on a platter to his brother Gunnarr, who notes with satisfaction that it hardly quivers—just as it never quivered at all in his brother's breast. Gunnarr is also relieved that no one but himself now knows the secret of where in the Rhine, the 'godsprung river' (Dronke [ed.] 1969: 9), the Niebelungs' treasure-hoard lies. Gunnarr is placed in a snake-pit, where he harps defiantly, hate in his heart, and the secret dies with him. Guðrún takes grisly revenge by serving her husband Atli with their two sons, chopped up into morsels to eat with ale, telling him what he has just eaten, scattering gold about the hall and killing him in his bed. She then sets fire to the hall, and later attempts to drown herself.

That is not the end of Guðrún's tragic story, but before continuing it, three points are worth emphasizing. First, in terms of plot, tragic death by the sword evidently satisfied the imagination of early Germanic poets better than death by nose-bleed, and similarly *Atlakviða*'s portrayal of Gunnarr's death in the snake-pit at the command of Attila is probably a

---

1.   In the Norse sources, Atli is taken to be the brother of Brynhildr.

2.   A useful introduction to the Old Norse poems and sagas referred to throughout this paper is Kristjánsson 1988; and further information and bibliography can be found in Clover and Lindow (eds.) 1985 and Pulsiano (ed.) 1993.

transformation of the fate of the historical Gundicarius, king of the Burgundians, who fell in pitched battle against the Huns at a time when Attila was at the other end of Europe.

Secondly, the tragic heroes of the early poetry are motivated by the need for displays of courage and by the sacred duty of revenge. The grief of a death can only be assuaged by the shedding of blood, and family honour must be satisfied. The protagonists, male and female, take horrific courses of action in the grim but serene knowledge that they are doing the right thing, driven by fate and a relentless code of honour. They almost collude in their own deaths. Gunnarr and Hǫgni have some warning of Atli's treachery, but proudly spurn their counsellors' caution and speed off through trackless Mirkwood, knowing that the way is wolfish (*Atlakviða* 8, 9 and 13). When Guðrún produces another two sons, Hamðir and Sǫrli, by a further marriage and incites them to despatch another vicious tyrant, Jǫrmunrekr (the legendary counterpart of Ermaneric the Ostrogoth), the motive is again revenge—he has put their half-sister Svanhildr to a horrible death—and again they die with heroic panache:

> We have fought well,
> we stand on slaughtered Goths,
> surmounting sword-weary dead
> like eagles on a bough.
> We have got good fame
> whether we die now or another day.
> No man outlives the evening
> after the Norns' decree (*Hamðismál* 30; Dronke [ed.] 1969: 167).[1]

To these heroes, avenging the dead is better than mourning them, and death is better than a life of disgrace—both sentiments also articulated in the Old English epic *Beowulf* (ll. 1384–85 and 2890–91). We may note, thirdly, that dying with bravado is a cardinal point in the code of these legendary heroes, a means of securing immortality in the form of posthumous fame.

The old heroic stories of the Germanic migration age

---

1.   The Norns are female personifications of fate, rather like the Latin Parcae or Greek Moirae.

continued to circulate in the North for many centuries. They were favourite subjects for stone or wood carvings (Davidson 1967: 126-29) and were sufficiently well known to be alluded to cryptically in the elaborate diction of Norse skaldic poetry; for instance the armour of any warrior can conventionally be referred to as 'Hamðir's shirt' or 'Hamðir's clothing' or 'Sǫrli's garments'. On a grander scale, when the poet Illugi Bryndœlaskáld eulogizes the conquests of Haraldr harðráði 'the Hard-ruler' of Norway in the mid-eleventh century, he interweaves his praises with the exploits of Sigurðr and Atli. Although details may change and emphases shift, these stories survive the passage of time with their values—of courage, resignation to fate and the defence of personal and family honour—more or less intact. As romance begins to displace the heroic as the dominant ethos of medieval literature throughout Europe, the pathos of Guðrún's suffering is explored, as well as her ruthlessness,[1] and the male paradigms are also modified, but the old world still informs the new.

In and around the thirteenth century, Icelandic writers produced an array of vernacular prose works, the greatest and most characteristic of which, the 'Sagas of Icelanders', were inspired by traditions about their country's early history. They focused mainly on the period from Iceland's settlement in the six decades beginning c. 870 to shortly after its official conversion to Christianity c. 1000, and they were concerned above all with problems of social disruption in the new republic, viewing these at least in part in an idealized way which reflects the old heroic modes of thought. One of these sagas, *Laxdœla saga*, has a plot clearly derived from the Volsung–Niebelung cycle, having at its centre a pair of couples whose situation corresponds closely to the tragic quartet of Sigurðr, Guðrún, Gunnarr and Brynhildr in that phase of the cycle which precedes Guðrún's marriage to Atli/Attila. Here the wife of the lesser hero feels, like Brynhildr, that she has been cheated of the man she loved and deserved, and arranges his death, her cool deliberation masking the passion she feels.

But almost every plot in these Sagas of Icelanders revolves

---

1. Notably in the first two 'Lays of Guðrún', *Guðrúnarkviða* I and II.

around a blood feud set in motion by some kind of affront to family or individual honour, in which killings spiral to a tragic climax, followed by violent retaliation or legal proceedings, and eventually dying away to a resolution (see Andersson 1967, Bycock 1982). The characters often find themselves in the same kind of dilemmas as those in the Volsung–Niebelung story—torn between loyalty to their family and to their kin by marriage, their sworn brothers or friends; and they generally make the same kind of choices, though often with regret. In *Njáls saga*, for instance, Flosi is the most prominent of several men of wisdom and goodwill who are drawn against their will into acts of terrible violence. He is invited to the home of his niece Hildigunnr, who treats him with ostentatious honour, and stages a magnificent inciting scene, placing on Flosi the responsibility for avenging her husband Hǫskuldr, a fine man and a protégé of Njáll, who has been killed by the sons of Njáll. Flosi's attempt to settle the matter peacefully comes to nothing after he is made the target of an unforgivable sexual insult, and so he becomes the leader of the party which attacks the farmstead of Njáll and burns him and his family inside. The women and children are allowed out, but the only male member of the family to escape is Njáll's son-in-law Kári, who takes prolonged and terrible revenge before eventually making a pilgrimage to Rome, as Flosi also does, to receive absolution from the Pope. Flosi and Kári are eventually reconciled, Kári marrying Flosi's niece Hildigunnr.

The idea of laughing in the face of death that we observed in the story of Gunnarr and Hǫgni is another motif that has many incarnations in the later literature. The legendary Jomsvikings, a warrior elite based on the southern Baltic coast, were, according to tradition, defeated c. 994 by Earl Hákon of Norway in a sea-battle at the beautiful inlet now called Hjørundfjord. In *Jómsvíkinga saga*, 'The Saga of the Jomsvikings', ch. 36, seventy of them are captured, taken ashore, and tied onto a long rope to await execution; a man called Þorkell is appointed to do the job. Among the vows the Jomsvikings as a company have taken is never to fear death or speak cowardly words, and their captors, having eaten a meal and bragged about the battle, are eager to test their valour. The saga catalogues the beheading of ten Jomsvikings, until the Norwegians are so impressed that the remainder are spared. Some of the executions are grotesque or indecent, but this is one of the pleasanter ones:

> Then the seventh man was led forward, and Þorkell asked as usual [how he felt about dying]. 'I am quite content to die. But strike at me quickly. I am holding a dagger, because we Jomsvikings have often discussed whether a man is conscious when he's suddenly beheaded, even after the head is off. And the proof will be that I will point the dagger up if I am conscious; if not, the dagger will drop.' Þorkell struck at him and his head flew off, but the knife dropped.

One particular variation on the theme of the heroic death is the hero who literally will not be polite to save his life. In the aftermath of another sea-battle, fought in 1062 off the southwest coast of Sweden, the Norwegian Finnr Árnason, who has defected, for fairly good reason, to the Danes, is captured by the victorious Norwegians and brought before King Haraldr harðráði 'Hard-ruler'. After some opening abuse, Finnr is asked by the king if he wants to be given his life. 'Not by you, you dog', he replies. He then refuses to receive it from Haraldr's son Magnús, 'that puppy', and finally, offered it from Þóra, his own niece and Haraldr's mistress, he remarks, 'It's not surprising that you've fought well, if the mare was with you'. His life is spared nevertheless (*Haralds saga Sigurðarsonar* ch. 66).

The home-grown heroes in the Sagas of Icelanders are capable of meeting death with wonderful nonchalance. Heroic bravado has clearly become a literary cliché, though doubtless also partly grounded in reality. One of the classic examples occurs early in the account in *Njáls saga* ch. 77 of the lone defence of his farmstead by the co-hero, Gunnarr of Hlíðarendi. One of the attackers, a Norwegian called Þorgrímr, climbs up on the building to establish whether Gunnarr is at home. From within, Gunnarr glimpses a red tunic through the window and lunges out with his halberd, so that Þorgrímr, wounded, loses his footing and slips to the ground. He walks over to his companions, who are sitting nearby. 'Gizurr looked at him and said, "Is Gunnarr at home?". Þorgrímr answered, "You can find that out for yourselves, but I found this out: his halberd was at home". With this he fell down dead.' Gunnarr goes on to kill another man and wound a further sixteen before finally succumbing to exhaustion and loss of blood. Gizurr, leader of the attackers, pays tribute to his valour, declaring that 'his defence will be remembered as long as this land is inhabited'.

Amid the heroics of poetry and saga, it is easy to forget that in reality the vast majority of deaths must have been from accident, disease or simply old age, the mourners bereft of redress or the comfort of glorious last words or deeds. Many of these mundane deaths occur in the sagas, and although they are rarely themselves the focus of the narrative, it is fortunate that at least once this kind of bereavement found a voice, that of the tenth-century poet Egill Skalla-Grímsson. In fact, his life and poetry give insights into both sides: the heroic ideology of the warrior and the experience of the ordinary Icelandic farmer. One of the Egill's early ventures was to fight for the English king Athelstan[1] against a mainly Celtic confederacy at the battle of Vínheiðr (often identified with the battle of Brunanburh, commemorated in verse in the *Anglo-Saxon Chronicle* for 937). His beloved brother Þórolfr fought and fell in the same battle, and Egill, according to the saga composed about him in the thirteenth century, buried him there on the battlefield, with all his weapons and clothing, and he spoke two verses over him, in the elaborately intertwining style characteristic of the *dróttkvætt* metre. The first one reads:

> He advanced, afraid of nothing,
> the earl's killer, swiftly
> —fierce-hearted he fell—into
> the mighty din of Óðinn [battle].
> The land burgeons (but I must)
> by the Vína over my
> (—mortal grief is that—conceal
> my sorrow) excellent brother (*Egils saga* ch. 55).

The poetry itself allows the expression of emotions that may have been difficult to manage in a culture that cherished heroic stoicism to an almost absurd extent, and shortly after this the

1. Old English Æðelstān; in the saga Old Icelandic Aðalsteinn.

extremely depressed Egill of the saga allows himself to be cheered up by two chests of silver and an arm-ring which King Athelstan gives to the family in compensation for the loss of Þórolfr.

In later life, however, Egill suffered a harsher blow that almost drove him to suicide: the loss of two of his sons, his favourite, Bǫðvarr, by drowning and another, Gunnarr, apparently from sickness. The saga (ch. 78) tells how Egill, on learning of Bǫðvarr's death, buries his body in his father Skalla-Grímr's burial-mound, rides home, silent but physically swollen with grief, and locks himself in the panelled bed which was a traditional part of Icelandic farmhouses. He refuses to speak, to come out, or to eat or drink, until on the third day his favourite daughter, the wise Þorgerðr, is summoned. She pretends to join her father's suicide plot, lying down on the other bed in the panelled closet, but then manages to trick him into sharing with her a drink from a large horn. Just like his old self, Egill takes an enormous swig, only to find that it is milk, not water. Þorgerðr suggests that, since their suicide attempt has failed, Egill should compose a poem in memory of Bǫðvarr, which she will carve in runes on a piece of wood, and Egill agrees to this. What he composes is a remarkable poem, *Sonatorrek*, 'The Grievous Loss of Sons'. Speaking at first with difficulty, straining to wring words from his heavy heart, he tells of his grief. He remembers the deaths of mother, father, brother, and then his recent loss:

> Grim to me is the gap
> that the wave tore
> in the fence of my
> father's kin.
> I know that unfilled
> and open stands
> the gaping lack of a son
> that the sea has dealt to me (v. 6).

Without Bǫðvarr he lacks a friend and defender in his cantankerous old age, and he is tormented by his impotence. If he could take up sword and fight against his son's slayer, the god of the sea, he would do so, but he has not the strength, and all can see the old warrior's isolation (vv. 7-9). Óðinn (Odin) has stolen his son, and it is joylessly that Egill will make offerings to his patron god, but Óðinn also has given him the gift of poetry, and it is that which allows Egill to work through his grief and face his own death with a glad heart. The saga relates that, having composed this poem, he recites it to the household, takes his place in his high seat and arranges the funeral feast for his sons.

Egill is living in the twilight phase, when Christianity is well known in the Nordic lands but not yet universally accepted. One of his comforts, obscurely alluded to in the poem, is that his son has departed on a pleasant path to some kind of dwelling with Óðinn (vv. 10 and 18). As for himself, he has no fear of the personified death—the goddess Hel—who stands awaiting him on a headland (v. 25).

We have seen, so far, that the heroic ideals of courage and honour manifest themselves in early poems and stories in a grim and exultant stoicism in the face of death. The examples given were mainly solitary deaths, but many more could be supplied from battle descriptions. Such behaviour is surely driven partly by the certainty of some kind of reward after death, and it is to this question that I now turn, with the caveat that it is not realistic to make grand generalizations about the Nordic view of death and the afterlife. The literary and archaeological evidence from the period around the ninth and tenth centuries affords glimpses of a varied array of beliefs and burial practices, and of a pagan mythology which is far from systematic; and all that can be attempted here is a brief survey of some of the possibilities.[1]

What is fairly consistent throughout early Germanic literature is the importance of posthumous fame as a form of immortality. This idea is classically expressed in v. 77 of *Hávamál*, 'Sayings of the High One [Óðinn]':

---

1. Further information and bibliography on early Nordic burial practices and attitudes to death and the afterlife can be found in Ström 1958, 1961; Turville-Petre 1964: 269-74; Davidson 1967: 111-32; Simpson 1967: 190-200; Foote and Wilson 1970: 406-14; Roesdahl 1991: 154-58; and Müller-White 1993.

Cattle die, kinsmen die,
each man will die the same;
I know one thing that never dies:
the renown of every dead man.

Life, in this light, is partly a matter of storing up deeds which one's relatives will recall with pride after one's death. As Beowulf, himself a Dark Age Scandinavian, even if an imaginary one, says:

Every one of us must experience the end
of this world's life; let him who can earn
glory before death; that, for a noble liegeman
unliving, is the best (*Beowulf* ll. 1386–89).

The verbal memorials surviving from medieval Scandinavia most characteristically take the form of highly elaborate encomiastic poems in praise of rulers of Norway, Denmark, Orkney or, more rarely, Sweden. They were declaimed before the descendants and retainers of the deceased ruler, and must have played an important role in preserving morale and political cohesion at a difficult time. One of these poems was composed by the Icelander Arnórr Þórðarson jarlaskáld 'Earls'-Poet' in memory of Haraldr harðráði 'Hard-Ruler', after his ambitious bid for conquest ended in defeat at Stamford Bridge near York in 1066. The poem contains many traditional images of heroic valour: the king's heart never trembles in the din of battle, thousands fall, and the enemy leaders thunder off to the safety of the city of York as the Norwegians win an opening victory. But soon afterwards, Arnórr has to admit, the king's excess of heroic spirit leads to his death. His men, in the time-honoured way, choose death rather than accepting quarter:[1]

They chose, the liegemen of the gracious
liege, much rather than wishing quarter,
beside the battle-keen captain
to fall, every one (*Memorial poem for Haraldr harðráði* v. 15b).

---

1.   Cf. Tacitus, writing of the continental Germanic tribes of the first century AD in *Germania* ch. 14: 'Indeed it is infamy and disgrace for any man who survives his chieftain and leaves the battle-line... Chieftains fight for victory, retainers for their chieftain'.

The poem itself confers a kind of immortality on Haraldr; but Arnórr, a Christian, is also careful to pray for the soul of his patron; he evidently believes in the power of intercession for the dead, through that sociable doctrine of purgatory to which reference is made in the first essay in this collection.

A lasting memorial of a material kind was often provided for deceased heroes. Beowulf, at the end of his epic, slain in a dragon-fight reminiscent of Sigurðr's, is cremated along with his weapons, amid much lamentation. His people also spend ten days building a huge barrow on a headland, as he had requested, and in it they deposit his ashes, together with the treasure-hoard he had won from the dragon. The poem closes as twelve warriors ride around it praising him as the most generous and beneficent of kings and the most eager for glory (*lofgeornost; Beowulf* ll. 3169-82).

This magnificent landmark is reminiscent of actual barrows associated with royal sites at Jelling in Jutland and Borre in south Norway, and with many others throughout Scandinavia. Another lavish funeral in *Beowulf*, that of the Danish king Scyld, launched out to sea in a ship laden with treasure, by definition finds no counterpart in the archaeological record, and ship- or boat-burials of any kind are extremely rare in Denmark, but hundreds of these, in mounds or trenches, are known from the other Nordic lands, including the spectacularly opulent Viking Age examples from Oseberg and Gokstad.[1] The Sutton Hoo ship-burial in Suffolk, dated early seventh century, is the most famous of a handful of examples from East Anglia. These finds contained an impressive array of goods, including jewellery, carved items, weaponry, textiles, furniture and domestic utensils in varying amounts. Food is also a common element in these and other 'accompanied burials', as is the presence of other human or animal bones alongside the deceased. The precise religious significance of these and the other diverse

---

1.   Both finds were located in Vestfold, south Norway, and after painstaking restoration are on view at the Viking Ship Hall, Bygdøy, Oslo. The date of the Gokstad find is presumed to be c. 850, that of Oseberg c. 900. For brief discussions and further bibliography see Christensen 1993a, 1993b.

inhumation and cremation practices of the pagan North is difficult to establish. Ship-burials (or the common alternative of ship-shaped arrangements of stones over cremated remains, as at Lindholm Høje in Denmark) have, for instance, normally been interpreted as implying a notion of a journey to the afterlife, and this may well be correct, but they may well also make statements about the ethnic, social, political or economic status of the deceased, of the surviving kin or of the community at large.

Less ostentatious memorials are also available for those of more slender means. Thousands of Viking Age gravestones or memorial-stones are to be found in Scandinavia, the most notable including the picture-stones from the Baltic island of Gotland and the Swedish rune-stones bearing messages such as that on the Gripsholm stone: 'Tola had this stone raised for her son Haraldr, the brother of Yngvarr. Bravely they fared out, far after gold, and in the east they fed the eagles [i.e. made carrion of their enemies]. They died in the south in Serkland' (cited in Shepard 1984–85: 233). This kind of monument is mentioned in *Hávamál* v. 72:

> A son is a blessing, even if born late,
> for a man after death.
> Rarely do memorial stones stand by the road,
> unless a son has raised them for a father.

The literary sources provide a fascinating, if not entirely dependable, complement to the archaeological material. A concept found in many saga narratives is that the occupants of burial mounds may continue to interact with the living, having asked beforehand to be buried in some suitable spot— overlooking the fjord, where they can watch the ships go by, or on a hill where they can keep an eye on the district. A famous example is Gunnarr of Hlíðarendi, encountered above as the co-hero of the first half of *Njáls saga*. A pagan at a time when Christianity is on the horizon, he is given a traditional burial in a mound, sitting upright, but his influence on events is not over, for the servants claim that they hear him chanting verses blithely inside the mound. His son Hǫgni is not told, being of a sceptical disposition, but one night he and his friend

Skarp-Heðinn, son of Njáll, are standing outside. It seems to them that the mound stands open, lit by shifting moonlight and four lights burning within. Gunnarr turns to the moon and declaims a verse exulting in his warrior prowess and affirming that he would die rather than yield. The mound then closes, and the companions immediately recognize that they are being spurred to revenge (ch. 78).

Gunnarr's posthumous role may not be benign, but it is reasonably dignified, and hardly out of line with the ethics of the saga age, or even out of line with the laws of Christian Iceland, which sanctioned killing for revenge in some circumstances. In some cases, though, the undead dead make their presence felt in a palpable, entirely unghostly way which can hover between the frightening, the grotesque and the comic. One of the thoroughly malevolent revenants is Þórolfr bægifótr, 'Lame-foot', in *Eyrbyggja saga* (a saga full of ghosts, berserks, sorcerers and heathen practices). A disagreeable bully in life, Þórolfr in death brings havoc and destruction to people and animals in the neighbourhood to such an extent that the valley containing his grave mound is depopulated. Moving his body, heavy, ugly, but uncorrupt, to a more remote place provides temporary relief, but then the trouble begins again, and Þórolfr is only finally despatched by being levered out of his second grave, rolled to the shore and burned in a huge pyre. Even then, his evil magic lives on in the form of a bull calf born to a cow who has licked the stones on which Þórolfr's ashes have blown about, and the cycle only ends when the bull has destroyed its owner and plunged into a quagmire (chs. 34 and 63).

About the otherworldly destination of soul and body after death there is no unanimity. One poem makes mention of Niflhel, the dark realm of the dead, and below it a further nine worlds into which the dead depart (*Vafþrúðnismál*, 'The Sayings of Vafþrúðnir [a giant]', v. 43), although the same poem also mentions Valhalla, about which more will be said below. There seems to be little or no idea here of reward or retribution in the pagan afterlife, but this does colour the world-view of the poem *Vǫluspá* ('The Prophecy of the Seeress'), which is thought to belong to the same tenth-century twilight period as Egill Skalla-Grímsson. The poet of *Vǫluspá* seems to envisage various destinations. The beautiful Gimlé, for instance, roofed with gold, will appear after the great cataclysm, and there the just will enjoy eternal bliss (v. 64), while earlier in the poem we see a macabre vision of oath-breakers, murderers and adulterers tormented on Nástrǫnd ('Corpse-strand') in a hall woven out of serpents (v. 38). The influence of Christian ideas here and elsewhere is not surprising, given the long history of relations—amicable and otherwise—between Scandinavia and the Christian lands of Western Europe, and given the fact that several of the early settlers of Iceland, around 900, were of Norwegian stock but came to the new land via the British Isles, especially Ireland and the Hebrides.

However, if we think of the Nordic afterlife we tend to think first and foremost of Valhalla or Valhǫll, 'the Hall of the Slain', and rightly so. This is not, like horned helmets, a figment of the modern popular imagination about Vikings. According to the didactic poem *Grímnismál*, 'Sayings of Grímnir (Óðinn)' Valhǫll is thatched with spears and shields, and the benches are strewn with mail-coats (vv. 8-10). A wolf lurks west of the doorway, and an eagle hovers over it. There Óðinn chooses the slain, weapon-dead men, every day. Later in the poem (v. 14) it is said that the privilege of choosing the slain is shared with the goddess Freyja (an odd choice, since she is a fertility deity), and elsewhere we learn that the valkyries share this role; indeed the world 'valkyrie' (*valkyrja*) probably means 'chooser of the slain' (de Vries 1977: 641). When Eiríkr blóðøx, 'Bloodaxe', that infamous king of York and enemy of Egill Skalla-Grímsson, was slain on the Pennine moors at Stainmore, a memorial poem was composed for him which opens with a scene of great commotion in Valhǫll as the warrior occupants muster and the valkyries prepare drink to welcome Eiríkr to Óðinn's hall. Among the reception party are Sigmundr and Sinfjǫtli, father and brother of Sigurðr the dragon-slayer (*Eiríksmál* v. 5).

As to how the warriors in Valhǫll pass their time: predictably, they drink and fight. They feast on the meat of the boar Sæhrímnir which is cooked, eaten and made whole again every day, and they drink an endless supply of mead from the goat Heiðrún (*Gylfaginning* chs. 38–39 and *Grímnismál* 18 and 25). When not drinking, they spend their time killing each other, then rise for a meal, and start all over again the following day (*Vafþrúðnismál* v. 41; *Gylfaginning* ch. 41). This endless military training is in preparation for the great confrontation, when they will pour out of the five hundred and forty doors of Valhǫll, eight hundred abreast, and march to fight with the gods against the monstrous wolf and his giant allies (*Grímnismál* v. 23).

The gods of the pagan North are themselves not only fallible but also mortal. Not only is the death of the fair god Baldr prominent among the mythical stories, but all are doomed to be destroyed in the almighty cataclysm of Ragnarǫk, the 'Doom' or 'Twilight of the Gods', when the trickster god Loki will ally with the giants against the gods, when Þórr (Thor) and the World Serpent will engage in fatal single combat and Óðinn himself will be destroyed by a monstrous wolf. According to *Vǫluspá*, the whole earth will be destroyed:

> The sun will begin to blacken; earth will sink into the ocean;
> The bright stars will disappear from the heavens...

> Towering flame will sport against the very sky (loosely based on *Vǫluspá* v. 57).

The *Vǫluspá* poet envisages a period of regeneration after the old order has been swept away, but his vision concludes with a dark dragon flying, corpses in its wings.[1]

Valhǫll is not everyone's idea of heaven, but it is obviously the wish-fulfilment of a warrior elite, which must have served a serious ideological purpose in promoting death in battle as an attractive option. It leaves the majority of the population uncatered for, including the half who happen to be female, the peasant farmers quietly tending their land, and slaves. Lacking the prospect of anything but a vague and dark future after

---

1. Among the most accessible accounts of the mythology, including Ragnarǫk, are the thirteenth-century *Snorra Edda* (see *Snorri Sturluson: Edda* below), and modern works including Turville-Petre 1964 and Martin 1972).

death, these sections of society may well have sympathized with the anti-heroic view that life, even a diminished life, is worth holding on to. This gets a rare hearing in the poem *Hávamál*, v. 71:

> A lame man rides a horse, a handless man herds sheep,
> a deaf man fights, and well.
> Better to be blind than burned;
> no-one has use for a corpse.

According to Icelandic tradition, Christianity was formally accepted by the Alþingi or national assembly in 1000 AD. The conversion process in the other Nordic lands was roughly contemporaneous, though more protracted and bloody, and in Sweden pagan observances continued at least until the end of the eleventh century. Alongside its cultural contributions of literacy, Latin learning and a strongly chronological view of human history, Christianity brought to the North a new ethical system and a view of death and the afterlife more coherent than those previously available; burial customs tended correspondingly to be homogenized in favour of inhumation without grave-goods. In *Njáls saga*, the eponymous hero lives long enough to see Christianity officially established in Iceland, and his posture in death could hardly be more different than that of his friend Gunnarr. Knowing that the fate of death by burning is in store for him, and knowing too that if he lives he will be unable to take revenge for his sons, the old man resigns himself to the imminent conflagration as his attackers kindle fire around his home. He reassures his household with the words, 'Bear up well and speak no words of fear, for this one storm will come, but it will be long before another like it. And have faith that God is merciful, and will not let us burn both in this world and the next'. Njáll and his wife Bergþóra refuse the chance to escape from the house, and their young grandson Þórðr will not leave them. They cross themselves and the boy, entrusting their souls to God (ch. 129). When the blackened ruins of the house are investigated some time later, the bodies are found unmarked by the flames, except for one finger that the boy had stretched out from under the hide covers, and Njáll's face and body have an unusual radiance. Those who witness it see this as a great wonder and offer thanks to God (ch. 132).

It would be agreeable to be able to say that the saintly resignation of Njáll inspires those left behind to renounce the option of revenge. However, Njáll's own final speeches are not untouched by the old heroic values, and his son-in-law Kári, the father of little Þórðr, cannot express his grief in any but the old way, so that there is a great deal more blood-letting before resolution is reached. Indeed, an optimistic view of human behaviour could hardly be expected from the anonymous thirteenth-century author of *Njáls saga*, for he lived through times that were if anything more grim than this, when the old paranoia about personal honour had been compounded by mounting greed, and when whole neighbourhoods became sucked into the power struggles of the great chieftainly families. He knew that Christianity ought to, but did not, bring about a revolution in people's attitudes.

In fact the descriptions we have of thirteenth-century Iceland, in the great compilation *Sturlunga saga*, make agonizing reading, because its violence is more immediate and more vicious, and it is not excused by the demands of fate or an implacable code of honour. The killings in *Njáls saga* have a kind of stylized elegance about them—as when Gunnarr will catch a spear in mid-air and hurl it gracefully back at its sender (ch. 30)—which is lacking from the malicious and inept hackings so often portrayed in *Sturlunga saga*. Moreover, the references to Christian institutions and sentiments within accounts of thirteenth-century events add a grim irony to the narratives. When one man is ambushed on his way to meet the bishop and dealt a mortal blow near a pillar in the choir of the church (Jón Birnuson, in ch. 76 of *Íslendinga saga* within the *Sturlunga* collection), or when another chants prayers to the Virgin as he is horrifically tortured (Órækja Snorrason in ch. 115), we are reminded that things should be better now. A verse of exultation uttered after a raiding party against Bishop Guðmundr of Hólar had done its vicious work shows how easily the Christian religion was accommodated to the old ethics of killing (ch. 44):

The proud Sturla has
—the raven treads on carrion;
Christ deals glory and support—
avenged Tumi well.

The old ethics died hard, and authors in thirteenth-century
Iceland could not realistically envisage a society without strife,
but looking back at history, they did imagine one in which
deeds of violence were driven by high ideals and where the
state of things could be partly ascribed to the workings of fate.
The more thoughtful of them doubtless felt, as we do, that the
extremes of behaviour which spring from the old ideals of
honour and revenge were neither socially useful nor morally
acceptable, but they were prepared to admire energy, courage
and dignity in the face of the greatest test of all, death. Above
all, perhaps, they were stirred by stories of ancient times
whose emotive power outweighs and outlasts their particular
ethical frameworks.

It is fitting that the last word should be given to someone
who illustrates the notion that the best of these values do not
necessarily have to be attached to acts of violence. Here is a
heroic death indeed, so well stage-managed that few of us
could hope to do the same, unless we accede to the idea of
euthanasia. The arrangements for the estate of the deceased,
orderly but free from the modern proliferation of paper-work,
should also be noted. In this passage from *Laxdæla saga*, ch. 7,
Unnr, a great matriarch of Norwegian origin, has brought her
family to Iceland, via Ireland and the Hebrides, marrying off
female relatives along the way and, on arrival, dealing out land
to her family and servants. In her old age she arranges the
marriage of her favourite grandson, Óláfr feilan, and provides
a magnificent wedding feast. She welcomes the guests
decorously:

> Then she walked into the hall, attended by a large company.
> And when all were seated, people were impressed at the
> splendour of the banquet. Then Unnr said, 'I call my brother,
> Bjǫrn, to witness, and Helgi and my other kinsmen and
> friends, that I place this estate, with everything that belongs to it,
> in the hands of my grandson Óláfr, to own and manage'. After
> that, Unnr stood up and said she would retire to the room where

she usually slept. She said that everyone should enjoy themselves as they best pleased, and that all should be cheered with
drink. It is said that Unnr was tall and strongly built. She walked
firmly down the hall, and people remarked what a magnificent
woman she still was. The drinking went on throughout the
evening, until it was time to sleep. The next day Ólafr feilan
went to his grandmother Unnr's bedroom, and as he came into
the room, Unnr was sitting up against the pillows. She was dead.
Ólafr went back into the hall and announced the news. People
thought it remarkable how she had kept her dignity to her
dying day. Now the drinking went on in the joint honour of
Ólafr's wedding and Unnr's funeral. And on the last day of the
feast Unnr was moved to a burial mound which had been
prepared for her. She was placed in a ship in the mound, and a
great wealth of goods with her. Then the mound was closed.[1]

Bibliography

Primary Sources
Where possible, reference is made to a standard English translation of Old Norse
works. Where a reliable translation is lacking (as is the case for most of the
poetry), a standard edition of the original text is listed.

The Anglo-Saxon Chronicle (trans. G.N. Garmonsway; London: Dent, 1953).
Atlakviða, in Dronke (ed.) 1969.
Beowulf (ed. F. Klaeber; Lexington: Heath, 3rd edn, 1950).
Egils saga (trans. C. Fell; London: Dent, 1975).
Eiríksmál, in *Den norsk-islandske skjaldedigtning*, AI and BI (ed. F. Jónsson; repr.;
     Copenhagen: Rosenkilde & Bagger, 1967–73 [1912–15]).
Eyrbyggja saga (trans. H. Pálsson and P. Edwards; Harmondsworth: Penguin,
     1972).
Grímnismál, in H. Kuhn (ed.), *Die Lieder der Codex Regius*. I. *Text* (Heidelberg:
     Carl Winter, 1962).
Guðrúnarkviða I and II, in Kuhn (ed.), *Die Lieder der Codex Regius*. I. *Text*.
Gylfaginning (part of *Snorra Edda*), see *Snorri Sturluson: Edda*.
Hamðismál, in Dronke (ed.) 1969.
Haralds saga Sigurðarsonar (from Snorri Sturluson's *Heimskringla*): *King Haralds Saga*
     (trans. M. Magnusson and H. Pálsson; Harmondsworth: Penguin, 1966).

1.   This paper, albeit inadequate, is dedicated to the memory of my
brother Nick Edwards, who died on February 22 1993, in the week of the
paper's original delivery as a public lecture.

Hávamál, in Kuhn (ed.), *Die Lieder der Codex Regius. I. Text.*

Jómsvíkinga saga/The Saga of the Jomsvikings (ed. and trans. N.F. Blake; London: Nelson, 1962).

Laxdœla saga (trans. M. Magnusson and H. Pálsson; Harmondsworth: Penguin, 1969).

Memorial poem for Harald harðráði (Arnórr jarlaskáld), in Jónsson (ed.), *Den norsk-islandske skjaldedigtning.*

Njals saga (trans. M. Magnusson and H. Pálsson; Harmondsworth: Penguin, 1960).

Snorri Sturluson: Edda (trans. A. Faulkes; London: Dent, 1987).

Sonatorrek (Egill Skalla-Grímsson), in Jónsson (ed.), *Den norsk-islandske skjaldedigtning.*

Sturlunga saga (trans. J. McGrew and R.G. Thomas; New York: Twayne, 1970–74).

Tacitus I: Agricola, Germania, Dialogus (ed. and trans. W. Peterson; rev. M. Winterbottom; Cambridge, MA: Harvard University Press, 1970).

Vafþrúðnismál, in Kuhn (ed.), *Die Lieder der Codex Regius. I. Text.*

Vǫlsunga saga/The Saga of the Volsungs (ed. and trans. R.G. Finch; London: Nelson, 1965).

Vǫluspá, in Kuhn (ed.), *Die Lieder der Codex Regius. I. Text.*

Secondary Sources
Andersson, T.M.
1967   *The Icelandic Family Saga: An Analytic Reading* (Cambridge, MA: Harvard University Press).
Bycock, J.L.
1982   *Feud in the Icelandic Saga* (Berkeley: University of California Press).
Christensen, A.E.
1993a   'Gokstad', in Pulsiano (ed.) 1993: 232.
1993b   'Oseberg', in Pulsiano (ed.) 1993: 457-59.
Clover, C.J., and J. Lindow (eds.)
1985   *Old Norse–Icelandic Literature: A Critical Guide* (Ithaca, NY: Cornell University Press).
Davidson, H.R.E.
1967   *Pagan Scandinavia* (London: Thames & Hudson).
Dronke, U. (ed.)
1969   *The Poetic Edda. I. Heroic Poems* (Oxford: Clarendon Press).
Foote, P.G., and D.M. Wilson
1970   *The Viking Achievement* (London: Sidgwick & Jackson).
Kristjánsson, J.
1988   *Eddas and Sagas* (trans. P. Foote; Reykjavík: Hið íslenska bókmenntafélag).
Martin, J.S.
1972   *Ragnarǫk: An Investigation into Old Norse Concepts of the Fate of the Gods* (Assen: Van Gorcum).

Müller-White, M.
   1993   'Burial Mounds and Burial Practices', in Pulsiano (ed.) 1993: 58-
               60.
Pulsiano, P. (ed.)
   1993   *Medieval Scandinavia: An Encyclopedia* (New York: Garland).
Roesdahl, E.
   1991   *The Vikings* (trans. S. Margeson and K. Williams; London: Guild).
Shepard, J.
   1984–85   'Yngvarr's Expedition to the East and a Russian Inscribed Stone
               Cross', *Saga-Book of the Viking Society* 21: 222-92.
Simpson, J.
   1967   *Everyday Life in the Viking Age* (London: Batsford).
Ström, F.
   1958   'Döden och de döda', in *Kulturhistorisk leksikon for nordisk
               middelalder* (Copenhagen: Rosenkilde & Bagger), III: 432-38.
   1961   *Nordisk Hedendom* (Göteborg: Akademiförlaget-Gumperts).
Turville-Petre, G.
   1964   *Myth and Religion of the North* (London: Weidenfeld & Nicholson).
Vries, J. de
   1977   *Altnordisches Etymologisches Wörterbuch* (Leiden: Brill, 2nd edn).

Part III

Disposing of the Dead

A Job for Life

Andrew Bardgett

Introduction

When people discover that I am a funeral director, their reaction often takes the form of a joke: 'Oh, you work in a dying trade', or 'I suppose people are always dying to meet you'. On a more serious note I am often told 'Well, recession won't affect you, you won't ever be short of business', or 'You've got a job for life'. A job for life it may be, but what exactly is my job?

A few years ago a woman for whose relative I had arranged a funeral commented that her job and mine were very similar—she was a travel agent. My first reaction was to laugh but a little reflection made me realize that similarities between our occupations are quite strong. We both consult the client[1] offering the various choices, discussing their obligations and giving financial advice. We both need to consider how timescales are affected by the various documents required and how soon the 'client' can be ready. We organize the holiday or the funeral according to the client's wishes and the availability of transport and facilities—for example the hotel room or time at the crematorium. We both prepare documentation and itineraries for our, or our sub-contractor's, staff and we both provide supervision of what has been organized, either with our own staff, in the funeral director's case, or by a courier in the travel agent's case. There are of course differences: notably

---

1. Although the deceased person is my client in the sense that it is on his or her behalf that the arrangements are made, obviously the arrangements are made *with* the family (or executor) of the deceased and so they are, strictly speaking, the client.

the funeral director sends a bill after the event whereas the travel agent receives payment in advance; the travel agent's client wants to make the journey whereas the funeral director's usually does not; and the funeral director, unlike the travel agent, cannot arrange return tickets!

One way of looking at my job, then, is as 'travel agent to the dead'. As an illustration of this, the 'In Memoriam' columns of newspapers (discussed by Jon Davies in this volume) often have entries very similar to the sort of letters that might be written to a person who had gone far away from home. The dead person is perceived as having made a journey.

However, although most people could provide a fairly detailed answer to the question 'what does a travel agent do?', the same question posed about a funeral director usually produces a vague answer. Perhaps this is because 'society' does not like to contemplate death or the practicalities associated with it. A good indication of this is the very low percentage of the population who write wills. 'Signing your own death warrant' is the objection commonly made.

Our reluctance to consider death is summed up for me by an inscription on a headstone in America which has two lines. The first reads 'I had expected this' and the second 'but not so soon'. We pay lip service to the fact that we are going to die— but not today!

This reluctance to consider death means, as I suggested above, that we do not consider the practicalities associated with it either. The funeral director's job is very much to do with these practicalities and most people therefore remain ignorant of what it involves. This article is meant to change that.

Arranging a Funeral in Consultation with the Family

The funeral director's job can be described in terms of a set of tasks, typically arranged in serial form, one task or set of tasks after another. In practice some of the tasks will be carried out in parallel with others and the tasks may be carried out in a different order. But, to begin with, how does one arrange a funeral?

Do-it-yourself guides are available for all manner of tasks, including arranging funerals. These guides are often drawn up by people who have some knowledge of the subject, are well intentioned but are clearly *not* funeral directors! They contain errors and omissions and no funeral director would follow the advice in exactly the way it is described, since this would probably result in the funeral being delayed several days. Such guides are usually either too simplistic to be helpful or so complicated that they illustrate why most people do use the services of a funeral director and why there are so few DIY funerals!

Basically the funeral director's job is to try to carry out the wishes of the bereaved family. Since they have often not thought about death, however, the family's wishes may not be clear. The starting point, therefore, is a two-way exchange, with the funeral director providing advice and in return discovering the wishes of the family together with basic factual information such as the age and address of the deceased, the date of death and so on.

The advice covers four areas: the choices that can be made, the obligations of the family, financial advice and, if required, sources of assistance with the cost of the funeral.

There is a wide range of choices but the fundamental choice is between burial or cremation. Is there to be a service in a church, temple or mosque or a service in the crematorium or cemetery chapel (including non-religious, humanist services)? There are questions about the type of coffin, choice of cemetery and type of grave. If a cremation is chosen there is the matter of disposal of the ashes: they may be buried in a family grave or special plot, scattered in the Garden of Remembrance, or taken to be scattered elsewhere. At some crematoria there are columbaria where urns are kept as memorials. Crematoria usually have a book of remembrance to commemorate the dead.

Included in the advice given is an estimate of cost, and to a certain extent choices can be made on this basis. Funeral costs will be discussed below. Having discussed the choices with the family the funeral director in return obtains their wishes and a 'blueprint' for the funeral.

Secondly, advice is given on the obligations facing the family. These are primarily the obligations to register the death and to follow the procedures in which the coroner is involved. This can be very complicated.

Thirdly, the funeral director would normally give some basic advice on the administration of the dead person's estate, dealing with banks, building societies and insurance companies together with information on obtaining Grants of Probate if the person has left a valid will or Letters of Administration if not.

The fourth area of advice concerns the assistance that is available to help with the cost of the funeral. Help is available from the Department of Social Security (DSS), social services departments and from hospital authorities. This information is frequently needed.

As a result of this exchange of information with the family the funeral director now has a blueprint for the funeral, and the next step is to turn this into an actual funeral.

Minimum Timescale and Limiting Factors

The first stage is to look at those factors which set the minimum timescale and involve liaison with the hospital or doctor. Death, like so many things in life, has its paperwork and the availability of the necessary documents sets the earliest date for the funeral. If a postmortem examination is to be performed this may determine how soon the body will be available.

Another factor to consider is the size of the body. A large coffin may be too big to fit into a cremator and therefore must be buried. Moving a very heavy person may need extra staff or even lifting equipment. Funeral directors are only too well aware of the origin of the expression 'a dead weight'.

Other factors to consider include infection risks, for instance from hepatitis or AIDS, which might affect what is to be arranged. It may seem incredible but until recently when the dangers of AIDS became reasonably well known the medical profession was under no obligation to warn a funeral director that a body could pose an infection risk.

The time and manner of the removal of the body may also

have to be considered, particularly if the death has occurred at home or in a nursing home.

The Day and Time of the Funeral

Having checked on those factors which set the minimum timescale and on other factors which may have a bearing on exactly what is to be arranged, the funeral director's next task is to set the day and time of the funeral. There are five factors which have to be considered. The central considerations are the wishes of the family. These are usually established during the initial discussions although the involvement of the coroner or other uncertainties may result in the preference for the day of the funeral becoming 'as soon as possible' rather than a particular day.

The liaison with the hospital or doctor, together with the timing of the registration of the death, will establish the availability of the documentation.

The other factors which have to be considered are the availability of a time at the crematorium or cemetery, the availability of a minister and a church and lastly the funeral director's own staff and vehicles. Getting all five factors together is usually straightforward but at times can be very difficult. Public holidays are difficult times to arrange funerals, with Easter usually being the worst. Good Friday and Easter Monday are public holidays and so most crematoria and cemeteries do not operate. The same applies on Saturday and Sunday at Easter, so that there are four days when no funerals can take place. The week prior to Easter is only four days long for the funeral director, Monday to Thursday. This is a busy time for ministers with more services than usual so they are less able to take funerals. Five days' worth of funerals have to be fitted into four days, and so the crematoria and cemeteries become very busy. Since the family may well be unhappy with the thought of a four-day delay, from Thursday to Tuesday, there is a lot of pressure on the funeral director to arrange the funeral before Easter, making this a difficult week. The same considerations apply to the week after Easter, which some ministers like to take as holiday.

Collection, Preparation and Submission of Documents

It is usual for the funeral director to arrange the documents necessary for the funeral. One part of the documentation which the funeral director cannot arrange, however, is the registration of the death. Where a doctor has been attending a person before death then that doctor would normally issue a 'medical cause of death' certificate together with a 'notice to informant'. These are taken to the Registrar of Births, Deaths and Marriages in the area where the death occurred. The relatives need to provide information to register the death, as indicated on the 'notice to informant'. After registering the death the registrar issues a certificate of registration of death (Form BD8) for the DSS, any copy certificates required (these are what most people would call 'death certificates') and a certificate for burial or cremation, often referred to as a 'disposal' certificate. This certificate is usually passed to the funeral director who submits it, together with the other documents required, to the crematorium or cemetery authorities.

For cremation a statutory application, Form A, has to be completed and signed by the person applying for the cremation and then witnessed. Most crematoria and cemeteries also require an additional formal notice of a cremation or burial.

Cremation law requires the completion of a set of medical forms B and C. The doctor attending the deceased normally completes part B and a second, independent, doctor completes part C. These are rather old-fashioned forms and it is relatively easy to miss parts of questions. Coupled with the fact that completing such forms is not normally part of a doctor's training, it is easy to see why so many of these forms are incorrectly completed. Having them corrected can form an appreciable part of a funeral director's job.

The documents for cremation are scrutinized by a 'Medical Referee' who has to ensure that the legalities surrounding the cremation of a body are adhered to. Once satisfied the Medical Referee signs Form F, the authority to cremate.

Collection, Preparation and Presentation of the Body

The next stage of the funeral director's work is that concerned with the body. The first priority is to identify the body. Even in cases of death at home, some form of identity label is required so that there can be no doubt of the identity at any stage. Checks are made on any valuables on the body and instructions sought. In some cases, but not always, jewellery is removed.

Funeral directors' awareness of the origin of the expression 'a dead weight' was mentioned earlier. A human body is a difficult thing to lift or move but if we add to this society's unwillingness to consider the practical side of death some real problems are produced. Even where one might expect death to be considered, such as in elderly people's nursing homes built in recent years, the moving of bodies is rarely considered. Even the most modern nursing homes often have lifts which are too small to allow easy removal of bodies or which have access from inappropriate rooms, for instance the residents' lounge.

Once the body has been moved to the funeral director's premises it can be prepared. In the past, when deaths more usually occurred at home, there were normally one or two people in each street who would 'lay out' bodies. This is now rare, and even hospital nurses often do not know how best to lay out a body. This can be very important if the family intend to view the body.

A practice which has come into increasing use is that of arterial embalming. The word 'embalming' frequently conjures up thoughts of mummification. The only thing mummification and embalming have in common is the objective of preserving the body. The big difference is in the time scales of the two methods of preservation. Embalming is aimed at preserving the body but it is not carried out to preserve the body for a long time. Embalmers talk of the 'three Ps' of embalming: preservation, protection and presentation.

Embalming aims at a short-term preservation so that the changes which would normally occur in a body after death are slowed down, preventing their becoming noticeable between the time of death and the funeral. Embalming provides protection from disease for the funeral director's staff as well as relatives and friends who might visit the body. Even if the cause of death is a non-infectious one such as a stroke or heart attack, the human body is an ideal breeding ground for bacteria. A body can rapidly become very unpleasant and pose a health risk. The chemical solutions used for embalming kill the bacteria which are present in the body and so prevent the action these bacteria would have on the body. This leaves the body in a hygienic condition which makes it safer and more pleasant to handle or touch. Although it may seem an odd aim, the embalmer is trying to present the dead person in a lifelike way so that he or she seems peacefully asleep. Embalming helps this and, by returning the skin to a more lifelike colour, can help to take away some of the strangeness of death.

The simplest description of arterial embalming is that it is the same basic process as a blood transfusion, but where in the case of a living person the heart would normally circulate the blood, in this case a small pump is required to circulate the embalming solution. Embalming is not used in every case, and some funeral directors do not offer this service.

After embalming the body is placed in the coffin which is then dressed so that the person can be viewed in the chapel of rest. The question of whether or not to view may be a most difficult one. Where someone has died after a long period of pain it may be a help to the relatives to see the person free from pain and looking at peace. On the other hand, if a death has been very sudden the relatives may have great difficulty in accepting that the person has died, and seeing the person afterwards may help the acceptance of death. In all cases the decision of whether or not to view is a very personal choice.

Organization of Sub-Contractors

The final section of preparation work is the organization of sub-contractors. Funeral directors often place notices in newspapers on their clients' behalf. They organize flowers, catering and printing. If a burial is to take place in a churchyard it will be necessary to employ a gravedigger; not many churches employ a regular gravedigger nowadays. It is usual for the funeral director to arrange these sub-contractors and to pay them. These costs then appear in the funeral director's bill as disbursements, payments on the client's behalf.

That completes the funeral director's preparatory work. In summary, there is an initial two-way consultation with the family to obtain a 'blueprint' for the funeral. The funeral director checks on the factors which set the minimum timescale for the funeral and any factors which might affect what is to be arranged. The day and time of the funeral are fixed and the documentation seen to. The body is attended to and the sub-contracted parts of the funeral arranged.

Having seen to all the preparatory arrangements the funeral director then has the work associated with the actual funeral service. Rather like a parachutist, the funeral director must get things right at the first attempt! Careful preparations have to be made on the day.

The staff need to be given their instructions so that they know exactly where they need to be, at what time and with which vehicles. Directions to particular addresses and special instructions, such as the route to follow or how to care for passengers who may be disabled, need to be given. A final check is made on the identity of the body and on any valuables which may need to be dealt with. The funeral director often receives flowers for the funeral and these are listed and held until the time of the funeral. At the appropriate time the coffin is placed in the hearse together with its flowers and the cortège starts its journey.

Although the funeral director may take all the care in the world, 'Murphy's Law' or the law that 'whatever can go wrong will' applies as much to funerals as to any other human activity. Vehicle breakdowns, accidents and even deaths during funerals can all make the funeral director's life fraught. Imagine arriving at a church to be told by an obviously flustered vicar that the bell-ringer has just collapsed and died in the bell tower. 'I've phoned for the emergency services,' says the vicar. The words have hardly left his lips when, in the distance, the familiar sound of a siren heralds the approach of an ambulance. The ambulance, complete with both siren and flashing lights, stops behind the cortège waiting outside the church. The ambulance crew, knowing as the funeral director does that moving the dead person might prove difficult, tell us that they have summoned the help of the fire brigade. Again, in the distance, we hear sirens and moments later two fire engines and a control van stop behind the ambulance, the limousines and the hearse. An emergency call relating to a sudden death is always passed to the police and inevitably two panda cars, sirens and lights flashing, join the rather unusual cortège now assembled outside the church. Although it may seem amusing now, no one outside the church was laughing.

The vast majority of funerals, however, are not as exciting as the one described and having safely arrived at the cemetery or crematorium, the funeral service takes place. This is the final farewell and the travel analogy often finds its way into the funeral service. A well-known reading from St John's Gospel has Thomas asking, 'We don't know where you are going, how can we know the way?' Another reading makes the analogy between death and a ship setting sail and being lost from sight over the horizon only to be greeted on a distant shore.

The service over, the funeral director's staff return the family to their home or a hotel or restaurant.

After the Funeral

After the funeral the funeral director may have several 'follow up' tasks to complete. Acknowledgments are sometimes placed for clients or thank-you cards provided. Grave memorials may need organizing or additional inscriptions added. Flowers are often sent to hospitals or nursing homes and the flower cards or list are returned to the family. The flowers are sometimes kept if there is to be a burial of ashes within a few days of a cremation but ashes are sometimes buried or scattered months or years later. There are instances where ashes are kept until a spouse dies so that both sets of ashes may be buried or scattered together.

Cremation is sometimes used as a way of overcoming problems regarding a burial. If a family grave has insufficient

room for a full burial there will still be room for several sets of
ashes. It may not, because of cost or distance, be practicable to
have a burial in another part of the country, but having a
cremation and a subsequent burial of ashes can overcome this
problem. Similarly burial at sea, which is very expensive and
takes weeks to organize, is often replaced by cremation and a
scattering or burial of ashes at sea. A cautionary tale for
anyone considering this option came about some years ago. A
family collected their father's ashes which were contained in a
simple metal urn with a name plate on it. They put out to sea
and at a fair distance from the coast dispatched the urn into
the water, returning home satisfied that they had carried out
their father's wishes. Some weeks later the bomb disposal
squad were called to deal with a suspected mine washed up on
on the beach only to discover that the 'mine' had a name! It is
preferable either to scatter the ashes or to prepare the urn to
ensure that it will sink!

The last task for the funeral director is to make up and send
the bill. Funeral directors are often subject to quite vitriolic
criticism from the media on the question of funeral costs.
Because funerals cost a lot the media assume that funeral
directors make huge profits. Both the DSS and the Office of
Fair Trading, when looking at the funeral business, came to the
conclusion that this was not the case and that only in the very
large funeral directing groups were profit margins at levels
other service industries would find acceptable. Profit levels in
smaller firms were below those of similarly sized non-funeral
businesses. In blissful ignorance the media continue to produce
articles which invariably contain the well-worn phrase 'it's a
RIP off', while consistently refusing to take a serious look at
how the cost of a funeral is arrived at.

A funeral bill has two distinct parts. The funeral director's
own charges account for between two thirds and three
quarters of the total bill. The fees the funeral director pays on
the client's behalf make up the remaining quarter to a third of
the bill and include crematorium or cemetery fees, the
minister's fees and doctors' fees for cremation certificates. This
is money which the funeral director loans to the client to
enable the funeral to go ahead. Any similarity with travel

agents disappears at this point; travel agents never pay for their clients' holidays and send them bills when they come home. But this is effectively what the funeral director does. The funeral director's charges cover providing and preparing a coffin, moving and attending to the body, seeing to all the documentation, arranging and supervising the funeral and paying all disbursements. Being able to provide this service requires staff on call at all times, specialized premises and very specialized (and hence expensive) equipment. A new hearse for example can cost between £40,000 and £60,000. It is estimated that, on average, there are around 40 hours of labour per funeral. Even a few moments' thought and some simple mathematics will show that funerals are not going to be cheap. Funerals do cost a lot but it can be seen that there is a lot of background work involved and that the cost of providing the service is also high. Even so, in comparison with the average weekly wage, funeral costs have fallen steadily since the war.

In this article I have attempted to give an insight into the work of a funeral director by describing the main tasks involved. There are other areas of the work but these are less common, including for example dealing with deaths or funerals at a distance and the transferral of bodies to and from this country. Dealing with foreign countries involves completely different documents and procedures and even within the European Union there is no standardization of the documentation. Other less usual tasks include the exhumation of bodies either for reburial or for cremation, and last but not least dealing with the increasing numbers of people who are now pre-paying for or pre-arranging funerals.

I made the point at the beginning of my article that some people see a funeral director's job as a 'job for life'. Death in our society is a highly organized and well documented affair, and the archeologists of the future should be left in little doubt as to how we regarded and disposed of our dead. The job of a funeral director, though, is not so lacking in surprises as to deprive those archeologists of reasonable room for varied interpretations of our funeral practices!

Law after Death, or 'Whose Body Is It?'
The Legal Framework for the Disposal and Remembrance of the Dead

J.D.C. Harte*

Property and the Quest for Immortality: The Legal Significance of Human Remains and their Remembrance

From its early recorded days, English law, like other ancient systems of law, has been a battleground between the dead and the living. The history of property law, particularly land law, has demonstrated the efforts of successive generations to tie up their property after they have gone the way of all flesh. Property is a fundamental legal concept which involves rights over land, moveable things, or intangible matters such as original ideas. Much law is concerned with identifying who has rights over particular property, how those rights may be transferred to others and how they may be protected through legal proceedings. Those who have inherited property have struggled to loosen the restrictions imposed by their forebears, so that they in their turn can dictate what will become of their possessions when they pass them on.

Many volumes have been written on property law, and particularly on the law of succession, as it has been moulded and remoulded in this shifting struggle. Today, in very general terms, where they would be free to do so during their lifetime, the living are also free to decide to whom their property will

* I am very grateful for the help of a British Academy small grant to help an Investigation of the Legal Protection of Moveable Items of Artistic and Historical Importance. This made possible the accumulation of material included on funeral artefacts in this chapter and the illustrations to the text.

pass on their death, provided they comply with the law of wills. Historically this may be a freedom peculiar to modern societies which stress either autonomy of the individual or commercial flexibility, even though, in practice, this concentrates economic power in the hands of the few. If a person fails to make an effective will, statute lays down rules of intestacy to fill the gap, generally ensuring that the property passed on is shared between the closest members of the family, as recognized by the law.

In the longer term, trusts and other devices may be used to exert control far beyond the grave, but as time goes on that power becomes weaker. In particular, indefinite control of property by the dead is generally prevented by the Perpetuities and Accumulations Act 1964, a favourite source of difficult examination problems in legal education. The law allows a person to dispose of his or her property by dictating a series of rights for others to benefit from in turn, while preventing these beneficiaries from actually disposing of the property. They must pass it on in turn to the next person on the list. However, the 1964 Act provides that the person left holding the parcel after a set period of time will no longer be prevented from dealing with it by the original owner as he or she chooses. The maximum period is 80 years or the lifetime of some existing individual plus a further 21 years.[1]

A similar time principle is applied to preserve a person's creative identity under the law of copyright, now in the Copyright Act 1988. A person who produces any original work in writing or in any other permanent form, whether a book or a musical score or a painting, is entitled to property in it and may therefore control who copies it. This right normally lasts for 50 years after the death of the person who created the work, so the right to exploit it survives for 50 years for the benefit of those who inherit it.[2] People may wish to tie up their property after their death for many motives. Some testators

1. For a clear explanation of the relevant rules, see Sir R. Meggary and M.P. Thompson, *Meggary's Manual of Real Property* (London: Sweet & Maxwell, 7th edn, 1993).

2. See generally W.R. Cornish, *Intellectual Property* (London: Sweet & Maxwell, 2nd edn, 1989).

may want to make the best provision for their families. They may seek to ensure the survival of the family as a dynasty, aiming to provide grandchildren and greatgrandchildren with a fair share each; or some with a fairer share than others! Other property owners, with a wider sense of community than the immediate family, may wish to protect the property itself as part of the national heritage, keeping intact a well managed country estate or a collection of works of art. Some may be driven by the desire to perpetuate their own memory.

Striving to preserve one's identity after death, through one's possessions, may be a pathetic attempt to engineer immortality. On the other hand, it may represent an effort to express affection and concern for those whom one leaves behind. It may be a quest to maintain, for the benefit of others, what one has created or the values one has held during life. For the bereaved, a death may lead to unseemly squabbling over possessions, and here the law may come fully into play. However, for those who cared more for the person who has died than for his or her property, what may be most important is the law relating to the disposal of the mortal remains and the provision made for perpetuating the memory of that person.

It is a truism of English law that a human being cannot be treated as property. Nevertheless, it is salutary to remember that, historically, many legal systems have taken a very different approach. The Athenian city state which was the source of modern concepts of democracy was built on slavery. Sizeable parts of Roman law, which were included in the staple fare of English law students, certainly into the 1960s, treated human beings as property, not only slaves but children as well. Even the common law tradition has taken slavery for granted. The original Constitution of the United States of America allowed for slavery and it was the norm in remaining British colonies until the reforms which were started, virtually single-handed, by William Wilberforce at the end of the eighteenth century. However, in England itself, by the beginning of the eighteenth century slavery was regarded as legally impossible. Lord Mansfield, a generally far from radical Lord Chief Justice, concluded his judgment in the case of James Somerset, dealing with whether a negro slave could be claimed as property, with the famous words: 'the state of slavery is of such a nature that it is incapable of being introduced on any reason, moral or political... Whatever inconvenience may follow from this decision...the black must be discharged'.[1]

As living human beings cannot be subject to property rights in English law, neither can the dead. The principle that no one may own the dead would seem to be consistent with the same concern to respect the status of human beings as is shown by the legal rejection of slavery. However, the parallel may be misleading. First, the living may claim rights over their own bodies, so as to protect them, though these rights are restricted in the case of certain human beings, such as children and the mentally disabled. By contrast, rights over a corpse may not be claimed in the name of the dead person in any circumstances.

Secondly, it is significant that the law is chary of treating even parts of the human body or human tissue as property. This still appears to reflect a respect for the human body as a unique, indeed a holy, part of creation, in the Judaeo-Christian tradition. There is an inherent legal principle that human remains should be protected and accorded respect, quite apart from the existence of particular individual rights.

The law provides a framework for disposing of human remains, and for the long-term protection of the places where remains are interred and memories preserved. This framework may be seen as demonstrating the established Christian tradition which is still embodied in English law, while accommodating changed and increasingly diverse beliefs and needs in a pluralist society. For those with a merely materialist outlook, the law enables survivors to cope with the reality of death by recognizing their interest in the memory of the dead.

This paper seeks to explore who has legal rights in English law to dispose of human remains and how English law provides for their protection. It also considers the protection of places of interment and monuments to the dead both in terms of private property rights and the public interest.

---

1.   (1772) 20 State Trials 1 at p. 82.

The Legal Identity and the Status of the Dead

The identity of a human being is difficult to define legally. Thus, it is significant that English criminal law has consistently treated a foetus, however advanced, as less than a human being. Killing a foetus has been treated as a serious criminal offence and still is, unless approved under the Abortion Acts. However, it is not homicide.[1] Similarly, the foetus is not regarded at common law as a legal person entitled to bring a claim for damages in respect of injury sustained in the womb, although if it survives, under the Congenital Disabilities (Civil Liability) Act 1976, it may now bring a claim for its disabilities. The mother may have a cause of action on her own part which will include damages for the loss of the foetus.

Although there may be difficulty in identifying who has rights to protect them, there is a basic principle of English law that all human remains should be treated with dignity. Thus, under burial law, cremated remains tend to be treated with the same respect as a body. However, it may be difficult to decide exactly what are parts of a human being and what are merely products of a body. Similarly, it may be difficult to determine when a substance or an item has acquired a new independent identity.

Historically, limbs and organs might be interred in different places. At one extreme, pieces of enemies of the state who were beheaded and quartered could be displayed at different ends of the land. Sympathizers who rescued the remains might well only be able to inter part of the body. The final resting place of the head of Oliver Cromwell is reputedly a wall in the chapel of Sidney Sussex College, Cambridge.

By contrast, the hearts and entrails of kings were not infrequently interred in different places from their bodies. The bodies of saints were scattered across Europe. The more famous the saint, the greater the desire to acquire a fragment so as to assist devotion. The number of fragments available had a tendency to increase so as to meet demand. At the other

1. See J.C. Smith and B. Hogan, *Smith and Hogan: Criminal Law* (London: Butterworths, 7th edn, 1992).

extreme, it has been taken for granted that a person may be charged with stealing a specimen of his or her own urine. In *R. v. Welsh,* a driver was convicted for pouring a urine sample down the sink after handing it over for its alcohol content to be analysed.[1]

Modern science has raised many new problems. Cells may be 'immortalized' by being cultured and put into mice or other animals. Genetic engineering raises many ethically contentious possibilities, which are bound to lead to an increasing number of legal questions, not least with regard to material from the dead. Practices such as cryogenics, the freezing of entire bodies in the hope that they may be revived at some future date, may offer little realistic prospect of a renewed life in this world for the dead individuals concerned, but such bodies provide potential laboratory subjects for future scientists. This use is likely to be the last thing that the dead person would have authorized if asked.

Although a dead person or parts of a human being cannot belong to anyone, human tissue may so change its identity that it becomes part of other property. Cells fused in a microscope slide or bones set in a piece of macabre furniture may be protected by the property rights of whoever owns the slide or the furniture. Specimens of human bodies of historic as well as scientific interest may be the centre of controversy, particularly where they were put into collections and museums in Britain during the colonial era and are now demanded back for cultural or religious reasons by the governments of the countries in which they originated.

Problems which apply where material is taken from the living may be compounded if it is taken from the dead. Material taken for scientific experiments is subject to careful ethical controls but complications may arise. For example, a deceased person may have signed a consent form for tissue to be used for research generally, but the surviving spouse may object to tissue saved from a postmortem examination being used for a particular purpose.

1.   [1974] Road Traffic Reports 478.

Property in the Dead and the Power to Dispose of Human Remains

Protection of a body must be through individuals with recognized legal personalities, who have the power to bring appropriate legal proceedings: that is, adults of sound mind. Corporate persons are also recognized at law, such as a local authority or an undertaker's business which is registered as a limited company under the Companies Acts. These may act as parties in legal proceedings to resolve the fate of human remains. Such proceedings are most likely to be initiated by relatives but may take many different forms; for example challenging a high-handed action by a burial authority or disputing an undertaker's claim for fees.

No one may have property in a body, so it may not be stolen or be the subject of a civil wrong of trespass or conversion. Similarly, no one may defame the dead. The sons of the prime minister W.E. Gladstone realized this when they wanted to protect their father's name from a book which had made scurrilous allegations that charitable work he had performed among 'fallen women' had an ulterior motive. The sons devised an effective way out of the impasse by publishing their own vitriolic attack on the author of the book. The author was forced to sue them in libel. He lost and the name of the prime minister was vindicated.

Relatives may, in certain cases, bring claims in contract or in tort in their own right in respect of painful events surrounding the dead. In *Vigers v. Cook*, a contract claim resulted from the mishandling of the funeral of a First World War casualty,[1] and in *Owens v. Liverpool Corporation*, relatives sued for the nervous shock resulting from a traffic accident involving the hearse.[2]

Although it is not regarded as capable of being property, a corpse is not entirely in a state of legal limbo. Relatives and others may find means of bringing legal proceedings to protect the dead in private law. Human remains are also safeguarded by public law provisions. These also take account of the interests of relatives, although they do not always give them

1.   [1919] 2 KB 475.
2.   [1939] 1 KB 394.

priority. Generally it is difficult for any individual who does not actually have custody of a body to insist on a particular course of action unless this is specifically provided for by statute.

The use of organs for transplants is regulated under the Anatomy Act 1984. To a large extent this Act enables individuals to provide in advance that their remains may be used for purposes which will benefit others. Although contention can arise, sensitive application of the Act may be helpful, both to the family and to society at large. Hospitals are desperate to obtain organs for transplants, and relatives may find it comforting if they can authorize such transplants. However, they may be profoundly hurt emotionally if they are not involved in the decision and feel that their relation's remains have been abused or desecrated.

The use of material from the dead for scientific or medical purposes may clearly be justified in the public interest. However, it is sometimes difficult to balance this interest against respect for the sensitivities of the bereaved and for the wishes of the dead themselves. Thus, it has been argued that there should be a presumption that dead people have consented to their bodies being used for medical purposes, although it would be possible to declare that one's body was not to be used in this way. The difficulty lies in ensuring that such a declaration is known to those who have to deal with the decision, for example, to remove an organ after a road accident. This could not be ensured unless a person carried a document at all times stating his or her objection. Even then, a document could easily be mislaid in a fatal accident.

In some cases, the wishes of relatives may certainly be overridden in the public interest. Thus, there are clear arrangements for investigating suspicious deaths. These may involve an autopsy, which may be ordered by a coroner, under the Coroners Acts 1887 and 1926, despite the wishes of the deceased and the sensitivities of relatives, including any religious objections. In practice, it is fair to say that decisions here are likely to be made so as to avoid adding to the pain of bereavement wherever possible.

On the other hand, abuse of the dead is likely to be a

criminal offence, whether it is by a stranger or by someone with lawful custody of the body. Most obvious abuses would be covered by the common law offence of unlawfully disinterring human remains. This would include removing a body for the purposes of witchcraft, although that ceased to be a specific criminal offence when witchcraft was decriminalized in 1735.

Unauthorized anatomical dissection is specifically prohibited by statute, currently the Anatomy Act 1984. Abuse of the dead also includes preventing proper burial. This is condemned by the law, both in the interests of the general public, for health reasons, and to prevent the hiding of crime, but also to relieve the distress of relatives. Thus the common law offence of conspiring to prevent the burial of a corpse was upheld by the Court of Appeal where three youths, two of them mentally disabled, were present when a young girl died on a playing field. They hid her body under some paving stones, where it was discovered four months later. The three youths were initially convicted of manslaughter and theft. They successfully appealed against these convictions but their further conviction on a charge of conspiring to prevent burial was upheld. It did not have to be proved that they had intended to prevent proper burial but only that they had agreed to conceal the body and that this had in fact prevented burial. Sentences of three years were justified by the Court of Appeal, specifically because relatives had suffered for four months without knowing the fate of the victim.[1]

A further well-established principle is that the disposal of a body must not be carried out in such a manner as to cause public offence. However, what one person regards as offensive another may regard as decent and respectful. This was demonstrated in Price's case, where a well-known Welsh freethinker was acquitted on a charge of public nuisance for cremating the body of his infant child in a keg of kerosene on an open hillside, watched by a crowd which had gathered out of morbid interest.[2]

Because a body is not regarded as property, it cannot be

1. *R. v. Hunter and others* [1974] QB 95.
2. *R. v. Price* (1884) 12 QBD 247.

stolen. For this reason, those who in the past abused dead bodies were sometimes prosecuted for theft of the grave goods, such as the shroud or coffin fittings.[1] These were treated as the property of the executors or administrators of the estate of the deceased. Even an anatomy student's teaching skeleton may not be regarded as property, although a plastic facsimile or the skeleton of a gorilla would. Strictly, the student might only be able to sue or prosecute someone who took the real specimen for appropriating the wire which held it together. However, it may also be that, if expensive work had been carried out in cleaning the bones, this would have converted the skeleton itself into property.

A person with custody of a body may be free to dispose of it against the wishes of both the deceased and surviving relatives, in particular by arranging a speedy burial, but this does not give him or her power to make money out of the situation by holding the body to ransom, even to recover debts which are believed to be properly owed. What may seem surprising is that relatives do not necessarily have the power to determine how a body is finally disposed of. The person who has lawful custody of the body after death has a duty to dispose of the body and a power to do so in the manner which they regard as most suitable. This rule may have been established so as to avoid any risk to health if the body could not be interred quickly. It might also be expected to avoid unseemly disputes over who is entitled to decide how and where a body is to be disposed of. There are some restrictions laid down both at common law and in statute which regulate the procedure, but these will not necessarily satisfy relatives.

The person who has custody of a body following the death has a primary responsibility at common law to dispose of it.[2] If a person dies in a hospital or in the care of a public authority, that public authority is responsible for disposing of the remains. In certain cases this is spelled out by an express statutory provision. That is so, under the Children Act 1989, with children who have died in local authority care. There is also a residuary duty on the local authority, under the

1. *Haynes* case (1613) 12 Co. Rep. 113.
2. *R. v. Byers* (1907) 71 JP 205.

National Assistance Act 1948, to arrange disposal if a person dies in the street or if no one else has made the necessary arrangements.

Today, if the power to dispose of a body is abused by a public official, such as a hospital administrator or a mortuary attendant, it could be possible for a public law action to be brought in the High Court, in particular by relatives claiming damages for administrative abuse. However, no practical remedy would really be available, especially if a body had been cremated. A person with no official position, such as a funeral director, could abuse his or her position, for example by carrying out the burial at a time or in a place against the wishes of the family. Their only redress would be to refuse to pay the funeral director's fees, and they would have a good defence if they were sued for the fees.

There is a duty on any executors who accept responsibility under the will to provide for disposal. However, even though executors are named in the will they are under no obligation to agree to act, and if they do formally take out probate under the will they may not be formally authorized until after disposal has already taken place. Their responsibility then may simply be that of paying expenses which have already been incurred. In practice, where executors are named, they are often the closest relatives and will probably take over responsibility for the funeral before they are formally appointed. If there is no will or no executors appointed, the deceased may well have died at home, where a surviving spouse will have responsibility to dispose of the remains as householder. In other cases, the body will normally be released to the spouse, if he or she wishes, to make the necessary arrangements. However, there seems to be no duty on a spouse to deal with the remains, and, correspondingly, there would seem to be no right to do so. The old rule was that a husband was liable for the expenses of his wife's funeral but this was implicitly abolished when married women were empowered to hold any sort of property in their own right and therefore to appoint executors for all purposes under the Married Women's Property Act 1882.

In Rees's case, in 1946, a married woman had been looked

after for the last three months of her life in the home of her sister and brother-in-law. She made them her executors and they tried to recover the funeral expenses from her husband. The Court of Appeal ruled that the expenses were the responsibility of the executors and not of the husband.[1] The other side of the coin is that, in such a situation, it would seem likely that the husband would not be able to prevent the executors disposing of the body contrary to his wishes, for example by cremation instead of burial or in a different cemetery from the one he would have preferred. The same would apply in the case of the body of a dead husband being dealt with by executors against the wishes of his wife.

If a deceased person leaves insufficient means to cover burial expenses, it is possible that a surviving spouse might be under a duty to provide for disposal. The spouse would not be likely to have to reimburse an undertaker who had arranged the funeral on someone else's instructions, but might be bound to repay reasonable expenses to the 'Good Samaritan' who gave the instructions. Normally, an undertaker who deals with funeral arrangements may recover expenses from any executors if there are adequate funds, even if it is not possible to show an actual contract between an executor and the undertaker. In the absence of executors, undertakers may even apply to the court to be made administrators of estates in their own right so as to recover their expenses.[2]

There may be a legal obligation on a parent to provide for the burial of a child and, if so, it may be that the parent will have a legal right to override the plans of anyone else who has custody. The child, as a minor, could not provide for his or her own executors. A similar principle might apply where an elderly person who had not provided for executors became incapable of managing his or her own affairs and adult children or other relatives had been made guardians. Otherwise, a child will probably have no right or duty to dispose of the remains of a parent.[3]

A number of the issues discussed above were raised in the

1. *Rees v. Hughes* [1946] KB 517.
2. *Newcombe v. Belowe* (1867) LR 1 P & D 314.
3. *Chapple v. Cooper* (1884) 13 M & W 252.

case of *R. v. Gwynedd County Council, ex p B.*[1] Mr and Mrs B, who
then lived in North Wales, fostered a little girl suffering from
Down's Syndrome and a systolic heart condition when she was
three and a half weeks old, because her natural parents were
unable to look after her. Mr and Mrs B moved to Lincoln and
Gwynedd County Council assumed parental rights and duties
for the child. Nevertheless her natural mother regularly visited
her in Lincoln. The natural father died and was buried in
Holyhead. When she was aged four, the little girl also died.
Gwynedd County Council had statutory power to deal with
the burial, under section 25 of the Child Care Act 1980, but
declined to use this, and decided that the natural mother had
the right to arrange for the child to be buried in the same plot
as her father. The foster parents wanted the child to be buried
in Lincoln, where she had lived most of her life and had many
friends. They sought judicial review of the council's decision,
in the High Court. The case was dealt with extremely rapidly.
On 7 March 1991, leave was given by Sir Stephen Brown,
President of the Family Division, for the foster parents to
challenge the council. On the morning of 8 March the case was
heard by Eastham J., who ruled in favour of the council,
upholding the natural mother's rights. His decision was con-
firmed the same afternoon by the Court of Appeal. The basis of
the decision was that, as a matter of statutory interpretation,
the local authorities' assumption of parental powers expired
when the child died and therefore the natural parents' rights
revived. Under section 25 of the Act, the council could have
overridden those rights, but it was free not to do so. The case
recognized the underlying rights of the natural parents and also
the principle that the local authority could be challenged in
the courts as to its exercise of powers in respect of human
remains.

It is normal practice for a will to include directions as to
funeral arrangements. Under the Anatomy Act 1984 such
directions will be binding if they provide for the use of the
body for public purpose. Otherwise, there is no legal
obligation for executors or others to comply with the wishes of

---

1.   [1991] 2 Fam LR 365.

the deceased as to how or where the body is to be disposed of.[1] However, it may be that in the circumstances, the moral incentive to follow the wishes of the deceased is usually more effective in ensuring that those wishes are carried out than any legal duty would be.

Rites and Methods of Disposal

Cremation is a very recent revival. It has been approved by statute and is an acceptable practice under the canon law of the Church of England. Especially in urban areas, it is now by far the most popular method of disposal, being used after some 80 per cent of deaths in the UK. However, it poses obvious legal problems. In particular, it is likely to destroy any evidence of foul play. There are special safeguards against this under the Cremation Act 1902 and successive Cremation Regulations, such as a requirement for two medical practitioners to certify the cause of death. However, burial is still regarded as the traditional Christian form of committal and, legally, is treated as the norm. Thus, under the National Assistance Act 1948 a local authority may not normally cremate a body contrary to the expressed wishes of the deceased, or, under the Children's Act 1989, the body of a child contrary to the wishes of a parent.

Breach of the cremation regulations is a criminal offence. Generally, the penalty is a small one and is geared to the public nuisance inherent in burning a corpse without proper safeguards rather than to covering up foul play. The offence of burning a corpse is now one of strict liability. At common law, as we have seen in the case of the Welsh freethinker Price, the practice was permissible, provided it was not done in a manner calculated to cause public offence. A more severe sentence of up to two years' imprisonment is available for making false statements so as to procure cremation.

Although it is difficult, in theory, to challenge a person with custody of a body as to the method of its disposal, in practice a body will normally be handed over to the nearest relatives

---

1.   *Williams v. Williams* (1882) 20 Ch D 659.

or to the executors. They are then in a position to claim certain rights, both as to a funeral and as to the means of disposal. It is here that the survival of an established Christian church may continue to be valued by many who rarely, if ever, attend services, but who still refer to themselves as 'Church of England' on various official forms. The Church of England is described by opponents of establishmentarianism as a privileged institution. It would be more accurate to describe it as providing certain privileges for citizens who choose to use them. Two of these are burial in consecrated ground and Anglican funeral services.

England is divided into ecclesiastical parishes of the Church of England. Where there is a churchyard open for use in a parish, there is a right of burial in the churchyard for anyone who dies in the parish, is normally resident there, or is on the electoral roll of the parish church as a regular worshipper. The right is enforceable in either the special church courts or the civil courts. At least where there is also a right to an Anglican burial service, the right to burial will apply both to bodies and to cremated remains. An incumbent may authorize other persons to be interred in the churchyard, if the Parochial Church Council has been consulted and provided the future rights of parishioners are not adversely affected.

Where there is no churchyard in the parish, effectively there will still be a right to burial. Normally, the local authority will provide a cemetery, if necessary in a nearby area, and, normally, part of such a cemetery will be consecrated. As local authorities have a residual duty to provide for the disposal of remains not dealt with otherwise, and must respect the preference of the deceased for burial rather than cremation, where burial is desired they must ensure that it takes place somewhere.

The right to an Anglican burial service is not so general as the right to burial. It only applies to those who have been baptized, although baptism need not have been in the Anglican church and may have been by any lay person, provided it was in the name of the Trinity. This entitles for example Methodists and Baptists to have a Church of England service said at their burial. However, suicides and those who have lived notoriously

immoral lives may be denied a burial service. The incumbent
of a parish is obliged to provide the funeral service of anyone
entitled to a Church of England burial in his or her parish. He
or she may be compelled to do so by an order of mandamus
obtained on Judicial Review from the High Court.[1] The
incumbent may even be liable in damages if he or she refuses to
act and thereby causes expense to those who have brought the
body for the service.[2]

Although there is a right for a Church of England service to
be used for burials in a churchyard, equally, under section 6 of
the Burial Laws Amendment Act 1880, there is a right to burial
without any service, or with any Christian service; that is any
'religious service used by any church, denomination or person
professing to be Christian'. This allows exotic services and
expressions of belief to be carried out publicly in churchyards
of Anglican churches, although not in church buildings.
However, it would not permit an avowedly non-Christian rite,
such as a Muslim burial service or an atheist burial ceremony.
On the other hand, a non-Anglican Christian service may be
used for someone in respect of whom there is no right to an
Anglican service. Indeed, an Anglican service may be used in
such a case, even though the incumbent may refuse to conduct
it.

Although the rights of non-Anglican Christians are guaranteed
in the burial grounds of the national church, there are
reasonable restraints. The incumbent must be notified of a
proposed burial and may vary the time if he or she chooses.
There will be a criminal offence, punishable by a fine or
imprisonment, if the right to burial is abused by violent, riotous
or indecent behaviour, and, in particular, if the occasion is
used in a wilful attempt to bring into contempt or obloquy the
Christian religion or the belief or worship of any denomination
or the members or any minister of any such church or denomination or any other person. Because no penalty is prescribed
by the statute, the punishment is in the discretion of the Crown
Court.[3]

1. *R v. Vicar of Bassingbourne* (1845) 9 JP Jo 83.
2. *Davis v. Black* (1841) 1 QB 900.
3. *R v. Morris* [1951] 1 KB 394 at 398.

On the face of it, it would be an offence for anyone, including an incumbent, to use the occasion of a funeral address at the graveside to make a personal attack, even on anyone who seemed responsible for the death of the individual being buried. Certainly, the rule not only protects the Church of England, but any Christians, from unpleasant sectarian attacks in what could be very inflammatory circumstances. The potential for unrest on such an occasion may seem remote in an English country churchyard, but would certainly be very real at the burial of the victim of a South African riot or, nearer home, at the burial of the victim of a sectarian killing in Northern Ireland.

Burial Grounds

When human remains have been interred, the law treats them, in theory at least, with exceptional respect. Before the nineteenth century virtually all the dead were interred in Anglican churchyards. Those of a higher social class might be found room in the church itself. A right to burial in the local parish churchyard was a practical necessity. However, in the mid-nineteenth century, with the spread of large cities, commercial cemetery companies were set up. The first commercial cemetery in England is believed to have been Liverpool Necropolis in 1825. The first to be set up expressly by statute was Kensal Green in London. Such cemeteries continue to be regulated by individual acts of parliament, normally incorporating the Cemeteries Clauses Act 1847. Generally, burial grounds were provided by local authority Burial Boards, under successive statutory powers, in twelve Burial Acts from 1852 to 1906. In addition, the Public Health (Interments) Act 1879 provided a simpler regime for municipal cemeteries. These all now operate under the Local Government Act 1972.

A churchyard will normally be consecrated. This applies to any extension, even if it is physically separate, for example because it lies on the other side of a road. A private cemetery, or part of a municipal one, may also be consecrated under ecclesiastical law, which is part of the general law of the land.

The effect of consecration is that the land is subject to the Faculty Jurisdiction which is exercised by the diocesan chancellor. He or she is the judge appointed by the diocesan bishop who is the 'ordinary', that is the person with 'ordinary ecclesiastical jurisdiction'. A faculty from the chancellor, or in some cases now the archdeacon, is required for any significant addition to, or removal from, consecrated land, including the removal of human remains outside the boundaries of the consecrated land in question.[1] The consent of the Secretary of State is also normally required. However, under Section 25 of the Burial Act 1857, a coroner may order a body to be disinterred for the purpose of inquiring into the cause of death.

Parliament assumed that, just like the old parish churchyard, the modern cemetery would remain undisturbed in perpetuity. Whether or not there was a residual idea that the dead were literally waiting to be raised in their original bodies where they had been interred, it was certainly intended that respect for the dead should not lightly be sacrificed to commercial development. The Disused Burial Grounds Acts 1884 and 1981 still severely restrict any sort of building on burial grounds. There are provisions which allow Church of England burial grounds to be declared redundant and developed, but generally only if there has been no burial within the last 50 years, and even then only if suitable arrangements are made for moving both remains and memorials. Under the Town and Country Planning Act 1990, other burial grounds may also be developed by local or central government, although they too are expected to show sensitivity to any surviving relatives.

In the past, dissenters and non-Christian religious minorities, such as Jews, were able to provide their own burial grounds, because there was nothing to stop an individual being buried on his or her own land. This is still the case, provided the death has been properly registered. A person who wants to be buried in a back garden, or to inter a relative there, would be advised to obtain planning permission, although it might possibly be argued that a family burial is a domestic use,

---

1. *Norfolk County Council v. Knights and Caister-on-Sea Joint Burial Committee* [1958] 1 All ER 394.

ancillary to a dwelling, and, therefore, is outside normal planning controls. This may seem a farfetched suggestion in the garden of a suburban semi-detached house but not necessarily in the case of a large country house. Many such mansions from the past are still replete with chapels and mausolea. It would seem that if there is no need for planning consent there will be no restriction on burying, provided no hazard to public health is involved. For larger private burial grounds planning consent is required. Recently, for example, planning permission was granted for a private cemetery in an estate of 19 acres at Tideswell in Derbyshire.[1]

Burial Practices

Although no one may hold property rights in a human body, the law does recognize legal rights in burial places. However, their status is not entirely clear and may vary, depending on whether the burial place is in a churchyard, or a municipal or commercial cemetery.

Most burials are in churchyards or public cemeteries. Occasionally, cremated remains, at any rate, may still be allowed in a church.[2] Even where there is a right to interment, the incumbent, in the case of a churchyard, and the burial authority, in the case of a municipal cemetery, may determine the exact place of burial, except where a plot has been acquired in advance. Future burial rights may be reserved, under a faculty in the case of a churchyard, or under a grant in the case of a municipal cemetery burial. A faculty will not be granted to a non-parishioner without the concurrence of the incumbent or if there is a serious risk that parishioners will be deprived of grave spaces. However, the fact that all space will be exhausted in a period as short as seven years does not preclude reservation of individual spaces, as the effect will be marginal.[3]

In both churchyards and municipal cemeteries, rights to

---

1.   P. Sparkes, 'Exclusive Burial Rights' (1991) 2 Ecc LJ 133, at p. 138.
2.   *St Peter's Folkestone* [1982] 1 WLR 1283.
3.   *Re St John the Baptist, Werrington* (1992) 2 Ecc LJ 319, Peterborough Consistory Court.

burial now last for 100 years. The form of burial may also be determined by the relevant authority, including whether a vault may be constructed or a special sort of coffin used.[1] Unless there is a family vault or a faculty or grant reserving specific places, there is no right for someone to be buried close to his or her ancestors.[2] Church authorities are reluctant to consent to non-parishioners being buried in attractive churchyards for fear they will be swamped.[3]

The reservation of family burial places can give rise to distressing litigation where mistakes are made later and a space is inadvertently used for someone for whom it was not intended. In a private cemetery, if a person is inadvertently buried when another is entitled to be there, the secular courts may be reluctant to order the removal of the body already interred.[4] By contrast, if a faculty has been granted, an order for removal is more likely. In *Re St Luke's, Holbeach Hurn*, an elderly lady who had been an active church member successfully petitioned for the removal of the body of another woman four months after it had been placed between their respective husbands. The petitioner declined to accept another space in the row below, saying that she had never been trampled on or bullied by her husband during his life and she did not like the idea of being under his feet now. The space had been reserved for her by faculty but the family concerned with the other burials, who were not churchgoers and were ignorant of the need for a faculty, had been informally led to believe that the space was theirs.[5]

Reburial

The desire of relatives for a loved one to be interred in a particular place may extend to wanting to move the body to another place so as to be near a spouse or other relative. This may be permitted even though the body is to be cremated, so

1. *Winstanley v. North Manchester Overseer* [1910] AC 7.
2. *Re Smith decd.* [1994] 1 All ER 90.
3. *Re St Nicholas, Baddesley Ensor* [1982] 2 All ER 351.
4. *Reed v. Madon* [1989] 2 All ER 431.
5. [1990] 2 All ER 749.

that it may be reinterred elsewhere more easily. Thus, a faculty has been granted to a son for the disinterring and cremation of his father's remains where the mother had died after moving away from the place where she had previously lived and had desired that she and her husband's body should be cremated and interred together.[1] However, if the burial occurred a long time before, or if what is proposed seems eccentric, permission is less likely. Thus, in one case, the widow of an army officer was refused permission to have his body exhumed after 18 years, cremated and reinterred in the same mausoleum.[2]

A chancellor will be reluctant to allow remains to be moved around the country with a surviving spouse. Although Home Office consent has been obtained, the fact that, for example, a widow has moved and finds it difficult or impossible to visit the grave is normally an insufficient ground to allow removal of a body, especially where a headstone had been erected on the original grave, confirming its permanence.[3] The same principles apply to cremated remains which are in a casket and could easily be removed. The underlying policy was stated by Chancellor Lomas of Chester in the case of *Re Smith*;

> [I]t is clear that most men and women desire and hope that when after their death their remains have been decently and reverently interred they should remain undisturbed. Where the burial has taken place in ground consecrated in accordance with the rites of the Church of England it is clear that the intention of all those taking part is that the earthly remains of the deceased are to be finally laid at rest. Having reread the forms of service for the burial of the dead authorised for use in the Church of England I am satisfied that there is nothing provisional in those forms of service and that the whole intention and purpose is that the remains of the deceased should be laid at rest once and for all...[If it were to] become a matter of course for petitioners to obtain faculties for the exhumation of the remains of their relatives and their reinterment elsewhere whenever they moved from place to place...[i]t would lead to an unseemly procession of disintegrating corpses and ashes between burial

1.   *Re Matheson* [1958] 1 All ER 202.
2.   *Re Dixon* [1892] P 386.
3.   *Re St Mary Magdalene, Lyminster* (1990) 2 Ecc LJ 127.

grounds. I make no apology for referring to the matter in that way for it brings to mind the distress which has been caused to so many incumbents and others obliged to be present when disinterment has taken place.[1]

Even so, there may be exceptions, as where an area set aside for cremated remains has become overgrown and the identity of individual burial places is likely to be lost.[2] Consent has also been given to remove the remains of distinguished individuals to more appropriate places. Thus, in 1901, in *Re Talbot*, the remains of the principal of a Roman Catholic college were reburied under his college chapel.[3] More recently, in 1991, the London Consistory Court allowed the body of a Lt. Col. J.W. Boyle, a Canadian soldier 'of some public interest', to be moved to Canada, provided a new monument was erected, to mark the original grave.[4]

Family disputes may erupt over proposals to remove bodies, and these may have to be resolved by the diocesan chancellor. In 1988, the son of a woman buried in Cheddar churchyard petitioned to move her body to Epsom where her husband was buried. The petition was opposed by the dead woman's parents. The dead husband had expressed a wish for his wife to be buried with him, but the dead woman herself had expected to be buried at Cheddar. The chancellor refused the petition, holding that there was no general rule of law or practice that spouses should be buried together. He stressed the fact that there was opposition by close relatives and pointed out that the dead husband's body might be moved to Cheddar.

A chancellor will be reluctant to allow the removal of bodies for some reason unconnected with the deceased or their relatives, unless it is in furtherance of the work of the church, as where a site is needed for a church extension.[5] Church extensions are permitted under the Disused Burial Grounds Acts, and in *Re Jewson's Wills Trusts*, the Chancery Division of the High Court upheld, as consistent with the Acts, a gift in a

1. [1994] 1 All ER 90.
2. *Re Atkins* [1989] 1 All ER 14.
3. [1901] P 1.
4. *Re St James' Churchyard, Hampton Hill* (1991) 2 Ecc LJ 253.
5. *Re All Saints Melbourn* [1992] 2 All ER 786.

will to provide a caretaker's house in a burial ground which was still being used.[1] The proposal would not have involved moving human remains but that was not actually relevant to whether the Act applied. Other building is usually prohibited, except under specific statutory powers. Thus, a bus shelter was treated as unlawful because it would overhang a burial ground.[2] Changes on consecrated land which do not involve building, such as road schemes, may be authorized by faculty, even if removal of human remains is necessary to allow such public works. However, permission will only be given on weighty grounds such as preventing danger.

In *Norfolk County Council v. Knights*, a faculty was refused to construct a four-feet wide path on the edge of a cemetery at Caister-On-Sea in Norfolk and beside a busy main road, because it was not established that it was vital for the safety of pedestrians using the road.[3] The scheme would have involved removal, from consecrated land, of some 400 bodies and a lifeboat memorial of national importance (see Figure 1). The case was of particular interest because the church authorities remained studiously neutral and the local authority petition was defeated by the opponents, twenty-seven of whom were represented at the hearing, in seven groups.

Where bodies do have to be removed from consecrated ground for health reasons, the faculty will authorize relatives to reinter them in other consecrated land nearby.[4]

Memorials

The aesthetic character of churchyards and their importance as part of the spiritual and cultural heritage of the nation are recognized by strict regulation under the Faculty Jurisdiction of the Church of England. This system of regulation requires the permission of the chancellor, that is the diocesan bishop's judge or in some cases the archdeacon, for any alterations to

1.   [1961] 3 All ER 1022.
2.   *Re St Mark's Church, Lincoln* [1956] P 336.
3.   [1958] 1 All ER 394.
4.   *Rector of St Helen's Bishopsgate, with St Mary Outwich v. Parishioners of the same* [1892] P 259.

Figure 1. *Cemetery on Ormesby Road, Caister-on-Sea, Norfolk. The graves which were to be moved and the lifeboat memorial are in the narrow strip of land separated from the remainder of the cemetery by trees.*

the church, churchyard, fixtures or even loose furnishing. The secular system of listed building control in the Planning (Listed Buildings and Conservation Areas) Act 1990 does not apply to church buildings in use, even though they are listed nationally as of major historic and architectural interest. This concession was introduced originally so as to avoid secular authorities' interfering with the freedom of churches to order their buildings for worship. It was justified because the Faculty Jurisdiction of the Church of England provided an alternative system of protection which still compares very favourably with that operated by the state. The importance and interest of this area of law has recently been recognized by the publication of new textbooks, notably *The Faculty Jurisdiction of the Church of England* by George Newsom,[1] and the appearance of the *Ecclesiastical Law Journal* which publishes regular case summaries. These provide many of the illustrations contained below.

A major anomaly in the ecclesiastical exemption from listed building control was that the greatest churches, namely cathedrals, were each a law to themselves, operating under their own statutes, with their administrative chapters, largely free from outside interference. This gap has now been filled by the Care of Cathedrals Measure 1990 with a national system for approving alterations to cathedrals. This system will apply where new memorials are added or old ones moved or altered. Certain other major Anglican churches are not cathedrals but are also outside the Faculty Jurisdiction. Technically known as 'peculiars', these include the great royal chapels of Westminster Abbey and St George's Chapel at Windsor which contain many of the monuments to the dead of greatest national significance. Discussions are at present being held within the Church of England as to possible means of providing a greater public say in any alterations to these buildings.

To avoid allegations of partiality, the ecclesiastical exemption was, from the start, given to all non-Anglican churches. It applies to 'ecclesiastical buildings in use' and this would probably now be interpreted by the courts as including

1. London: Sweet & Maxwell, 2nd edn, 1993.

synagogues, mosques and other non-Christian religious buildings. To meet pressure from conservationists, non-Anglican religious bodies have developed more publicly accountable systems for authorizing alterations to their buildings which are likely to safeguard the relatively few important memorials which they contain.

A major advantage of the Faculty Jurisdiction and the provisions of the Cathedrals Measure over the secular system of listed building control is that the Church of England arrangements protect items inside a church which are not fixtures. Also, the church system regulates interior additions. New memorials in churches are strictly controlled, although exceptions may be allowed. Memorials in churches can be a considerable source of interest for visitors and new examples do continue to be added. For example, in 1990 the Rochester Consistory Court allowed a plaque to be fixed in an inconspicuous place in the Church of All Saints, Brenchley, to commemorate a young boy tragically killed playing cricket. The plaque had originally been in the boy's school but this had now closed. The family worshippped in the church and would contribute £100 towards the maintenance of the building.

In churchyards, the Faculty Jurisdiction provides a major control over memorials and, to a lesser extent, over burials. However, ordinary planning controls also apply, which means that planning permission would be required to take extra ground into the churchyard and also, probably, for any large new monument. Existing monuments of architectural or historic interest may be individually listed.

There are three practical considerations which face many parish churches concerning their churchyards: monitoring the quality of monuments, dealing with cremated remains and providing long-term maintenance for memorials. First, it is difficult to monitor the quality of new monuments. This is most important where a churchyard has a distinctive character. It applies far less to municipal cemeteries, which are generally much larger and are landscaped in quite different ways. Diocesan chancellors delegate to incumbents the power to authorize standard headstones. Normally, the standards followed are those in the *Churchyards Handbook*, published by the Church of England Church Information Office.[1] These are restrictive, although it is stressed that chancellors will consider favourably well-designed alternatives, and a quantity of recent case law has accumulated over what is and is not acceptable.

The churchyard rules may be criticized for tending to encourage uniform and mass-produced monuments. They can upset relatives who want some personal inscription or an unacceptable embellishment such as a photograph set in the stone. Being necessarily negative, no standard rules are able to ensure the richness of design shown in eighteenth- and nineteenth-century monuments. In fact, however, very high quality work is available at a cost not necessarily much greater than that for a mass-produced stone and advice will readily be given by the highly qualified Diocesan Advisory Committees which advise chancellors on their exercise of the faculty jurisdiction (see Figures 2 and 3).

Restrictions which seem surprising to some include a tendency to forbid free-standing crosses, particularly because these are vulnerable to damage. Where the character of a churchyard has already been impaired by incongruous monuments, chancellors may be willing to permit other less striking exceptions to the rules, for example a larger than normal headstone. Generally, polished black or red granite headstones, which are commercially produced in great numbers by monumental masons and proliferate in municipal cemeteries, are strongly discouraged in churchyards, as are kerbstones, which make maintenance difficult. In *Re St Breoke, Wadebridge*, Truro Consistory Court permitted a polished black granite stone which was not visible from the church because several such stones had recently been erected in the vicinity.[2] The petitioners were rewarded for making a proper application for a monument not covered by the rules. However, the parish was punished for the earlier abuses by the withdrawal of the incumbent's delegated power to approve stones.

1.   Eds. H. Stapleton and P. Burman, 3rd edn, 1988.
2.   (1993) 2 Ecc LJ 59.

Figure 2. *A fine example of a modern churchyard memorial, carved by Richard Grasby FSD-C FRSA. The photograph was kindly provided by Mr Grasby.*

Figure 3. *Another churchyard memorial by Richard Grasby, who kindly provided the photograph.*

Inscriptions are particularly likely to give rise to problems where those who are brought for burial, and their relatives, have only a nominal church connection. The *Churchyards Handbook* discourages anything but short inscriptions and advises that biblical verses should be carved without references, somewhat disingenuously assuming that these will be too well known to require adding to the text. Chancellors will certainly be reluctant to approve the display of inappropriate wording, such as 'toodle', which a daughter wished to put on her mother's headstone as an affectionate form of farewell. In another case, a monumental mason was ordered by the Carlisle Consistory Court to remove an unauthorized headstone he had put up which included an 'x' representing a kiss, a red rose and a picture of a Jaguar car. The use of gilded lettering may also be regarded as inappropriate.

There is now a great accumulation of funereal monuments from the nineteenth and twentieth centuries. Often these give a churchyard or a cemetery its character, but they are far more permanent than the memorials of earlier eras. They use up precious resources if they are to be maintained and they hamper reuse of the ground for new burials.

The second, and particularly challenging, problem concerning churchyards is the question of how to treat cremated remains. The Church of England has never come to terms with the practice of cremation. Although there may be a funeral service in a parish church the committal does not take place in a church building but in a crematorium which has more affinities with an industrial plant than with a place of worship. The crematorium may also be a considerable distance from where the funeral took place. Even where there has been a church service, there is no normal assumption that the cremated remains will be returned to the church for interment. They may be scattered over open country or in the sea or be retained at home in a casket by a bereaved close relative. There is no separate approved form of service for the final disposal of the remains.

Where cremated remains are returned to a churchyard they are treated in certain respects like a body. In particular, normally, they must not be moved again without a faculty, although the secular consents which would be needed to move a body outside a churchyard would not seem to be required. What has proved most difficult has been to accommodate memorials for those whose cremated remains are interred in churchyards. The recommended churchyard rules do not permit any casket or permanent container. The remains should simply be emptied into a hole in the ground and decently covered over. Where there is already a family burial, the old grave may be used and permission may be obtained from the incumbent for an additional inscription on a headstone. This may be possible even though the burial ground has been closed. Indeed, in such circumstances, consent may be fairly easily obtained to replace an existing and relatively recent headstone.

The difficulty arises where there is no proper grave to use. A faculty will be required to set aside a special area for cremated remains. Small individual memorials are discouraged over the individual plots. There is difficulty in avoiding the appearance of a pets' cemetery and tiny stones give little scope for artistic design. Practices which have been suggested tend to ignore the problems of such areas, recommending the use of a book of remembrance in the church or an ossuary or columbarium beneath it. However, effectively designed areas for cremated remains could offer a new means of binding families to their ancestral parish church, even though they may have moved far away. From the church's point of view this offers a valuable opportunity to minister to many who are not churchgoers and, more materialistically, a possible source of funding for maintenance and improvements.

Maintaining Memorials

The long-term maintenance of memorials is more difficult to ensure than restricting their erection to start with. The law generally recognizes that it is much harder to enforce positive obligations than negative ones, and it mainly confines itself to punishing harmful acts rather than omissions. Certainly, criminal law normally punishes harmful actions, not failures to act. Thus, desecration of a grave would be an offence but failure to maintain one would certainly not be. The civil tort of negligence or a breach of duty under the Occupiers' Liability Acts 1957 and 1984 generally consist in doing things which a reasonable person would recognize as likely to cause harm. The custodians of an unsafe burial ground could be liable to someone who was injured by a collapsing tombstone but they could not normally be compelled to repair it, only to keep people away who might be injured.

It is difficult for a person to set up a fund to ensure that memorials will be permanently maintained, because of the rules against perpetuities. However, under the Local Authorities Cemeteries Order 1977, a local authority with responsibility for burials may enter into an agreement which will bind it for 100 years to maintain a monument in a cemetery. There are other legal devices which may be used. Certain charitable trusts are not subject to the normal restrictions on perpetuities. Provision for disposal of the dead is itself regarded as a charitable purpose of 'public utility' and 'beneficial to the community' irrespective of any religious sentiment. Therefore, funds may be restricted permanently for this purpose, whether in providing burial grounds or crematoria or for covering undertakers' costs.[1]

Providing funds for the maintenance of a parish churchyard is treated as charitable by the law. The same applies to funds for non-Anglican churchyards, such as a Quaker burial ground. This has been justified as a religious purpose on the grounds that there is no difference between a gift to repair 'God's House' and one to benefit 'God's Acre' and that one naturally connects the burial of the dead with religion.[2] However, charitable status has also been applied to the long-term maintenance of secular cemeteries.[3]

A fund to maintain an individual memorial is valid but it is not regarded as a charitable trust and so cannot be enforced.[4]

---

1. *Scottish Burial Reform and Cremation Society Ltd v. Glasgow Corporation* [1968] AC 138.

2. *Re Manser, A.G. v. Lucas* [1905] 1 Ch. 68.

3. *Re Eighmie, Colbourne v. Wilkes* [1935] Ch. 524.

4. See generally J.B. Clark, *Theobald on Wills* (London: Sweet & Maxwell, 14th edn, 1982).

However, a worthwhile sum may be given to one charity, subject to the condition that if it fails to maintain a memorial the money may be claimed by another charity. Sir James Tyler successfully used this device at the end of the nineteenth century to maintain a family vault in Highgate cemetery. He gave money to the London Missionary Society. The money was to pass to a school if the Missionary Society failed to keep up the tomb.[1]

Particularly in churchyards, a good way of ensuring that a monument is well maintained indefinitely is to have it made of simple, durable, material, as a fine piece which will be looked after as a work of art in its own right. However, although it is more likely to be maintained, a memorial which is itself a work of art may give rise to rather different problems. It may be vulnerable to theft. Insurance may be a problem and the church authorities may want to sell it to keep up the fabric of the church itself or pay for improvements. This may be particularly true of outstanding monuments inside a church and of artefacts such as ancient banners, hatchments or helmets. Such items initially belong to the person who erected them and subsequently to the descendants of the person commemorated. They may not be removed from the church without a faculty but a faculty may not authorize their sale unless the descendants who have rights in them consent. Even if there are no descendants with a claim, a faculty will not be granted unless there are special reasons, such as the need to provide for expanding demands of the church's ministry.[2] Thus, in *Re St Martin, Lothbury*, London Consistory Court refused the church permission to sell a seventeenth-century bust of Sir Peter le Maire, by Hubert le Sueur, worth some £25,000.[3]

Two major cases of funeral artefacts concerned Tudor helmets. In 1974 the Chancellor of the Diocese of Chichester granted a faculty for the sale of the helmet from the tomb of Thomas West, eighth Lord De La Warr, from the parish church at Broadwater in Sussex (see Figure 4).[4] The helm had been

1.   *Re Tyler* [1891] 3 Ch. 252.
2.   *Re St Gregory's Tredington* [1972] Fam 236.
3.   (1988) 1 Ecc LJ (4) 6.
4.   *St. Mary's Broadwater* [1976] Fam 222.

stored in a bank vault after its value was appreciated and the sale was authorized so as to finance pastoral work of the church, even though it was opposed by the Tower Armouries and the Diocesan Arts Council. Most significantly, the current Lord De La Warr raised no objection to the sale and appears to have been treated by the chancellor as renouncing all claims to the helm so that it became the property of the churchwardens. By contrast, the following year, the chancellor of Peterborough refused a faculty for the sale of another helmet which was still above the tomb of Sir William Russell, first Earl of Bedford, at Thornhaugh church.[1] Although the present Duke of Bedford had not formally intervened, it seemed likely that he was entitled to claim ownership and the Bedford family had recently refurbished the tomb. The chancellor took the view that, as the petitioners had failed to satisfy him that there was no present owner who could be identified or that if there was one he or she would consent to the sale, there was no jurisdiction to allow the sale. In 1990 a faculty was granted by the Chancellor of York for the sale, to the Tower Armouries, of a third helmet, on the tomb of Sir John de Melsa, in Aldborough church, dating back to 1377. The Earl of Huntingdon, who was the current descendant, agreed formally to transfer his rights in the helmet to the churchwardens so as to allow the sale, on terms that the church authorities should maintain the tombs of the de Melsa family (see Figure 5).[2]

Although Victorian cemeteries contain a riot of monumental statuary, and indeed architecture, as they have been filled the funds for general maintenance have dried up and local authorities tend to regard them as liabilities, or, at best, as potential open spaces or recreation areas where the monuments are largely an obstruction. By contrast, monuments in churches and older monuments in churchyards may be better maintained because of the continuing use of the church building. Monuments inside a church are largely protected from the elements and are likely to have local or wider historic interest which helps to guarantee their conservation.

---

1. *Re St Andrew Thornhaugh* [1976] Fam 230.
2. *Re St Bartholemew's Aldborough* [1990] 3 All ER 440.

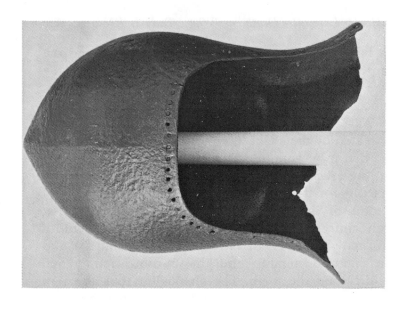

Figure 5. *The funeral helm of Sir John de Melsa from Aldborough church, Yorkshire. Reproduced by kind permission of the Board of Trustees of the Royal Armouries.*

Figure 4. *The funeral helm of Thomas West, Lord de la Warr, from Broadwater church, Sussex. Reproduced by kind permission of the Board of Trustees of the Royal Armouries.*

A Future Legal Framework for Remembrance of the Dead

Churchyards and cemeteries are increasingly recognized as an important part of the English cultural heritage. Churchyards provide the setting for some of the most evocative and historically fascinating of our ancient buildings. Many churchyards and cemeteries, whether in country or city, are havens for wild flora and fauna, important for their scientific value and prized for recreation. Funeral monuments, inside and outside of churches, provide an unparalleled series of sculpture galleries, including some of the finest statuary, such as busts by Rysbrack and the 'bale' tombs in a number of West Country churchyards. They are visible, visitable and verdant, a major proclamation of our ancestors.

Burial grounds are relatively well protected from despoliation although they are vulnerable to decay, especially where they have been officially closed. However, the very fact that they are not kept manicured and perfectly maintained adds both to their charm and to their scientific interest. This would be lost if they were cleared for public parks or reused on a regular basis. However, it may also be that much more use could be made of them which would justify their protection and help to ensure their maintenance. For example, churchyards could be advertised far more widely as tourist attractions. This has been done with a number of great municipal cemeteries such as Kensal Green in London and Attercliffe in Bradford, following the French example of Montmartre. Country churchyards have the additional attraction that they are commonly linked by ancient footpaths and bridleways and could be developed, along with parish churches, as points in a modern form of recreational steeplechase (see Figure 6). Urban cemeteries could feature more prominently in city heritage trails.

A burial ground is an emotive place. Even for those who eschew any religious dimension to life, it gives a sense of historical perspective and a sense of continuity with past generations. For the Christian believer, it is a *memento mori* and a place to reflect on immortality. The justification for the Church of England as a national church is that it serves all

Figure 6. *A traditional country churchyard at Rollesbury, near Caister-on-Sea, showing the original churchyard around the church and a larger extension to the west.*

citizens who wish to claim its ministrations. Funeral rites and burial grounds provide a remaining opportunity to present the Christian hope to a secular society. The legal restraints on change in churchyards have helped to preserve them. The law also provides a framework for new policies which could reaffirm people's connections with their forebears and with the land. The Faculty Jurisdiction could be used to make greater provision for family burial areas, particularly of cremated remains, which could encourage many who feel unchurched to find a new identity in this life, with intimations of the life beyond.

For minority groups, burial grounds provide a means for rooting their identity in British soil. Some long established groups can relate to burial grounds or individual graves which may already be of some antiquity. For all of us, churchyards and other burial grounds summarize our past, move us to reflect upon our present and invite us to consider the nature of our future. They address both the living and the dead.

Part IV

Matters of Life and Death

Choosing to Die

Bryan Vernon

This essay began in reaction to an article in the *Lancet* on
14th September 1991 entitled 'Euthanasia and Other Medical
Decisions concerning the End of Life'.[1] This presents results of
research conducted at the request of the Dutch government to
inform debate on possible legislation about euthanasia. It
showed that in 38% of all deaths and 54% of all non-acute
deaths, some medical decisions had been taken which affected
the time of death. In 17.5% of cases high doses of painkillers
had shortened life while alleviating pain and symptoms. In
17.5% of cases a non-treatment decision had affected the time
of death. In 2.9% of cases drugs were administered with the
explicit intention of shortening life, including euthanasia at the
patient's request, assisted suicide and life-terminating acts
without explicit and persistent request. I am not aware of a
similarly far-reaching study in this country, but an admission of
ignorance is often a prelude to the provision of information.
The authors of the Dutch report call for greater public debate
about the choices at the end of life. This is my contribution to
this debate—which is in reality a complex set of issues.

A phrase like 'medical decisions concerning the end of life'
can evoke fears that doctors are playing God. Such a thought
attracts understandable antagonism from followers of most
major religions—and indeed from others who fear that doctors
exercise too great a power in decisions about life and death.
We should face the possibility that this is a game which a

1. P.J. Van de Maas *et al*, 'Euthanasia and Other Medical Decisions
concerning the End of Life', *The Lancet* 338 (September 14 1991), pp. 669-75.

playful God had invited us to play. Or if there is no God, it may be a game which we are free to play.

The question raised by the title 'Choosing to Die' goes to the heart of the value system we choose to adopt. The question 'whose life is it anyway?' has been used to predetermine the answer, but it remains a question. There follows the question of whether life is the most important value of all. What of autonomy? What of justice? What of doing good and its partner, avoiding harm? These problems form what Harry Moody describes as the dominant model of medical ethics.[1]

There are several circumstances in which a person might be prepared to choose to die. These range from martyrdom to suicide to euthanasia. There are times when the choice of a painkiller implies at the very least a willingness to accept death, for it may be hastened when the dose is high. The rejection of life-saving treatment is another way in which death can be chosen. In many instances death may be the outcome but it is not a foregone conclusion. There may need to be an element of risk assessment to determine whether an individual intends the natural and foreseeable consequences of his or her actions, whether he or she is reckless or merely negligent. Our view of the situation will naturally be influenced by the degree of conviction shown by the individual in expressing the wish to die.

A major portion of this article explores the ethics of suicide. This is perhaps the most extreme form of the choice of death, and therefore useful for looking at the principles involved. I then look at euthanasia, where the mitigating factor of serious illness plays a part, and finally look at the case of declining life-saving treatment, which may embrace the acceptance of death. I shall be looking at questions such as whether, if some choices of death can be justified, we can avoid the shift which Margaret Pabst Battin highlights in *Suicide*: from suicide as a rational act to societal manipulation of individuals into taking their own lives when they would not otherwise have chosen to

---

1.   H. Moody, *Ethics in an Aging Society* (Baltimore: Johns Hopkins University Press, 1992).

do so.[1] Can we sustain a truly pluralistic society in which you can 'turn off' your elderly mother at the first hint of dementia while I cling tenaciously to my deaf-blind quadraplegic maiden aunt? There are obviously large areas of debate here and the issues will necessarily be treated fairly briefly. However, the purpose of an essay such as this is not to provide a series of ready-made answers but to stimulate readers to think about the issues.

Blackstone summed up the traditional antipathy to taking one's own life when he wrote: 'The suicide is guilty of a double offence: one spiritual, in invading the prerogative of the Almighty and rushing into his presence uncalled for, and the other temporal, against the King, who hath an interest in the preservation of all his subjects'.[2] If what Jon Davies writes in the first essay in this volume is true, then the king, like the rest of us, has an interest in the death of his subjects, to make room for their replacements.

Apparently the main impetus for Augustine's sharp condemnation of suicide was that many Christians of his time had actively sought martyrdom with excessive enthusiasm, convinced that they would immediately be translated into an eternal life of bliss. No doubt the conditions of fifth-century slavery were such that many of us might well have made a similar choice. Life was cheap. No circus was a good one without extensive loss of life. Perhaps the media attention given to the mauling of Ben Silcock[3] is a sign that we have developed a heightened moral sensitivity. The Old Testament records a number of suicides without condemnation. There is an injunction against killing in the Ten Commandments, but it is not entirely clear what this means. It seems to forbid unlawful

1.   M.P. Battin, 'Manipulated Suicide', in M.P. Battin and D. Mayo (eds.), *Suicide: The Philosophical Issues* (London: Peter Owen, 1980), pp. 169ff.

2.   W. Blackstone, *Commentaries on the Laws of England* (ed. A. Ryland; London: Sweet, Pheney, Maxwell, Stevens & Sons, 1829), IV, p. 189.

3.   Ben Silcock was a young schizophrenic man who climbed into a lion's cage at London Zoo in December 1992 and captured media attention, leading to a debate about community treatment orders. Ironically he had been refused admission to hospital despite seeking it.

killing, but is not specific as to what that includes. It did not deter some notable slaughters. The only suicide in the New Testament is that of Judas Iscariot, and it is possible to read this as an attempt at expiation and a realization of the magnitude of his offence. Certainly no moral is drawn by the evangelist (Mt. 27.3-5).

It is not clear that suicide was forbidden by the church before Augustine, though admittedly it is also not clear that it was permitted. I am wary of arguments resting on the premise that suicide is unnatural. As David Hume said, 'Were the disposal of human life so much reserved as the peculiar providence of the Almighty, that it were an encroachment on his right, for men to dispose of their own lives; it would be equally criminal to act for the preservation of life as for its destruction'.[1] Joseph Fletcher makes a similar point in 'Ethics and Euthanasia' when he deals with the concept of playing God. 'Yes, we are playing God', he admits:

> But the real question is: which or whose God are we playing? The old God who is believed to have monopoly control of birth and death, allowing for no human responsibility in either initiating or terminating a life, was a primitive 'God of the gaps'—a mysterious and awesome deity, who filled in the gaps of our knowledge and of the control which our knowledge gives us. 'He' was, so to speak, an hypothecation of human ignorance and helplessness.[2]

Talk about God always risks being divisive: those of us who believe in him are not of one mind in our description of his characteristics. As a simple example I would not want to lay undue stress on the word 'his'. For those who do not acknowledge God such talk can be alienating.

Both believers and unbelievers, however, share the perception that our lives are not our own creation. I can call life a gift, because I can detect a giver, and I hope that those who cannot

1. In A. MacIntyre (ed.), *Hume's Ethical Writings* (New York: Collier, 1965).

2. J. Fletcher, 'Ethics and Euthanasia', in D.J. Horan and D. Mall (eds.), *Death, Dying and Euthanasia* (Westport, CT: Greenwood Publications, 1980), p. 296.

detect a giver will allow me the phrase. It certainly seems possible for people to feel grateful for their lives without having an object for their gratitude. If life comes to us a gift, then surely it becomes ours. Narveson argues for such a view of self-ownership.[1] He cites the example of Brahms, who is said to have destroyed several of his works because in his judgment they were not good enough. They would surely find a place on Classic FM if not Radio 3 had they survived, and we all suffer from their loss, or at least the world lacks an enrichment it could have enjoyed; nonetheless, no one would dispute his right to destroy his work. Similarly, for Narveson the view of our lives as 'owned' by us permits suicide.

We might want to modify the word 'gift'; rather than simply saying that life has been given to us, we could say that we are stewards of it. This has an echo in our experience of the world, for the abortion debate has highlighted the difficulty in saying that life has a definite beginning. Each one of the particular combination of molecules that combine to form the person whose name you bear has had an existence before its association with you, and will have an existence afterwards. If you are a steward of your life, we might think you have a duty to the 'owner' to behave in a way of which the 'owner' would approve—but that does not show conclusively that suicide is wrong, for the 'owner' might approve of such a course of action. Suppose I went to work abroad for a period of time and entrusted you with the care of my dog. If it developed cancer, I might be quite content with your asking the vet to put it down, and might not see this as an abuse of your stewardship.

The decision to take one's own life is described by one writer as irrational on the grounds that we do not know what lies beyond the act of dying. The cheerful confidence of the authors of the 'in memoriam' notices in the *Evening Chronicle*[2]

1. J. Narveson, 'Self-Ownership and the Ethics of Suicide', in M.P. Battin and D.W. Maris (eds.), *Suicide and Ethics* (New York: Human Sciences Press, 1983).

2. See Jon Davies' article 'One Hundred Billion Dead: A General Theology of Death', in this volume.

owes more to faith and hope than to irrefutable evidence. How can a rational choice be made when the outcome is so uncertain? Oates writes:

> But can one freely choose a condition, a state of being, that has never been experienced except in the imagination, and there, only in metaphor?... Rationally one cannot 'choose' Death, because Death is an unknown experience, and perhaps it isn't even an 'experience'—perhaps it is simply nothing; and one cannot imagine nothing.[1]

This has been countered by the point that we often choose things of which we have no experience, and these choices may be rational.

A stronger argument may be that death is irreversible. To be sure there are many choices in life which cannot be unchosen, although the effects of some choices can be reversed. To choose death, though, is to foreclose on all future choices. Indeed, if we aim to create autonomy as Jeremy Seedhouse advocates in his useful textbooks on medical ethics,[2] we might want to oppose suicide. It might seem paradoxical to refuse to allow the autonomous agent to kill himself or herself in the interests of safeguarding autonomy, but it would be foolish to dismiss this idea so lightly.

Until now little debate in this area has been of a practical nature. As a hospital manager as defined by the Mental Health Act 1983, I see patients who are detained against their will. Some of these are suicidal. The professional advice that we receive about such cases is that the patients are mentally ill and that, if not detained, they may be at serious risk of self-harm. The rationale for such detentions is that there are those whose view of the world is temporarily jaundiced. With time and treatment the prospect of continuing with life will, it is hoped, become tolerable. There are, however, times when the disjunction between what people were and what they are now is so great that they are not themselves or not in their right minds.

---

1. J.C. Oates, 'The Art of Suicide', in Battin and Mayo (eds.), *Suicide: The Philosophical Issues*, p. 167.
2. J. Seedhouse, *Ethics: The Heart of Health* (Chichester: John Wiley, 1988), and *Liberating Medicine* (Chichester: John Wiley, 1991).

There are libertarians who would argue that people in these circumstances should be allowed to kill themselves, and who would see interference as an unjustifiable violation of autonomy. It may be the case, as they argue, that left to themselves fewer people would attempt to kill themselves if they knew that there was no legal structure to prevent them—but the only way to establish this would be to embark on a hazardous social experiment which risked human life for a goal that is not clearly desirable.

While there is a debate about the possibility of rational suicide it seems that society has accepted the concept of irrational suicide in the provisions of the Mental Health Act. In this way of thinking there is an interesting assumption that to act rationally is better than to act emotionally. This is very different from the pervasive Western view of the selection of marriage partners where the reverse is usually the case.

Certainly the act of suicide is a denial of hope for the future life of the individual who performs it. This might be thought to be a conclusive objection for a Christian, yet I would question this. Hope is certainly central to a Christian way of life, but perhaps the suicide can carry out this task in hope. Often choices in life are made on the basis that one option is hopeless, so the other must be selected.

One problem for those who would see the choice of death as inherently wrong is that death has often been seen as better than some alternatives. There has been a long tradition of people dying for their country on the basis that this was a lesser evil than the loss of a war. People have courted martyrdom, although not always with the excessive zeal that Augustine sought to curb. Indeed suicide was thought preferable to rape for a virgin. T.S. Eliot evokes our sympathy for the sanctity of Thomas in *Murder in the Cathedral* with the lines 'The last temptation is the greatest treason; to do the right deed for the wrong reason'.[1] At the very least Jesus was reckless in going to Jerusalem and behaving as he did.

Staying alive then does not seem to be the sole reason for life. Regan chides both Kantians and utilitarians for not

---

1. T.S. Eliot, *Murder in the Cathedral* (London: Faber & Faber, 1962), p. 30.

producing a reason for living.[1] The followers of Kant fail to say
what we need to be free for. Utilitarians seek to maximize
happiness or well-being but fail to give a rationale for particular preferences. I suppose that any discussion about choosing
to die ought to explore what the meaning of life is. At the very
least the decision to die must mean that life has no further
meaning for the person who rejects it. The question 'what are
people for?' can lead us to define people by their function
alone, and, interestingly, suicide rates are higher among those
who lack a clearly-defined function in our society: the
unemployed and the elderly. In a pluralist society it is a
question we have difficulty in answering. The response of
Ignatius that our aim and purpose is to glorify God[2] would not
satisfy everyone. Even if this were to be adopted it would not
necessarily be a counter to suicide. To make the point, let me
quote a moving piece by Stewart Alsop, quoted by James
Rachels in *The End of Life*:

> The third night that I roomed with Jack in our tiny double room
> in the solid-tumour ward of the cancer clinic of the National
> Institutes of Health in Bethesda, Md., a terrible thought occurred
> to me.
>   Jack had a melanoma in his belly, a malignant solid tumour
> that the doctors guessed was about the size of a softball. The
> cancer had started a few months before with a small tumour in
> his left shoulder, and there had been several operations since.
> The doctors planned to remove the softball-sized tumour, but they
> knew Jack would soon die. The cancer had metastasized—it had
> spread beyond control.
>   Jack was good-looking, about 28, and brave. He was in constant
> pain, and his doctor had prescribed an intravenous shot of a
> synthetic opiate—a pain-killer, or analgesic—every four hours.
> His wife spent many of the daylight hours with him, and she
> would sit or lie on his bed and pat him all over, as one pats a
> child, only more methodically, and this seemed to help control
> the pain. But at night when his pretty wife had left (wives cannot

---

1.   D.H. Regan, 'Suicide and the Failure of Modern Moral Theory', in
Battin and Maris (eds.), *Suicide and Ethics*, p. 63.
2.   See L.J. Puhl, *The Spiritual Exercises of St. Ignatius* (New York: Loyola
University Press, 1951), p. 12.

stay overnight at the NIH clinic) and darkness fell, the pain would attack without pity.

At the prescribed hour, a nurse would give Jack a shot of the synthetic analgesic, and this would control the pain for perhaps two hours or a bit more. Then he would begin to moan, or whimper, very low, as though he didn't want me to wake him up. Then he would begin to howl, like a dog.

When this happened, either he or I would ring for a nurse, and ask for a pain-killer. She would give him some codeine or the like by mouth, but it never did any real good—it affected him no more than half an aspirin might affect a man who had just broken his arm. Always the nurse would explain as encouragingly as she could that there was not long to go before the next intravenous shot—'only about 50 minutes now'. And always poor Jack's whimpers and howls became more loud and frequent until at last the blessed relief came.

The third night of this routine, the terrible thought occurred to me. 'If Jack were a dog,' I thought, 'what would be done with him?' The answer was obvious: the pound, and chloroform. No human being with a spark of pity could let a living thing suffer so, to no good end.[1]

Jack's wife, the nurses and Stewart Alsop himself could all be said to glorify God—but does the continuation of Jack's life necessarily do so? Such undeserved suffering is not always thought of as a reason for glorifying God. Indeed it often has the opposite effect. Since all unbearable suffering does eventually end in death, is it permissible to bring that death forward? It might be that human intervention to end a life at this point is precisely what God is calling for and that we are too deaf to hear. Early in this article I alluded to Blackstone, who gave two reasons for objecting to suicide. His second was the interest of the king. Perhaps this should be widened to include the whole of society.

It may seem that so far I have been advocating acceptance of suicide. I have concentrated on general arguments against suicide, many of which I do not find to be robust. However, most of us, most of the time, are not fighting a fierce internal battle about whether or not to stay alive. We choose life. Some

1. Quoted in J. Rachels, *The End of Life* (Oxford: Oxford University Press, 1986), p. 153.

of us may be inspired by the words attributed to Moses in Deuteronomy 30:

> Today I offer you the choice of life and good or death and evil. If you obey the commandments of the Lord your God which I give you this day, by loving the Lord your God, conforming to his ways, and keeping his commandments, statutes and laws, then you will live and increase, and the Lord your God will bless you in the land which you are about to enter to occupy... I offer you the choice of life or death, blessing or curse (Deut. 30.15, 16, 19)

We do not start each day with a resolution to stay alive. Much of the time it is an unexplored assumption. There are those who would argue that were more people to explore this assumption rationally the suicide rate might rise considerably. Perhaps the pursuit of pleasure, often alleged to be what life is for, is too simple an account after all. Staying alive despite a lack of pleasure is the lot of many people. Is there a deeper pleasure, a sense of pride, which derives from coping against the odds?

There is certainly a sense of solidarity with others who suffer the 'slings and arrows of outrageous fortune'. It is this solidarity with the rest of humanity which the suicide breaks. The suicide of someone we know challenges us deeply. If he or she has gone, we feel, why should we stay? Indeed life may seem that much less worth living after such a person's suicide. It is often the case that the elderly members of a family seem to support one another, so that if one person dies others may quickly follow. A high proportion of spouses die within a year of their partners. In short we make life worth living for one another. The 'king' feels deprived by the untimely loss of one of his subjects.

Most of those who are prepared to sanction suicide in principle believe that in practice many people are not justified in choosing it because it would break relationships that they have with spouses, children, other family members and friends. These are valuable bonds in society based on trust and cemented by promises both explicit and implicit, and which should therefore not be destroyed. The case of the hypothetical isolate who has none of these ties is then raised.

I once attended a conference in London for which a

colleague arrived late. She explained that her train had been delayed by what British Rail described as a fatality on the line. It seemed that someone had committed suicide. Although neither of us knew anything about the identity of this person we were both affected by this death, as were other passengers. I do not mean that we were inconvenienced, but that our emotions were engaged, albeit for an anonymous stranger. Our slight distress was of course nothing compared to the trauma of the train driver, the emergency services and the undertaker who were all involved. This may argue against standing in front of a train to kill oneself, but I think that we can draw wider conclusions that relate to all methods of suicide. Even the isolate who dies cannot avoid leaving a body behind. It requires disposal and, in a country that likes to know who lives there, registration. To describe our registration system as evidence of our care for one another is to claim too much, but it is a sign of our mutual belonging in a shared society. The growth of the emphasis on the principle of autonomy over against beneficence has been a symptom of a growing sense of the importance of the individual. Alvarez makes the interesting point that 'the Church's condemnation of self-murder, however brutal, was based at least on a concern for the suicide's soul. In contrast a great deal of scientific tolerance appears to be founded on human indifference'.[1] Indeed, of late a great deal of the church's concern for the soul has focused on the individual, at the cost of the fertile images of the body of Christ, the true vine and the living stones which emphasize our interconnectedness. To those brought up in the Thatcher years we must keep on asserting that there is such a thing as society. Of course, there are also individuals and a denial of this can lead to the abuses and excesses of the former Soviet system. Both need to be sustained in a creative tension.

Undue emphasis on the principle of autonomy fails to take account of our interconnectedness. This point raises objections from those who say that if we keep alive the potential suicide for the benefit of others we are treating him or her as a means

1. A. Alvarez, 'The Background', in Battin and Mayo (eds.), *Suicide: The Philosophical Issues*, p. 30.

rather than an end. My particular brand of facile optimism, so the criticism goes, fails to take seriously the suicide's desperate sense of hopelessness: I am not treating the person with the respect that he or she deserves. It is important to listen to this criticism, but rather than meekly accepting it and letting the potential suicide carry out his or her intention, I think that the appropriate response is to accept some responsibility for making life less intolerable. Interconnectedness must imply mutuality. If I can have a claim on you to stay alive, then you must have a claim on me to make this a worthwhile option.

The story of a suicide which most impressed me was of a man whose funeral I conducted. Nine months before he had attempted suicide but had been unsuccessful. He awoke in the Accident and Emergency room of his local hospital, was furious to learn of his failure and was abusive to the staff and intolerant of his care. His family were upset, and he spent the next months explaining to them why he felt that suicide was the right option. When he eventually took his life, although they were distressed, they understood why he had taken this action. They realized that they were unable to make life bearable for him, and were better equipped to accept his death. This is an unusual case of a suicide acknowledging his interconnectedness. Such a strong sense of mutuality may be anathema to the champions of autonomy, but I suspect that it makes for a more bearable society. Again we return to the question about what life is for: to be free or to relate? Indeed I am who I am by virtue of the relationships in which I am involved. I am someone's husband, father, employer, employee, friend, neighbour. I am part of a complex web of relationships that both define and transform me. Each of these individual relationships is dispensable, though clearly not without enormous cost, as those who have experienced bereavement, unemployment or divorce can testify. It is even possible to survive the loss of all of these relationships—although the subsequent suicide of many Holocaust survivors suggests that this is a difficult transformation to achieve. But to achieve a meaningful sustainable life devoid of all relationships would seem to be an insuperable challenge.

The importance of relating is stressed by those who would

like the option of euthanasia to be available. James Rachels draws the distinction between being alive and have a life in *The End of Life*. It is more important to us to have a biographical life than to have mere biological existence. Courts in jurisdictions which do not recognize mercy-killing as a defence to a charge of murder are often in practice merciful in the way they deal with those who have practised euthanasia. In the case of Robert Weskin, who killed his mother when she was dying in great pain from leukaemia, the jury found him not guilty. Legally they were wrong, but in this way they were able to signal their disapproval of the law, as juries in this country had done before the offence of infanticide was recognized. The very term 'mercy-killing' is used to distance this act form murder.

For whose benefit is the mercy operating? People testify that they could no longer bear to see their relative suffering further. Are we truly acting in the interests of the person whose life is terminated, or merely protecting ourselves? I remember a firefighter telling me that he was unable to believe in God because he had seen too much suffering—ironically this was within weeks of the sudden death of my own son which had not deprived me of my faith. There is a difference between experiencing suffering and watching suffering, and in some ways the latter generates a greater feeling of impotence and therefore frustration.

At this point the euthanasia debate threatens to get very messy. While it is true that the bystanders may want to do something and that this is part of their motivation, they are also concerned for the person who is suffering. No one has a monopoly on compassion or self-interest in this debate, despite some eloquent claims to the contrary. It is not an adequate criticism of those who advocate euthanasia to say that they are only thinking of their own feelings. Nor is it satisfactory to say of opponents of euthanasia that they are more concerned with principles than with alleviating the suffering of someone in great distress. The story of Karen Quinlan demonstrates the difficulties here. This young woman suffered a lack of oxygen to the brain, probably as the result of a dangerous combination of alcohol and drugs. She suffered irreversible brain damage and was transferred to a respirator, requiring a tracheotomy.

She was not actually brain dead—that would have prevented the dilemma. After five months her parents went to court to ask that the respirator be turned off. Interestingly they had the support of their parish priest although they did not have the support of the Catholic hospital in which Karen was living. The hospital managed to wean Karen off the respirator before they were forced to accept the judgment of the New Jersey Supreme Court that it would be lawful to withdraw the respirator. It took Karen's body ten further years before it could submit to pneumonia. Hard cases made bad law, admittedly, but there are many unsatisfactory features to this case, which is well documented by Gregory Pence.[1] Even here, though, both sides had Karen's best interests at heart; the disagreement concerned what constituted her best interests.

Can it ever be in one's best interests for one's life to be ended prematurely? Perhaps a better way of phrasing the question is to ask whether it can be in one's interests for one's life to be ended before the time at which it would have ended but for the intervention. It is less elegant, but the word 'prematurely' prejudges. Much of the previous discussion about suicide is relevant here, but most instances of potential euthanasia occur when the end of life is in sight. Here I fear that the gap between public perception and the real possibilities of terminal care may encourage people to press for euthanasia in an ill-informed way. While a pain-free death without distressing symptoms cannot be guaranteed to everyone, there have been tremendous advances in palliative care in recent years. Anyone supporting euthanasia—either as a general principle or in a particular case—should make themselves aware of these developments before forming a judgment. Our most vivid images of death are of the deaths of those we have loved. If these occurred even five years ago, we should be aware that there have been further advances. Some of the responses to the case of Nigel Cox, the doctor who gave his patient Lilian Boyes

1. G. Pence, *Classic Cases in Medical Ethics* (New York: McGraw–Hill, 1990).

a lethal injection of potassium chloride,[1] came from experts in palliative care who would have administered much larger doses of painkillers than he had. This may explain why it was a condition of his reinstatement that he attend an update on palliative care. Such care, though, is not a panacea. Itching, the break-up of one's mouth and giving off a putrid smell can be just as distressing as pain, which still may not be relieved in every case. I stress this because it is just as possible to claim too much as too little for palliative care.

The prospect of euthanasia adds another morally relevant ingredient to the debate which is not present in suicide. Euthanasia requires the intervention of another person to enable death to take place. Traditionally the medical and nursing professions have been seen to exist to cure and to care, not to kill. A recent *Lancet* editorial concludes that it is unethical for doctors to take any part in execution by the state, because it contravenes the duty to preserve life.[2] The complication here is that the patient has actively sought euthanasia. We might point out, however, that the power of consumers is not generally so great that they can dictate what doctors provide. A sick note, an antibiotic for a virus or cosmetic surgery may all be refused by a doctor.

Is the difference here that euthanasia uniquely concerns values? If so, perhaps the person desiring euthanasia should seek to be treated by an ethicist rather than by a doctor. If euthanasia is about values, can we demand that we impose our value system on our doctor? A legal provision enables doctors to decline involvement in abortion. Surely there could be a similar conscience clause for euthanasia? But then the situation could arise in which a doctor would be content to perform euthanasia, his or her values coinciding with those of the patient. Both would feel that in this instance life has no further purpose. Consequentialists believe that to forbid euthanasia in this situation would be to maximize distress. Although I am not a consequentialist I think that this argument deserves to be

1.   Correspondence in the *British Medical Journal* 305 (October 17 1992), pp. 951-52.

2.   'Doctors and Death Row', *The Lancet* 341 (January 23 1993), p. 209.

answered on its own terms. It is impossible to predict all the consequences of a given action, but I would be concerned about the effects on the doctor of such a case. The decision to take one's own life, if successfully carried through, is not something that one has to live with. The decision to take another's, albeit with his or her consent if not insistence, may be harder to bear. It will affect future clinical decision-making, perhaps making the option of euthanasia easier. This is a reasonable fear, although a recent article showed that in Holland, many doctors who had performed one act of euthanasia would refuse to perform another.[1]

Another consequence is suggested by Margaret Battin in an article I mentioned earlier about suicide.[2] In a world in which euthanasia was generally permitted there would be a risk of manipulation. Such manipulation might not be apparent, but for instance might be less attentive, making euthanasia the more desirable choice. Ideological manipulation is also a possibility. Where euthanasia becomes more acceptable there is a hidden pressure to adopt it. If it is difficult to imagine a hard-pressed NHS manager trying to raise the euthanasia figures on a ward to balance the books at the year end, we can look to America, where administrators are deeply concerned about the enormous costs of keeping alive those who might have been persuaded to write a 'living will'.

I think that this argument is considerably more subtle than the slippery slope argument. In fact I find slippery slope arguments unconvincing. Although the possibility of abortion on demand exists in some places and on some incomes in the UK, this was not what Parliament appears to have intended, and is the result of loose drafting rather than a slippery slope. It would be possible to devise an Abortion Act which only permitted abortion in certain cases. The slope that is alleged to be slippery consists in fact of a large number of steps and it is disingenuous to say that it is a slippery slope from abortion to euthanasia.

The argument that I think has weight is that acceptance of

1. Van der Maas *et al.*, 'Euthanasia', p. 673.
2. See Battin, 'Manipulated Suicide'.

euthanasia would alter the moral climate and put pressure on some of the most vulnerable members of society to choose death. This does seem to me to be a foreseeable consequence of accepting euthanasia and too high a price to pay. Given an increase in pressure on people to be useful, such a change in the moral climate could prove irresistible.

Some of the momentum for a change in attitudes to euthanasia comes from the belief that we already allow a passive form of euthanasia. Nigel Cox would have faced no problems had he injected a very high dose of painkiller. He could have hidden behind the fiction that he only intended to kill the pain, not the patient. This is the doctrine of double effect, which the Catholic church employs to excuse those who cause death as an unintended but foreseen consequence of an action which had a justifiable motive. This can at times seem as though hairs are being split. James Rachels gives the example of a commander who orders a bombing raid on a civilian population during which a stray bomb destroys an ammunition dump. Had he ordered the destruction of the ammunition dump and a stray bomb hit the civilian population, the same people would be dead but the commander would be innocent.[1] I would argue that this conclusion is not as unreasonable as Rachels thinks. If we build up a series of cases where morally relevant factors vary by a small degree each time, we will eventually reach a point where our behaviour will change, and I think that the doctrine of double effect merely seeks to locate this point with some accuracy. It may be satisfactory in the armchair or the lecture theatre, but can be muddled at the bedside, where a doctor, patient and relatives are expecting death, are reconciled to it and perhaps hoping for it. In such a case the doctor knows the probable effect of a higher dose of painkiller, and may feel that he or she intends death because the prospect of death has become imminent and has become desirable.

This leads me to my final area of discussion: the refusal of further treatment where such refusal is expected to result in death. However vigorously we may fight to retain our life there is a point at which we shall lose. Most essays in this

1.   Rachels, *The End of Life*, pp. 15-16.

volume will no doubt allude to this fact. I do not understand why it is thought to be such bad form to remind an audience that they will not be here this time next century. It is probably the one statement in this book that is not contentious. Accepting death is something we all need to do in time. We may with Dylan Thomas say, 'Do not go gentle into that good night/Old age should burn and rage at close of day:/Rage, rage against the dying of the light'.[1] The work of Elizabeth Kübler-Rose has taught us to see this anger as one of the stages on the road to acceptance of death among the dying. Acceptance in the face of the inevitable seems ultimately to be the only mature and fruitful attitude. In an age which invites us to challenge fatalism and take control of our lives this is rather a downbeat message, but nonetheless realistic. We may even welcome death in our imagination, as Roger McGough does in his poem 'Let me Die a Youngman's Death':

> Let me die a youngman's death
> not a clean and inbetween
> the sheets holywater death
> not a famous-last-words
> peaceful out of breath death
>
> When I'm 73
> and in constant good tumour
> may I be mown down at dawn
> by a bright red sports car
> on my way home
> from an allnight party.
>
> Or when I'm 91
> with silver hair
> & sitting in a barber's chair
> may rival gangsters
> with hamfisted tommyguns burst in
> and give me a short back & insides
>
> Or when I'm 104
> & banned from the Cavern
> may my mistress
> catching me in bed with her daughter
> & fearing her son

1.   D. Thomas, *The Poems* (ed. D. Jones; London: Dent, 1971), p. 207.

cut me up in little pieces
& throw away every piece but one

Let me die a youngman's death
Not a free from sin tiptoe in
candle wax and waning death
not a curtain drawn by angels borne
'what a nice way to go' death.[1]

Fighting the inevitable to the end might seem to be perverse. When can we legitimately decline further treatment? This is a hard question to answer because we are often not in possession of all the facts, even now that the medical profession is prepared to discuss the possibility of death more openly. Non-treatment decisions by patients at an early stage in the course of a disease are a challenge to the profession because they reject it. At a later stage, however, the same doctors might feel happy with an instruction not to resuscitate. It is ironic that I can choose to affect my health status by my intake of nicotine or alcohol, by my choice of career or choice of sexual behaviour, yet I may be denied access to facts which would enable me to choose whether to embark on a course of life-saving treatment or not.

At a later stage, who should determine whether I should receive life-saving treatment? The living will has been perceived as the great solution to this problem, but it is not without difficulties. A family friend always said that people should die at the age of seventy. He is now in his late eighties. The problem is that although I can make a living will now I do not know how I will feel about treatment in the future, particularly in the distant future when I shall have changed markedly. The ability to accept dependence may well grow. An alternative is to appoint a proxy, but it is important that his or her interests do not clash with mine, and someone whose interests do not conflict with mine may not know me well enough to act as a proxy.

Should a doctor make these non-treatment decisions? In an ideal world the doctor–patient relationship is so strong that the

1. R. McGough, *Selected Poems, 1967–87* (London: Jonathan Cape, 1989), p. 15.

options have been discussed. In the imperfect world of the modern District General Hospital where the new house officer has to decide in the early hours of the morning whether to resuscitate an elderly patient, what factors must be taken into account? To a 24-year-old house officer, a 96-year-old patient may seem to have had a 'good innings'—but could this justify, say, taking away the patient's chance of seeing her great-granddaughter's first baby, due any day? If prognosis is poor, it may seem obscene to resuscitate the patient only to allow a lingering and more painful death a few days later. In the end perhaps we need to import the legal standard of the man on the Clapham omnibus. If he were the patient, would he want to be resuscitated?

There is a final point that I want to make, which brings me back to the observation that there would be more suicides if more people viewed their situations objectively. This of course only holds true if pleasure is their ultimate value. I sense, on the contrary, that there is a deep awareness that some suffering is part of the human lot. This point needs to be made with caution because suffering has been glorified in the past in ways that are tactless and offensive. But suffering can bring great dignity. I do not hold this up as an obligation, but as an important option to be considered by those who might otherwise choose to die.

I know that even a better expressed set of arguments will not dissuade some people from choosing to die. Although content with the refusal of treatment and the alleviation of pain I find myself unable to justify suicide or active euthanasia. Against those who feel that this violates autonomy, my defence is that autonomy alone is so basic, a kind of lowest common denominator of human existence. I prefer the enriched and enriching life of mutuality and interconnectedness with its greater demands and its greater rewards. My choice is to live life to the full.

'The Maid is not Dead but Sleepeth': Death and Revival in Writing by Women

Maria Manuel Lisboa

> And the Sybil, you know. I saw her with my own eyes at Cumae, hanging in a jar; and when the boys asked her, 'What would you, Sybil?' she answered, 'I would die.'[1]

The Sybil is the prototype for women who know too much, and her death wish as related by Petronius is therefore both prophetic and archetypal, encompassing a dimension which throughout literature, myth, social practice and existential experience has come to be regarded as women's sphere of expertise, namely death. Death, whether iconography or fact, whether naturally happening or unnaturally brought about by self or other, has emerged across boundaries of time, geography and culture curiously labelled as a metaphorically gender-specific activity, the prerogative of women; all the more curiously so, given the actual undeniably universal nature of the phenomenon.

The superstructure of gender-based ideology which throughout the last five millenia has sought to accredit the male with the traits of strength, activity, power, positive presence or life, has deemed it necessary on the whole to do so through the establishment of a binary opposition of culturally constructed femaleness as weakness, passivity, powerlessness, absence or death. The accompanying iconography of womanhood that has evolved across cultures and across centuries, depicting the

---

1. Petronius, 'A Fragment', in G. Macbeth (ed.), *The Penguin Book of Victorian Verse* (Harmondsworth: Penguin, 1987), p. 194.

female of the species as classifiable within one of two broad antithetical categories, the beautiful, fragile, dead angel, or the monstrous, fiendish, dangerously alive demon, links these diametric opposites through the shared assumption that each is better dead. The woman as Other, in the words of one critic, 'comes to represent the contingency of life, life that is made to be destroyed'.[1] Thus, whether more loved or less hated for it, a woman is more properly herself if dead, a tenet which stands whether its motivating impetus is seeming love or straight-forward misogyny.

Starting, then, with the misogynistic motivation underlying the 'beast must die' syndrome, we recall Germaine Greer's epoch-making statement that 'women have very little idea how much men hate them'.[2] Her statement finds substantiation almost anywhere one cares to look in the canons of fact and fiction, literature, art and history, medicine and religion, philosophy and community practice across the ages. When the outraged Orestes cries out to the Furies, 'Doest thou call me a blood relation of my mother?'[3] he unleashes the virulent prototype for a kind of misogyny which has exercised the minds of men throughout history, from Plato and Aristotle to newly-risen or never-abated masculinist thought today, and whose need for denying the frightening possibility of female power, or even female presence, begins with a denial of the womb which carried every man and continues throughout all areas of gender coexistence.

The obvious solution to the problem, for Orestes and his successors alike, was death for women, death metaphorical or literal, imagistic or factual, often both, and its implementation through the discourses of religion, literature, history and social institutions such as marriage, sexuality, medicine and psychiatry. Drawing upon examples from some of these, and

1.   S.M. Gilbert and S. Gubar, *The Madwoman in the Attic: The Woman Writer and the Nineteenth-Century Literary Imagination* (New Haven and London: Yale University Press, 1979), p. 34.

2.   G. Greer, *The Female Eunuch* (London: Grafton Books, 1985), p. 249.

3.   Aeschyllus, *Oresteia*. This particular translation, which differs from the Penguin Classics version, is quoted in M. Warner, *Alone of All Her Sex: The Myth and Cult of the Virgin Mary* (London: Picador, 1985), p. 41.

beginning with religion, feminist theologians and historians of religion have analysed the rise of the male-centred monotheisms which replaced the pluralist matriarchal religions and argue that

> man's self-elevation to a god did more than cut a woman down to normal size; it succeeded in subordinating her to a lower form of being. Each in its own way, the five major belief systems of Judaism, Buddhism, Confucianism, Christianity and Islam *by their very nature* insisted on the inferiority of women and demanded their subjection to values and imperatives devised to promote the supremacy of men... Individual patriarchs may indeed wriggle off the charge of woman-hating; the key to the gross inflictions laid on women in their names lies in the nature of the system itself. For a monotheism is not merely a religion—it is a *relation of power*... In the first and greatest act of discrimination, of deliberate *apartheid* in human history, women were made into *untermenschen*, a separate and inferior order of beings.[1]

Even forgetting actual practices such as the witch-burnings of the Middle Ages, whose casualties, estimated at an overall nine million, easily outnumber those of the Holocaust,[2] a perusal of the writings of the early Christian Fathers and their followers, not to mention of the Bible itself, makes harrowing reading for a woman. St Paul, for example, tells us that 'man... is the image and glory of God: but the woman is the glory of man... neither was the man created for the woman, but the woman for the man'.[3] This is so because, as St Augustine helpfully clarified, 'woman is not the image of God, whereas the man alone is the image of God'.[4] He also pointed out that 'the closeness of woman to all that is vile, lowly, corruptible and material'[5] is epitomized in such unspeakable goings-on as, for example, childbirth and menstruation, thus lending greater credence to the views of such as St John Chrysostom, who advised us that

1.   R. Miles, *The Women's History of the World* (London: Paladin, 1989), pp. 91-92, 102.

2.   J. Tweedie, *In the Name of Love* (London: Pan Books, 1988), pp. 35-36.

3.   2 Cor. 11.7, 9.

4.   Quoted in Miles, *Women's History*, p. 93.

5.   Quoted in Warner, *Alone of All Her Sex*, p. 58.

'the whole of [a woman's] body is nothing less than phlegm, blood, bile, rheum and the fluid of digested food',[1] or Odo of Cluny who interestingly argued that 'to embrace a woman is to embrace a sack of manure'.[2]

The above evidence is helpful in contextualizing the views of Thomas Aquinas, one of the most influential early Christian writers. The Angelic Doctor experienced some difficulty in reconciling woman with God's image, eventually concluding that woman, unlike man, was not made in God's image.[3] Tertullian, too, beginning with the conviction of female inferiority, gave vent in his writings to several instances of well-documented misogyny:

> Do you not realize that Eve is you? The curse God pronounced on your sex weighs still on the world. Guilty, you must bear its hardships. You are the devil's gateway, you desecrated the fatal tree, you first betrayed the law of God, you who softened up with your cajoling words the man against whom the devil could not prevail by force. The image of God, the man Adam, you broke him, it was child's play to you. *You* deserved death, and it was the son of God who had to die![4]

Tempting as it may be to regard the above examples as unpleasantnesses rendered aberrant by the passage of centuries, the authors of these utterances have found abundant echo in ready successors up to and including the present day, within and outside the Christian church. As Jill Tweedie succinctly remarks, just as St Augustine two thousand years ago believed that women's charms would damage his hope of heaven, today's footballers believe the same charms will put paid to their chances of winning a match.[5]

If the road to Damascus was undoubtedly women's Via Dolorosa, it was not the only one. The abyss which separates

1. St John Chrysostom, 'To the Fallen Monk Theodore', quoted in Warner, *Alone of All her Sex*, p. 58.

2. Quoted in Miles, *Women's History*, p. 98.

3. *Summa Theologiae* I, 93, 4 ad. I, quoted in Warner, *Alone of All Her Sex*, p. 179.

4. *Disciplinary, Moral and Ascetical Works*, quoted in Warner, *Alone of All Her Sex*, p. 58.

5. Tweedie, *In the Name of Love*, p. 45.

the various religions is bridged by the shared territory of misogyny. Muhammad, expanding on the Arab proverb which states that 'man is heaven, woman is hell',[1] explained that 'men are in charge because Allah has made one to exceed the other. So good women are obedient'.[2] Buddha, too, on the same topic, quizzically enquired of the Omnipotent, 'how are we to conduct ourselves, Lord, with regard to women? Women are full of passion...women are envious, women are stupid... That is the reason...that is the cause, why women have no place in public assemblies, do not carry on business, and do not earn a living by any profession'.[3] Elsewhere, even more pithily, he stated that 'the body of a woman is filthy, and not a vessel for the law'.[4] And every practising Jewish male thanks God daily in his prayers that he was not born a woman.

Philosophy, too, has had its say. Aristotle claimed that women were a deformity, although one that he admitted to occur in the course of nature.[5] Plato placed women between man and the brute beast because, according to him, their visceral parts were bigger than men's, whose cupidity is less violent[6]—a view possibly controversial in the light of the persistent gender discrepancy in violent crime statistics, both nowadays and historically. Whatever his hypothetical conclusions, Plato would nevertheless very likely have persisted in maintaining that men have larger heads and therefore more brains and sense than women.[7] It must have been partly from his acquaintance with Plato that Herbert Spencer supposed any learning for young ladies to risk 'excessive stimulation to their feeble mental parts', the ill-effects of 'brain-forcing' upon young women including nervousness, anaemia, hysteria, stunted growth, excessive thinness and sterility.[8]

1.   Quoted in Miles, *Women's History*, p. 100.
2.   Quoted in Miles, *Women's History*, p. 93.
3.   Quoted in Miles, *Women's History*, p. 134.
4.   Quoted in Miles, *Women's History*, p. 103.
5.   *On the Generation of Animals*, quoted in Warner, *Alone of All Her Sex*, pp. 40-41.
6.   Miles, *Women's History*, p. 135.
7.   Miles, *Women's History*, p. 135.
8.   H. Spencer, *Education: Intellectual, Moral and Physical*, quoted

In view of all this, it is not surprising that the concept of a man's loving a woman might prove difficult to countenance, as Plutarch eloquently explained:

> I certainly do not give the name 'love' to the feeling one has for women and girls, anymore than we would say flies are in love with milk, bees with honey or breeders with the calves and fowl they fatten in the dark...[1]

Plutarch, though, strikes a chivalrous note when contrasted with Roger de Caen, who, after expounding on the nature of a woman's body along the lines of the 'sack of manure' school of thought, reasonably inquired: 'if a fine crimson cloth covered a pile of foul dung, would anyone be foolish enough to love the dung because of it?'[2]

These examples lend credence to the social readings of contemporary writers such as Angela Carter and Joan Smith[3] who interpret misogyny as a founding tenet of contemporary society. Carter, in *The Sadeian Woman*, a treatise on pornography, suggests the latter to be emblematic of everyday gender relations, merely rendering explicit through quantitative but not qualitative distortion, the violence commonly committed by men against women in various walks of life, including the personal and the professional:

> Female castration is an imaginary fact that pervades the whole of men's attitude towards women and our attitude to ourselves, that transforms women from human beings into wounded creatures who were born to bleed.[4]

The everyday practice of this violence yields examples which may be drawn from every aspect of communal existence:

in Miles, *Women's History*, p. 228.

1. *Dialogue on Love*, quoted in Miles, *Women's History*, p. 68.
2. Quoted in Miles, *Women's History*, p. 98.
3. See J. Smith, *Misogynies* (London: Faber & Faber, 1989).
4. A. Carter, *The Sadeian Woman: An Exercise in Cultural History* (London: Virago, 1987), p. 23.

Under patriarchy, being female was a life sentence, but many
women never lived to serve it... For female infanticide was
pandemic. From the earliest existence of historical records to the
present day, to be born female in India, China or the Arab States,
indeed anywhere between Morocco and Shanghai, was
extremely dangerous. In pre-revolutionary China, childbirth
preparations for thousands of years included the provision of a
box of ashes next to the birthing bed, to suffocate a girl child as
soon as she was born. Throughout India...little girls...were
strangled, poisoned, thrown into the sea, exposed in the jungle,
fed to sharks as a sacrifice to the gods or drowned in milk with a
prayer that they would come again as sons. As late as 1808 a
British political commission found only half a dozen houses in
the whole of Cutch where the fathers had not had all daughters
born to them killed at birth.[1]

Marriage, too, for a variety of reasons has traditionally held
its dangers for women worldwide, as testified by two Indian
proverbs, 'early to marry and early to die', and 'the life of a
wife is two monsoons'.[2] But lest we should begin to con-
gratulate ourselves in Western superiority, let us cast our minds
to the symbolism of the Christian marriage ceremony, in the
course of which the woman, decked in the symbols of a
virginity without which she is judged worthless, is given away
by her father to her husband, stripped of her name and until
recently of her possessions, her rights over children, the right
to work or travel without her husband's permission, and
defined as the lesser part of a duo which is not man and
woman, nor husband and wife, but man and wife, thus effectively annihilating her autonomous identity and constricting her
to deadly invisibility. Or let us think of medical practice which
until this century commonly refused women anaesthetics in
childbirth in order that they fulfil the biblical edict that
women must give birth in anguish to atone for the sin of Eve.[3]
Or let us recall Martin Luther's lapsarian condemnation of

1.   Miles, *Women's History*, p. 117.
2.   Quoted in Miles, *Women's History*, p. 113.
3.   Gen. 3.16.

women, 'let them bear children till they die of it. That is what they are for'.[1]

Or, in a somewhat less grim context, let us recollect the words of one Professor Marshall to the socialist reformer Beatrice Webb upon her request for admission to university. He explained to her that

> a woman was a subordinate being, and that if she ceased to be subordinate there would be no object for a man to marry; that marriage was a sacrifice of masculine freedom and would only be tolerated by male creatures so long as it meant the devotion, body and soul, of the female and male! Hence the woman must not develop her faculties in any way unpleasant to the male; that strength, courage, independence were not attractive in women; that rivalry in men's pursuits was positively unpleasant... 'If you compete with us, we shan't marry you,' he summed up with a laugh.[2]

Or, in the words of another famous professor,

> Women are irrational,
> That's all there is to that,
> Their heads are full of cotton-hay and rags.
> They're nothing but exasperating,
> irritating, vacillating, calculating,
> agitating, maddening and infuriating hags.[3]

In literature, too, and in literary imagery, as some feminist critics have convincingly argued, woman has been compelled into conformity with a male-originated Ideal of the Eternal Feminine which iconographizes her as perfect and lovable only if meek, inactive, submissive, passive, silent, and above all dead:

> The aesthetic cult of ladylike fragility and delicate beauty... associated with the moral cult of the angel-woman...obliged 'genteel' women to 'kill' themselves...into art objects: slim, pale, passive beings whose 'charms' eerily recalled the snowy, porcelain immobility of the dead. Tight-lacing, fasting, vinegar-

1. *Kritische Gesamtausgabe*, II, quoted in Miles, *Women's History*, p. 103.
2. B. Webb, *My Apprenticeship*, quoted in Miles, *Women's History*, p. 224.
3. 'Why Can't a Woman Be Like a Man?', from *My Fair Lady*. Lyrics by A.J. Lerner, music by F. Loewe.

drinking, and similar cosmetic or dietary excesses were all parts
of a physical regimen that helped [preserve the image] of the
emblematic 'beautiful woman' whose *death*, thought Edgar Allan
Poe, 'is unquestionably the most poetical topic in the world.'
Whether she becomes an *objet d'art* or a saint, however, it is the
surrender of herself—of her personal comfort, her personal
desires, or both—that is the beautiful angel-woman's key act,
while it is precisely this sacrifice which dooms her both to death
and to heaven. For to be selfless is not only to be noble, it is to be
dead. A life that has no story...is really a life of death, a death-
in-life. The ideal of 'contemplative purity' evokes, finally, both
heaven and the grave.[1]

Faced with closed doors, no options and a dominant ethic
which, in Jean Baker Miller's words, 'induces women to view
themselves and their own attempts to know, and act on their
needs—or to enlarge their lives...as either attacking men or
trying to be like them',[2] women have grown in insecurity and
self-loathing, a living death which includes the awareness that
they 'speak on sufferance',[3] that their access to socialization
involves a 'graceful obligation of silence'.[4]

Metaphors of female writing, therefore, frequently allude to
the courage needed to break these barriers of externally
imposed silence and to risk the ostracism and punishment that
so often befell those few women who, in Sandra Gilbert's and
Susan Gubar's words, 'attempted the pen',[5] and 'bled into
print'[6] upon the blank page. Virginia Woolf warned us of these
lost literary foremothers whose trails have been historically
covered again and again by a patriarchal *status quo* covetous of
the monopoly of voice:

1.   Gilbert and Gubar, *The Madwoman in the Attic*, p. 25.
2.   J. Baker Miller, *Toward a New Psychology of Women* (Harmondsworth:
Penguin, 1979), p. 18.
3.   C. Kaplan, *Sea Changes: Culture and Feminism* (London: Verso, 1986).
4.   S.M. Gilbert, 'What do Feminist Critics Want? A Postcard from the
Volcano', in E. Showalter (ed.), *The New Feminist Criticism: Essays on
Women, Literature and Theory* (London: Virago, 1986), p. 34.
5.   Gilbert and Gubar, *The Madwoman in the Attic*, p. 7.
6.   S. Gubar, 'The Blank Page and Issues of Female Creativity', in
Showalter (ed.), *The New Feminist Criticism*, p. 302.

When…one reads of a witch being ducked, of a woman possessed by devils, of a wise woman selling herbs, or even of a very remarkable man who had a mother, then I think we are on the track of a lost novelist, a suppressed poet, of some mute and inglorious Jane Austen, some Emily Brontë who dashed her brains out on the moor or mopped and mowed about the highways, crazed with the torture that her gift had put her to. Indeed, I would venture to guess that Anon, who wrote so many poems without signing them, was often a woman.[1]

Woolf herself eventually committed suicide, and suicide as an act either of despair or rebellion, defeat or defiance, has become a central metaphor in the lives and writings of women for whom death has in any case always been held out as the realm *par excellence* of true femininity. Kim Chernin, writing on one particular form of female self-destruction today, the literal self-effacement into invisibility of anorexia nervosa, says the following:

We have seen the way [women] break down at the moment they might prosper and develop; we have observed the way they torture themselves with starvation and make their bodies their enemies, the way they attack their female flesh…

Women today seem to be practicing genocide against their female body precisely because there are no indications that the female body has been invited to enter culture…

[C]ulture, after opening the doors [of] its most prized institutions [to women] does not really welcome female development after all.[2]

Psychiatric illness, then, in many of its female manifestations, be it the clichéd hysteria whose very name (derived from the Greek word for womb, and traditionally believed to be caused by a wandering womb) is imprinted upon the Western psyche in connection with the image of the housebound Victorian wife or daughter, or be it the recently diagnosed eating disorders whose principal victims are high-achieving young women, can,

1. V. Woolf, *A Room of One's Own* (London: Granada Publishing, 1983), p. 48.
2. K. Chernin, *The Hungry Self: Women, Eating and Identity* (London: Virago, 1986), pp. 93, 186-87.

throughout the history of psychiatry as analysed by feminist medical historians, be largely linked to the female experience of confinement.[1] Alice Walker describes an extreme version of this kind of confinement, that of black women under slavery:

> Did you have a genius of a great-great-grandmother who died under some ignorant and depraved white overseer's lash? Or was she required to bake biscuits for a lazy backwater tramp, when she cried out in her soul to paint watercolours of sunsets, or the rain falling on the green and peaceful pasturelands? Or was her body broken and forced to bear children (who were more often than not sold away from her)—eight, ten, fifteen, twenty children—when her one joy was the thought of modelling heroic figures of rebellion, in stone or clay?... Then you may begin to comprehend the lives of our 'crazy', 'Sainted' mothers and grandmothers. The agony of the lives of women who might have been Poets, Novelists, Essayists and Short Story Writers (over a period of centuries), who died with their real gifts stifled within them.[2]

Walker is referring to the specific plight of black slave women; as other feminist writers on the subject have discussed, however, in relation to indexes of existential freedom, the dividing line between the plantation slave traded under the auction block and the southern belle or bride exchanged between father and husband in the matrimonial market stakes becomes at times disturbingly thin, and the difference in the consequences with regard to the mental health of the respective victims virtually negligible.[3]

Throughout the writing and the lives of women there echoes this sound of silence and madness, the muffled scream of those with something to say but under an injunction to muteness. Their suffering must often have led them to wreak revenge, first upon themselves and their own bodies, and then, sometimes, in writing and in reality, against too-powerful others. Karen Blixen articulates the pain of women confined to roles forcibly assigned to them by the incantations of pseudo-

---

1.   S. Orbach, *Fat is a Feminist Issue* (London: Arrow Books, 1989).

2.   A. Walker, 'In Search of our Mothers' Gardens', in *In Search of our Mothers' Gardens* (London: The Women's Press, 1985), pp. 233-35.

3.   O. Banks, *Faces of Feminism* (Oxford: Basil Blackwell, 1986).

biologistic dictates about a woman's rightful place, the suffering of women permitted no choice and forced to live in one way when they would rather live in another, women forced into a hypocritically exalted domestic role and told how marvellously they do it by those who would not consider doing it themselves:

> It is terrible and unbearable to an artist...to be encouraged to do, to be applauded for doing...second best... Throughout the world there goes one long cry from the heart of the artist: Give me leave to do my utmost![1]

Barred from the basic human right of doing one's very best, women, in Elaine Showalter's words, 'wake to worlds which offer no places for [who] they wish to become; and rather than struggling, they die'.[2]

Destined for death by the decrees of others, women may have historically rushed into it in their lives and in their fictions, but there are alternatives to self-destruction. When the fifteenth-century Portuguese cartographers drew maps of the world, at the edge of the known territories they would pencil in the words, 'from here onwards there be dragons'. Dragons are the unknown quantities at the edge of worlds which, in the process of pushing their frontiers ever further, leave the inhabitants of the margins no space to exist. And without space to exist, one dies, but one may also go mad, or bad. Similarly, without room to be, without 'a room of one's own', women in patriarchal culture may steer previously self-directed destructiveness towards the sources of their existential discomfort. Jules Henry remarked that 'psychopathology is the final outcome of all that is wrong with a culture';[3] in female culture, the twin figures of the madwoman and the murderous she-devil become alternative roles to the deathly silence of the angel-woman, and, in the words of Gilbert and Gubar, the violence of these doubles is the means by which 'the female author

---

1. K. Blixen, 'Babette's Feast', in *Anecdotes of Destiny* (London: Penguin, 1986), p. 68.
2. E. Showalter, 'Towards a Feminist Poetics', in M. Jacobus (ed.), *Women Writing and Writing about Women* (London: Croom Helm, 1978).
3. J. Henry, *Culture against Man* (New York: Knopf, 1963).

enacts her own raging desire to escape male houses and male texts, while at the same time it is through the double's violence that [the] anxious author articulates for herself the costly destructiveness of anger repressed until it can no longer be contained'.[1]

Jean Baudrillard, writing about the murderous capacity of icons and images to conceal, or murder, the reality they purport to represent, says of the iconoclasts that 'their rage to destroy images rose precisely because they sensed this omnipotence of simulacra, this facility they have of erasing God [or the reality in whose place they stand] from the consciousness of people', whereas the iconolaters, 'underneath the idea of the apparition of God [or reality] in the mirror of images... already enacted his [or its] death and...disappearance in the epiphany of his [or its] representations (which they perhaps knew no longer represented anything)'.[2] When reality is made to disappear behind the armature of icons and images of male authorship, woman becomes 'the focal point for male fantasies about women', an 'icon of female passivity',[3] the blank page upon which the images of male fantasy may be inscribed with no more than a perfunctory nod towards the reality which they brush aside.

This concept may provide the key to one motivation apparent in much recent writing by women, the punitive, perhaps vindictive if often hilarious writing of women such as Angela Carter, Fay Weldon and Margaret Atwood, which may be seen according to these parameters as the iconoclastic voice of what (for the sake of a better definition) I will call authors in transition, authors who have understood and resented the dangers of centuries of literary imagery enamoured with female death, but who have as yet only metaphors of anger and madness to replace the established ones of angelic death or unsuccessful fiendishness, rather than genuinely new alternatives which it

---

1.   Gilbert and Gubar, *The Madwoman in the Attic*, p. 85.

2.   J. Baudrillard, 'Simulacra and Simulations', in *Selected Writings* (ed. M. Poster; Cambridge and Oxford: Polity Press with Basil Blackwell, 1989), p. 169.

3.   Smith, *Misogynies*, pp. 82-83.

may be, for them, too early to envisage. If the death of the self has haunted the lives and minds of women as a central trope in their experience of existence and in the exercise of their imaginations, from the nineteenth century onwards and rapidly escalating in our century a new kind of voice has begun to be heard, and a new icon to be visible: that of the woman writer as a sort of Antigone at the crossroads, seeking to lay the ghost of past necrophiliac memorabilia through the fictional killing of the murderous imagination of the forefathers. This is certainly an icon destined to be itself torn down, eventually, in the very process of creative self-reinvention, but it is at present effective and necessary in the discovery and invention of new matrilinear literary inheritances.

Sarah Grimké, one of the early American feminists, coined the famous slogan, 'we ask no special favours for our sex. All we ask is that you take your feet off our necks'.[1] When the feet persist on female necks rendered recalcitrant by too much oppression, women barred from their share of power and voice may turn to violent fantasies of male annihilation, and female writing may be transfigured from the death of the self bleeding into print into the death by murder of the male other. And male writing, unsurprisingly, frequently discloses unease at its own originatory images of womanhood and the underlying fear that the dichotomy of the angel and the monster may fuse its terms to unveil the further nightmare of a lurking fiend underneath the angelic facade, a fear which finds its counterpart in the writing of women in the form of wish-fulfilment.[2] Nina Auerbach, writing about Victorian literature and its cultural creations, expressed this:

> Her heroine's demonic anger and rage for power—in other words, her soul...stays true to an angel face... It requires only the fire of an altered palette to bring out the contours of one latent in the face of the other... the angel becomes a demon by realizing the implications of her being.[3]

1. Quoted in Miles, *Women's History*, p. 242.
2. Gilbert and Gubar, *The Madwoman in the Attic*, pp. 3-44.
3. Mary Elizabeth Braddon, quoted in N. Auerbach, *Woman and the Demon: The Life of a Victorian Myth* (London: Harvard University Press, 1982), p. 107.

Elsewhere, she expands on the disturbing thinness of the dividing line between the two:

> [The angel woman and her demonic counterpart] among other things...share a feminist despair at their dependency on little men... Victorian female demons...keep dangerous if hidden company with their angelic counterparts.[1]

The aphorisms, images, metaphors and fantasies that have grown around the figure of the downtrodden woman turned killer encompass the spheres of fact and fiction, fantasy and reality, fear and desire. 'Like any artist with no form, she became dangerous' writes Toni Morrison in *Sula*, a view historically articulated by other women writers before her.[2] Gwendolen Harleth, George Eliot's entrancingly imperfect heroine, sums it up:

> We women can't go in search of adventures—to find the North-West passage or the source of the Nile, or to hunt tigers in the East. We must stay where we grow, or where the gardeners like to transplant us. We are brought up like the flowers, to look as pretty as we can, and be dull without complaining. That is my notion about the plants: they are often bored, and that is the reason why some of them have got poisonous.[3]

The murderousness of the erstwhile victim thus becomes crime with an agenda, a programmatic loss of control, and the she-devil, female fiend, monster, demon, temptress, seductress, mermaid, the flower turned poisonous, the ball-breaker, castrator, cannibal, man-eater, are all the outcomes of a wisdom acquired from experience, which teaches women that if you can't beat them, you must eat them. The role inversion between victim and oppressor, as well as having the merit of novelty, ensures that the old familiar things that men have done to women historically now reappear newly visible, newly scandalous, through the defamiliarization that the new occupants of the roles bring to it. Edgar Z. Friedenberg said

1. Auerbach, *Woman and the Demon*, pp. 96-101.
2. T. Morrison, *Sula* (New York: Bantam Books, 1980), p. 105.
3. G. Eliot, *Daniel Deronda* (Harmondsworth: Penguin, 1980 [1876]), p. 171.

that 'all weakness corrupts and impotence corrupts absolutely'.[1] The crushed women of history and literature unleash themselves into the crime of murder in order to avoid themselves becoming its victims, and find, like William Blake, that 'the road of excess leads to the palace of wisdom'.[2] The 'deathtalk', the murderous writing of certain contemporary women, may perhaps be seen as just that, the anguished but also exhilarated expression of an awareness that this, for the moment, must be the extent of wisdom.

It would be consoling to conclude with a rosier panorama of future regenerative images, but utopias ultimately must carry in themselves the palimpsest of that which they seek to ameliorate in the future, and which they hope to consign to the past. In reality, the days of 'girls on top' are far away yet, and images, literary or otherwise, of conciliation, of alternative and emancipated, positive forms of womanhood probably remain largely utopian in our present. At best, consolation must be found in sporadic exceptions in individual experience, and in present awareness that any status quo grounded in tyranny carries along with its uglinesses the mechanism of its own future undoing. Henry Maudsley, the Victorian psychiatrist, remarked that

> Survival of the fittest does not always mean survival of the best... it means only the survival of that which is best suited to the circumstances, good or bad, in which it is placed—the survival of a savage in a savage social medium, of a rogue among rogues, of a parasite where a parasite alone can live.[3]

This is evidently less than ideal, but it is also, happily, the recognition of destruction ever-threatening at the heart of every autocracy. In Thornton Wilder's *The Ides of March* Caesar, living his last days in the foreboding of what is to

---

1. E.Z. Friedenberg, quoted in S. MacLeod, *The Art of Starvation* (London: Virago, 1983), p. 60.

2. W. Blake, *The Marriage of Heaven and Hell* (Oxford: Oxford University Press, 1990), p. xviii.

3. H. Maudsley, *Body and Will,* quoted in E. Showalter, *The Female Malady: Women, Madness and English Culture, 1830–1980* (London: Virago, 1988), p. 119.

come, expresses the fear which must haunt every tyrant, the awareness of the danger inherent in forcibly keeping down those who in their turn might rise to destroy their oppressors:

> Rome as I have shaped it, as I have had to shape it, is not a comfortable place for [those] whose genius is the genius for ruling at the top. If I were not Caesar now, I would be Caesar's assassin.[1]

1.　T. Wilder, *The Ides of March* (Harmondsworth: Penguin, 1986), p. 192.

INDEX OF SUBJECTS

INDEX OF NAMES